THE NUTTIS SCHELL

Essays on the Scots language

Professor A J Aitken
Photograph: Ian F Mackenzie, School of Scottish Studies

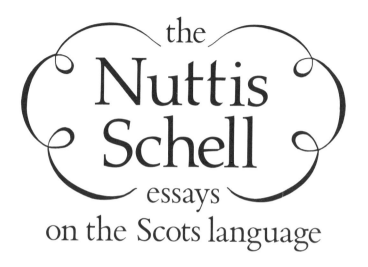

the Nuttis Schell

essays

on the Scots language

presented to A J Aitken

edited by Caroline Macafee and Iseabail Macleod

ABERDEEN UNIVERSITY PRESS

First published 1987
Aberdeen University Press
A member of the Pergamon Group

© The Contributors 1987

The publisher acknowledges subsidy from the Scottish
Arts Council towards the publication of this volume

British Library Cataloguing in Publication Data

The Nuttis Schell: essays on the Scots
  language presented to A J Aitken.
  1. English language—Dialects—Scotland
  I. Macafee, Caroline   II. Macleod, Iseabail
  III. Aitken, A J
  427′.9411   PE2102
  ISBN 0-08-034530-1

PRINTED IN GREAT BRITAIN
THE UNIVERSITY PRESS
ABERDEEN

CONTENTS

MODERN SCOTS

CONTRIBUTORS

Dr Alex Agutter, Lecturer, Department of English Language, University of Edinburgh

Professor Richard W Bailey, Department of English, University of Michigan

Priscilla Bawcutt, Liverpool

David Daiches, Emeritus Professor of English, University of Sussex, formerly Director, Institute for Advanced Studies, University of Edinburgh

The staff of DOST (Marace Dareau (editor), Eileen Finlayson, Marjorie McNeill, Lorna Pike (editorial assistants), Dr J A C Stevenson, Harry Watson (editors)

Dr Alexander Fenton, Research Director, National Museums of Scotland

Professor Denton Fox, Department of English, University of Toronto

John M Kirk, Lecturer, Department of English, Queen's University of Belfast

Caroline Macafee, Lecturer in English and Scottish language, University of Glasgow

J Derrick McClure, Lecturer, Department of English, University of Aberdeen

Angus McIntosh, Emeritus Professor of English Language, University of Edinburgh

Dr Margaret A Mackay, Lecturer in Scottish ethnology, School of Scottish Studies, University of Edinburgh

Iseabail Macleod, Editorial Director, Scottish National Dictionary Association, Edinburgh

Professor Dr Hans H Meier, Department of English, Vrije Universiteit, Amsterdam

David D Murison, Editor, Scottish National Dictionary

Mairi Robinson, Editor-in-chief, Concise Scots Dictionary

Dr Karl Inge Sandred, Reader, Department of English, University of Uppsala

Professor Arne Zettersten, Department of English, University of Copenhagen

PREFACE

The nuttis schell, thocht it be hard and teuch,
Haldis the kirnell, sueit and delectabill;
Sa lyis thair ane doctrine wyse eneuch
And full of frute, vnder ane fenȝeit fabill;
And clerkis sayis, it is richt profitabill
Amangis ernist to ming ane merie sport,
To blyth the spreit and gar the tyme be schort.
(from Henryson's Prologue to the *Morall Fabillis*)

Henryson's well-balanced view of scholarship is the source of our title. The metaphor has been applied before to *A Dictionary of the Older Scottish Tongue*, whose editor, A J Aitken, this volume honours. Unfamiliar and rather hard to crack, the Older Scots language, in which Henryson writes, is the repository of Lowland Scottish literary culture at its height. DOST, the record of that language, is likewise full of delights — both amusing and informative — in its wealth of quotations.

We are conscious in offering this volume of essays in honour of Jack Aitken that it is belated in that we have missed his 65th birthday and his retirement, which would have been suitable occasions; and short measure in that the contributions to this volume are only a small fraction of those who owe him intellectual, and indeed personal debts. Some whom we asked had to decline regretfully, or to drop out, equally regretfully; others we neglected to ask, not realizing the closeness of their association with him, and having only limited means of finding out without giving away the conspiracy. Sometimes we judged — perhaps wrongly — that their areas of work lay outside what we could hope to bring together in a single fairly cohesive volume. There was also the question of the length of the volume. We would like to apologize to anyone who would have liked to contribute and whom we overlooked.

What we *have* tried to do is to represent both those whose association with

AJA goes back a long time, and the younger generation now active in research, his students in spirit, and often in fact; both colleagues in Scotland and those who keep up an interest in Scots in other countries. We hope that the outcome also reflects to some extent the range of his own interests.

CAROLINE MACAFEE and ISEABAIL MACLEOD
February 1987

ABBREVIATIONS AND SYMBOLS

#	word boundary
/ /	encloses phonemes
[ ]	encloses phonetic realisations
⟨ ⟩	encloses graphemes
Abd	Aberdeen
a, adj	adjective
C	any consonant
CGEB	*A Comprehensive Grammar of the English Language*, Quirk *et al.* (1985)
CSD	*The Concise Scots Dictionary*
DOST	*A Dictionary of the Older Scottish Tongue*
EDD	*The English Dialect Dictionary*
e	early
f.	feminine
Gsw	Glasgow
GSc	Glasgow Scots, Glaswegian
L	Latin
la	late
LALME	*A Linguistic Atlas of Late Mediaeval English*, McIntosh *et al.* (1987)
LAS	*The Linguistic Atlas of Scotland*, Mather and Speitel (1975–86)
Loth	Lothian
ME	Middle English
MED	*Middle English Dictionary*
MLG	Middle Low German
ModDan	Modern Danish
ModE	Modern English
ModIcel	Modern Icelandic
ModSc	Modern Scots
ModSw	Modern Swedish
MSc	Middle Scots
m.	masculine
n, sb.	noun
ODan	Old Danish
ODS	*Ordbog over det danske Sprog*
OE	Old English, Anglo-Saxon
OED	*The Oxford English Dictionary*
OF	Old French
OHG	Old High German
OIcel	Old Icelandic
ON	Old Norse
OSc	Older Scots
OScand	Old Scandinavian
OSw	Old Swedish
Per	Perthshire
PrScand	Proto-Scandinavian
pple. a	participial adjective
SAOB	*Ordbok över svenska språket utg. av Svenska akademien*
sb.	substantive, noun
Sc	Scots
Scand.	Scandinavian
SND	*The Scottish National Dictionary*
SSRC	Social Science Research Council (now the Social and Economic Research Council)
StE	Standard English
TrSc	Traditional Scots
V	any vowel
v, vb	verb
vi	intransitive verb
vt	transitive verb
Wgt	Wigtownshire

A J AITKEN: BIOGRAPHICAL SKETCH AND LIST OF PUBLICATIONS

Adam Jack Aitken was born in 1921, in Edinburgh. He was educated at Lasswade Secondary School (Lasswade, Midlothian), and enrolled as an undergraduate at Edinburgh University in 1939. His studies were interrupted by the war: from 1941 to 1945 he served in the Royal Artillery. He returned to his Alma Mater in 1945 and graduated MA with First Class Honours in English Language and Literature in 1947. The following year he was Assistant Lecturer in English Language at Edinburgh University, and from 1948 to 1964 Research Fellow at the Universities of Glasgow, Aberdeen and Edinburgh.

From 1954 to 1965 he was Lecturer at the Universities of Glasgow and Edinburgh, Senior Lecturer at Edinburgh University from 1965 to 1975 (part-time 1971–5), and Reader there (part-time) from 1975 to 1979, when he resigned in order to devote his full time to lexicography. His lectures to undergraduates dealt with several subjects, including Lowland Scots, Middle Scots Language and Literature, Older Scots paleography, as well as various aspects of the English language.

Professor Aitken's long and active career as a lexicographer began shortly after graduation. From 1948 to 1956 he was assistant to Sir William Craigie, Editor of *A Dictionary of the Older Scottish Tongue*. When Sir William retired, he became Editor of the Dictionary, which post he held from 1956 to 1986 (part-time during the period 1971–79). It was during his editorship that he established (in collaboration with Paul Bratley and Neil Hamilton-Smith) the Older Scottish Textual Archive, a computer-readable archive (extending to over 1,000,000 running words) of certain key Older Scottish texts.

Professor Aitken has served on many academic councils and committees, including the Executive Council of the Scottish National Dictionary Association (since 1960); the Council of the Scottish Text Society (since 1962); the Council of the Association for Scottish Literary Studies (1972–82); the

Language Committee of the Association for Scottish Literary Studies (chairman 1971–76); the Editorial Committee of the Dictionary of Early Modern English Pronunciation (1972–76); and the Universities Forum for Research on the Languages of Scotland (chairman 1978–1981).

Since 1964, he has served as adviser or consultant on several dictionary projects: for an abortive plan for a projected Dictionary of Tudor English, University of Leeds (1964–68); the Dictionary of Sanscrit on Historical Principles, at Deccan College, Poona (1969); the Dictionary of Middle English, University of Michigan (1973); the Dictionary of Early Modern English Pronunciation (1972–74); and the Dictionary of Old English, Toronto University. Along with Mairi Robinson he was responsible for the detailed planning of the Scottish National Dictionary Association's *Concise Scots Dictionary* (published in 1985) and served as its Supervisory Consultant. Also, he acted as consultant for *Collins' English Dictionary* (1972–73) and for Chambers' *Twentieth Century Dictionary* (1973–77). And he has acted as Consultant to the Canada Council, the National Endowment for the Humanities and the Social Research Council for various projects involving Scots language and sociolinguistics, medieval Scots literature, lexicography and literary computing.

Professor Aitken has offered papers at a good many learned conferences dealing with Scots, lexicography, and other subjects in which he takes an active interest. And he has given lectures at numerous universities, at home and abroad, e.g. in Canada, the United States of America, Italy, France, Holland, Norway, Sweden Germany and India, where he was a visiting professor, at Deccan College, Poona, and at the University of Kerala.

In 1983 he was awarded a D Litt by Edinburgh University for his work on the *Dictionary of the Older Scottish Tongue* and other publications. In recognition of his outstanding academic achievements the University of Edinburgh appointed him Honorary Professor in 1985.

There follows a fairly complete list of the main publications of A J Aitken to 1986.

DOST, vols. III, IV, V, VI as sole or joint editor. Vol. II, letter G as assistant editor.

1953   Notice of *A Memoir and a List of the Published Writings of Sir William A Craigie, Scottish Historical Review* 32, 170–2.
         'The Older Scottish language', *Scotsman* 27 June.
1957   'A sixteenth century Scottish devotional anthology', review of J A W Bennett ed., *Devotional Pieces in Verse and Prose* (1955), *Scottish Historical Review* 36, 147–50.

1958   Notice of *Sir James A H Murray: A Self-Portrait* (1957), *Scottish Historical Review* **36**, 173–4.
       'On compiling the Older Scottish Dictionary', *The Periodical*, 234–6.

1961   'The Dictionary of the Older Scottish Tongue', *Scottish Genealogist* **8**, 3–12
       anonymously, 'Books over the Border', review of P D Hancock, *A Bibliography of Works Relating to Scotland* (1959–60), *Times Literary Supplement*, 30 June, 408.

1962   'Scottish language', *Chambers' Encyclopedia* (extensive revision of an article originally by W Craigie).

1964   'Completing the record of Scots', *Scottish Studies* **8**, 129–40.
       Review of C Elliott ed, *Robert Henryson, Poems* (1963), *Studia Neophilologica* **36**, 344–6.

1966   with Paul Bratley, 'An archive of Older Scottish texts for scanning by computer', *English Studies* **48**, 61–2 and *Studies in Scottish Literature* **4** (1967), 45–7.
       Review of D F C Coldwell, ed, *Selections from Gavin Douglas* (1964), *Studia Neophilologica* **38**, 152–4.

1969   Review of C Elliott ed, *Robert Henryson, Poems* (revised edition), *Studia Neophilologica* **41**, 427–8.

1971   'Historical dictionaries and the computer' in R A Wisbey ed, *The Computer in Literary and Linguistic Research* Cambridge University Press, 3–17
       co-editor with A McIntosh and H Pálsson, *Edinburgh Studies in English and Scots* London: Longman.
       'Variation and variety in written Middle Scots' in *Edinburgh Studies in English and Scots*, 177–209.
       'W A Craigie', *Dictionary of National Biography, Supplement, 1951–60* Oxford University Press.

1971–2 'The present state of Scottish language studies', *Scottish Literary News* **2**, 34–44.

1972   'The literary uses of computers', *Times Literary Supplement*, 21 April, 456.
       anonymously, 'A-Z, choosing a dictionary', *Times Literary Supplement*, 13 October, 1209–1212. Reprinted in *TLS 11, Essays and Reviews from the Times Literary Supplement 1972*, Oxford University Press, 209–25.
       'Gaelic, Scots and Gullane', *Scottish Literary News* **2**, 45–6.

1973   co-editor with R W Bailey and N Hamilton-Smith, *The Computer and Literary Studies* Edinburgh University Press.
       ed, *Lowland Scots* Association for Scottish Literary Studies, Occasional Papers no. 2

'Sense-analysis for a historical dictionary' in H Scholler and J Reidy eds, *Zeitschrift für Dialektologie und Linguistik* Beiheft, Neue Folge no. 9, 5–16.

'Definitions and citations in a period dictionary', in R I McDavid and A R Duckert eds., *Lexicography in English, New York Academy of Sciences*, vol. 211, 259–65.

'Le dictionnaire d'ancien écossais' in *Tavola Rotonda sui Grandi Lessici Storici*, Accademia della Crusca, Florence, 37–44.

'L'analyse des sens pour un dictionnaire historique', *ibid*, 91–5.

anonymously, 'Modern English from A to G', review of *A Supplement to the Oxford English Dictionary* vol. 1, *A-G*, ed R W Burchfield, *Times Literary Supplement* 26 January, 90.

1975   'The Scottish National Dictionary', *The Scottish Review* 1:1, 17–19.

1976   'DEMEP [Dictionary of Early Modern English Pronunciation]: Editorial procedure. A summary of A J Aitken's remarks, and other contributions to *DEMEP. English Pronunciation 1500–1800* Stockholm: Almqvist and Wiksell International, 88–102.

'The Scots language and the Teacher of English in Scotland' in *Scottish Literature in the Secondary School*, Scottish Central Committee on English, Edinburgh: HMSO, 48–55.

1977   co-editor with M P McDiarmid and D S Thomson, *Bards and Makars. Scottish Language and Literature, Medieval and Renaissance* University of Glasgow Press.

'How to pronounce Older Scots' in *Bards and Makars*, 1–21.

'Textual problems and the Dictionary of the Older Scottish Tongue' in P G J van Sterkenburg ed, *Lexicologie, een bundel opstellen voor F. de Tollenaere* Groningen: Walters-Noordhoff, 13–15.

1978   'Historical dictionaries, word frequency distributions and the computer', *Cahiers de lexicologie* **33**, 28–47.

'Oral narrative style in Middle Scots' in J-J Blanchot and C Graf eds, *Actes du 2e Colloque de Langue et de Littérature Ecossaises (Moyen Age et Renaissance)*, University of Strasbourg, 98–112.

1979   co-editor with T McArthur, *Languages of Scotland*, Edinburgh: Chambers, Association for Scottish Literary Studies, Occasional Papers no. 4.

'Scottish speech: a historical view with special reference to the Standard English of Scotland' in *Languages of Scotland*, 85–118.

'Studies on Scots and Scottish Standard English today', *ibid*, 137–60.

'The English of Scotland' in *Collins Dictionary of the English Language*, xxiv–xxv.

1980 with J D McClure and J T Low, *The Scots Language: Planning for Modern Usage* Edinburgh: Ramsay Head Press.

'New Scots: the problems' in *The Scots Language: Planning for Modern Usage*, 45–63.

'On some deficiences in our Scottish dictionaries' in W Pijnenburg and F de Tollenaere eds, *Proceedings of the Second International Round Table Conference on Historical Lexicography*, Dordrecht: Foris Publications, 33–56.

1981 'Angus McIntosh and Scottish Studies' in M Benskin and M L Samuels eds, *So meny people longages and tonges: Philological Essays in Scots and Mediaeval English Presented to Angus McIntosh* Edinburgh, xxix–xxvi.

'The Scottish Vowel Length Rule', *ibid*, 131–57.

'Foreword' in E Haugen, J D McClure and D Thomson eds, *Minority Languages Today*, Edinburgh University Press, vii–xii.

'The good old Scots tongue: Does Scots have an identity?' *ibid*, 72–90.

'DOST: How we made it and what's in it' in R J Lyall and F Riddy eds, *Proceedings of the Third International Conference on Scottish Language and Literature, Medieval and Renaissance*, University of Glasgow, 33–51. Expanded version, *Dictionaries* 4 (1982), 42–64.

'Scottish lexicography' in D Daiches, ed, *A Companion to Scottish Culture*, London: Edward Arnold.

1982 'Bad Scots: Some superstitions about Scots speech', *Scottish Language* 1, 30–44.

1983 'Foreword' in J D McClure, ed, *Scotland and the Lowland Tongue*, Aberdeen University Press, vii–xvii.

'The language of Older Scots poetry' *ibid*, 18–49.

'DOST and the computer: A hopeless Case?' in A Zampolli and A Cappelli eds, *Linguistica Computazionale III. The Possibilities and Limits of the Computer in Producing and Publishing Dictionaries. Proceedings of the European Science Foundation Workshop, Pisa, 1981*, 33–49.

1984 'Scottish accents and dialects' in P Trudgill ed, *Language in the British Isles* Cambridge University Press, 94–114.

'Scots and English in Scotland', *ibid*, 517–32. Also trans. into Japanese by Y Matsumura in *English Around the World*, Kenkyusha (1983).

'What's so special about Scots', *Northern Ireland Speech and Language Forum Journal* 10, 27–44.

1985 Pronunciation entries and contributions to front matter in CSD.

'Is Scots a language?', *English Today* 3, 41–5.

1986   'The pronunciation entries for the CSD' in D Strauss and H W Drescher eds, *Scottish Language and Literature Medieval and Renaissance* Germersheim, 35–46. Also *Dictionaries* 7 (1985). 134–50. 'Mapping the vowels', review of LAS III (1986), *Times Literary Supplement*, 9 May, 491.

forthcoming   'The period dictionaries' in R W Burchfield ed, *Studies in Lexicography* Oxford University Press, 94–115.

'The lexicography of Scots: the current position' in K Hyldgaard-Jensen ed, *Proceedings of the Third International Symposium on Lexicography* Tübingen: Niemeyer, Lexicographica, Series Maior.

'The extinction of Scotland in popular dictionaries of English?' in the Proceedings of the Dictionary Society of North America's Symposium on English Lexicography, University of Michigan Press.

ONE

Introduction

Caroline Macafee

In this Introduction I would like to review some of A J Aitken's major contributions to Scots and to lexicography. By and large, these are also the ones referred to by the authors of this book, so this will also serve as an introduction to the latter.

It will be seen from the list of publications on pp. xiv–xviii that AJA has been a prolific writer, quite apart from his 38 years on DOST. His doctorate was awarded on the basis of published work and I have a persistent image of him submitting this in a wheelbarrow. Anyone of his stature who is also an able and willing public speaker, as he has been, receives many invitations to speak and write on subjects on which they are known to hold opinions or to have special knowledge.

As well as writing on the methods and progress of DOST, he has turned the first sod in many areas of Scots studies, not only in the OSc period; and over a remarkable range of topics he has established an orthodoxy or at least a starting point for subsequent work. He has supervised and examined a large number of PhD theses, and is always prolific with ideas for research. With his ideas as with his time — in committee work, or helping individual scholars — he is unstintingly generous. As his student at Edinburgh, I learned a great deal from him that I was conscious of being taught, but it is only in retrospect that I can see that he was also communicating a certain philosophy of knowledge, which values theories according to their ability to create and organise empirical data, and in general makes theory the tool and not the master of work. The painstaking accumulation of data — in DOST and CSD as in SND and LAS — is the foundation of the subject for all future time. At the moment, when theoretical linguistics is undergoing an identity crisis, it is pleasing to reflect that work on and interest in Scots goes from strength to strength. This must surely be helped by the intellectual atmosphere of responsiveness to real-world questions which AJA has helped to foster. His approach, which might be called a pragmatic eclecticism, is grounded in his deep and wide-ranging interest in humanity and history.

Another aspect of AJA's teaching which I only became aware of later is his

1

complete indifference to the age, sex and nationality of students and colleagues, so long as they are interested in Scots. To somebody of my generation, this went unremarked, but looking back, I think he was far ahead of his time, and this may help to explain the disproportionate number of women academics who have flourished in Scots studies.

Likewise, he has made and kept up many international ties, thus helping to sustain the awareness of Scots amongst scholars of English language abroad, not only in the Scandinavian and Germanic countries, where it is long-established, but also, for instance, in the USA and Japan. His international influence has also been considerable in lexicography, through the Period Dictionaries (see below); international conferences, at the New York Academy of Sciences, Leiden, Pisa, Toronto and Ann Arbor, among other places; and advisory work, for instance on the *Dictionary of Sanscrit on Historical Principles*. He was a consultant to Robin Alston and Brør Danielsson in the mid-1960s on their proposed dictionary of Tudor-Stuart English, and later an external reviewer for the *Middle English Dictionary*.

His viewpoint is global in another sense: a comprehensive interest in Scots has led him to range over most branches of English linguistics. When new and promising approaches appear — such as computer-assisted methods in lexicography, or sociolinguistics — he is always keen to see them applied to Scots, and has helped to ensure the insertion of Scots data and Scottish issues into many contexts.

The linguistic articles by AJA which have proved most influential are those which he wrote while teaching undergraduate courses on Scots. This can hardly be an accident. Although it never actually cured him of a touch of long-windedness, teaching presumably provided the impetus for him to reduce to systematic tables and models the philological and etymological knowledge which informs DOST. Although a stickler for detail in editing, in teaching he has a talent for making the larger patterns clear. In an obvious way, the teaching was at the expense of DOST, but perhaps not really, since it must have multiplied many times over the number of people able to appreciate and benefit from the dictionary. Also, his courses were often attended by postgraduates and colleagues as well as undergraduates, and one sometimes sees published references to cyclostyled handouts which are no more than two or three pages long. Some of his material has also found its way into Kay's (1986) populist version of the history of Scots, as seen on television.

I have mentioned philology, so let me start with Aitken (1977a). This article provides a historical treatment of the entire vowel system — long and short monophthongs and diphthongs — taking ESc at *c.*1375 as being homogeneous and tracing the isolative developments plus some conditioned sound changes which have an extensive lexical base. This is done for Central Scots, plus some important dialect variants. It could, without much difficulty, be extended to include the dialects of England north of the

Humber, but if so, we would in a sense be annexing these to Scots, because the significance of Aitken's treatment is that it allows us to see the modern dialects branching off from a historical core (ESc), described without reference to the point of departure of StE.

As is conventional, the phonetic values are given for the starting point, ESc, as cardinal vowels or diphthongs close to the spellings. The detailed table (1977a: 7) attempts to reconstruct values intermediate between these and ModSc. The result (Jack Aitken as William Dunbar as a Morningside Irishman) can be heard on the privately produced Scotsway cassette tape 'Pronouncing Older Scots', and on some Scotsoun cassettes.

Clearly certain decisions and simplifications had to be made. In the phonology sections of the CSD Introduction (1985) Aitken has changed his mind about the intermediate stage of the diphthong *au*, e.g. *law* and also *caw* 'call'. The modern outcomes range from [ɔ] to [ɑ] and [a]. [ɒ], which he favoured in (1977a), is a phonetic compromise, but in the CSD he favours [ɑ], historically viable for OSc and still extant in dialect. The choice of [ɑ] in the CSD solves *the* descriptive problem of philology — hitting a moving target with a single name. In Aitken (1977a) the ESc vowels are numbered, and the numbers provide continuity through to ModSc (with mergers producing 12a, 12b, etc.), while the phonetic realization mutates. This is a very convenient presentation device, taken up by Catherine van Buuren (1982) whose Introduction is important as a description of fifteenth century Scots, replacing Girvan (1939).

Aitken (1977a) also gives a brief statement of the Scottish Vowel Length Rule (SVLR), sometimes called 'Aitken's Law', most notably by Roger Lass (1976). The allophony produced in the 'Aitken environment' — before voiced fricatives, / r / and morpheme boundaries — becomes phonemic when Central Scots / ø: /, vowel 7, splits into / ɪ / and / e /, e.g. *mune* and *muir*; and when vowel 1 splits into / əi / and / aɪ / (phonetic realisations as in CSD), e.g. *white* and *sky*. It remains doubtful whether vowel length in itself is ever phonemic in Scottish speech, despite pairs like *stayed* [e:] *staid* [e]; *wooed* [u:] *wood* [u]. The welter of phonetic detail now available in LAS Vol. III (1985) seems at first to cast doubt even on the length allophony generalized as the SVLR. The situation is complicated by the tendency in some accents, certainly in the West of Scotland, to length on the nuclear stress, which would affect words pronounced in isolation for the fieldworker. In fact, Hans Speitel had already allowed AJA to examine the raw data, and the results are published as Aitken (1981a). Several changes of mind and probably much discussion are concealed by the finished form of the article, but Aitken does succeed in discerning scales of vowels and environments with length increasingly likely as we go up the scale. He does not claim that these are implicational scales (where each less likely occurrence implies that all the more likely ones are already present), such as are associated with the (idealized) spread of sound changes through the lexicon, the phonological system and geographical space. Probably only recordings of connected speech from around the Lowlands can clarify this question.

I must mention before moving on, the pronunciation entries for the CSD, which AJA provided, including for the first time, reconstructed pronunciations (in a conservative ModSc model) for obsolete items. There are very few people who could have done this and even fewer broad-minded enough to include occasional well-established spelling pronunciations like *wally* ['wale] (s. v. *waw*2). (I notice, however, that auld lang syne [zaɪn] has not made it).

Aitken (1977a) also relates the vowel systems to OSc spellings. This is an area which Aitken (1971a) had covered in detail. Here, in describing OSc orthography, he uses a term which has since been anathemized by sociolinguists: 'free variation'. DOST illustrates again and again that every conceivable spelling of a given word will turn up somewhere. There is nevertheless an orthographic system, changing over time, which the article clarifies. And as he suggests, it may yet prove that the inconsistent usage of scribes shows some quantitative (i.e. sociolinguistic) preferences which might identify individuals or scribal dialects.

Now that *A Linguistic Atlas of Late Medieval English* is complete, it seems likely that the techniques which Angus McIntosh, Michael Samuels and others involved in that project have developed will be applied to OSc. McIntosh's article in this volume gives some idea of the potential in this area.

Aitken (1971a) also raises theoretical questions about what *kind* of spelling system OSc had. Alex Agutter (in this volume) develops these questions within a modern linguistic framework. This reflects AJA's own taste for typology, for instance his typologies of Scotticisms (forthcoming a) and of dictionary citation examples (1980a).

On OSc lexis, there exists an unpublished article by Aitken (1954), which is a very useful introduction. Although it consists largely of lists of examples (valuable in itself), it also establishes a general perspective in OSc lexis in relation to ME and ModSc. He points out, for instance that 'there exist *practically no Sc. borrowings from Scand. which are not also north. ME*' (excluding, of course, those derived from Norn) (p. 2). Likewise, 'some of the very common "grammatical" words of Scandinavian origin are never found in Scots' (p. 2). He suggests (while reviewing some place-name evidence of direct Scand, settlement) that this is because the Scand. influence was mainly at second hand via the Anglo-Danish of the north of England. In the CSD Introduction, he extends this view to see Northern ME, rather than the original OE of the south-east of Scotland, as the main ancestor of Scots. Karl Inge Sandred's article (in this volume) which examines four Scand. loan-words for measurement, illustrates how Scand. words have penetrated to the core of everyday Scots vocabulary.

The main part of Aitken (1954) is summarized as follows:

> Much of the vocabulary of Older Scots coincides with that of ME. generally, including: many words of Old English origin . . .; many Scandinavian words common to other ME. dialects also . . .; many French words which are common ME. . . . Some Scottish words of Old English origin have new meanings in Scots . . . Some Old English words which survived in Scots and the north fell out of use elsewhere . . . The Scandinavian element forms a comparatively large section of the vocabulary of Scots . . . Scots has a score or two of Low Dutch borrowings dating from the early medieval period which are not found in other dialects of English . . . In addition, Scots has a few 'popular' French adoptions of the medieval period, which occur only in Scots, and a number of nouns from Gaelic. A fair number of Scots words, including many which are found only in Scots and several which are 'popular' or slangy in connotation, have no ascertainable origin, and some of these were no doubt coined by ordinary speakers some time in the medieval period. The specially numerous Scandinavian and Low Dutch elements of Early Scots apparently reflect the social and political history of 12th and 13th century Scotland, the period of immigration of (amongst others) Anglo-Danish and Anglo-Flemish pioneer adventures. (pp 8,9)

He concludes:

> it will be obvious from the illustrations given that all the well-known general features which set off modern Scots from other English dialects were already established by the 15th century. (p 10)

There are various kinds of information about Scots lexis which he mentions as unavailable in 1954 — for instance the semantic fields into which loans fall, or the proportions of them entering the vocabulary at different periods — which have remained unavailable. But it now appears that with the CSD complete and stored on computer, it will be possible to generalize a great deal of additional information of this sort from it. This is the subject of Mairi Robinson's article in this volume.

In the area of syntax, there are a number of interesting points in Aitken (1978a), which examines three OSc texts whose language can reasonably be described as 'colloquial'. (This article also makes available in print 'John Campbell's Complaint', a short early seventeenth century deposition from Lanark, by an unpractised writer). It attempts to isolate colloquial features of language, Aitken's judgement here being much more cautious than that of many literary critics. One feature which he identifies is the narrative present tense, in which the -is inflection of the verb is generalized to all persons and numbers in all syntactic environments. (The normal rule is for only 2nd and 3rd singular to inflect when the subject is an adjacent personal prounoun). He has suggested that this also marks habitual aspect in ModSc and occasionally in OSc. Another short item with important comments on OSc prose style is his (1957) review of *Devotional Pieces in Verse and Prose* (Bennett ed., 1955).

Aitken's notes on style in OSc verse appeared in print in 1983. These establish the main parameters of stylistic variation, not only in diction, but in syntax, rhyme and metrics, to which everyone interested in the options of the OSc poet must refer. The flyting style — AJA tended to expose his students to bowdlerized extracts — is characterized by a high proportion of etymologically (sometimes semantically) obscure lexis. As Priscilla Bawcutt's article in this volume demonstrates, this obscurity has perhaps been exaggerated in the past by scribal and editorial transmission. Another unpublished work which is a very useful adjunct to Aitken (1983) is his *Older Scots: A First Reader*, which well deserves to see print, preferably in an expanded form and with the addition of a prose selection, which also already exists. A feature of the *Reader* is the glossary, which contains copious distributional and stylistic information on each word and idiom. This is what glossaries should all be like, although I have never seen another that comes anywhere near it. (If it ran to any length, it would tend to turn into the CSD; by the same token, the latter will revolutionize the study and teaching of Scottish Literature). Other editorial work on OSc which AJA has done has mainly been in connection with DOST, but the does claim some share, along with a fellow reviewer, Denton Fox, in the revised version of Elliott's (1963) edition of Henryson (Aitken, 1964a, 1969). The dependence of stylistics on lexicography is illustrated in this volume by Fox. The theme of authorship studies which he takes up is one which AJA has interested himself in — there are a number of studies of this kind in Aitken *et al.*, eds. (1973).

In the study of ModSc style, his main contribution is probably the 'five-column model' (partly derived from MacQueen's 1957 thesis) which can be found in Aitken (1979). This systematizes the choices which speakers and writers make between Scots and StE options. It draws attention to the large common core of material shared between Scots and (at least Scottish) StE (column 3). It distinguishes between Scots items with clearly identifiable StE equivalents, like *hame* = *home* (*hame* is column 2, its cognate is column 4), and distinctive Scots lexis, e.g. *clanjamphry* (Column 1, with StE equivalents in column 5). Writers in particular can create quite different effects by biasing their selection towards column 1 or column 2. This is a useful model for discussing ModSc style — much recent Glasgow writing, for instance, is distinguished by its use of non-standard spellings for essentially column 3 items, e.g. ⟨thingk⟩ *think*. For practical analysis, however, there is a problem in separating volumn 3 (the common core) from column 5 (StE items where Scots ones are available). This is in effect the problem of the non-standard status of Scots — there is no defined body of material which could be held to be 'available' or 'correct' as Scots. (Even our information on the currency of items in speech is very imperfect and out of date). Aitken (1979) uses the five-column model to give a historical description of the relationship between Scots and StE, puts this in a sociolinguistic context, and concludes by identifying various registers within ModSc speech. He also discusses the currency, even in educated middle-class speech, of 'covert Scotticisms'. Speakers are generally not aware that these *are* Scottish. He has been gleaning these from the reactions of the English for many years. The covert/overt distinction was investigated empirically by Sandred (1983, 1985). Aitken (1984b) is substantially a revised version of (1979). In the same volume he provides a brief description of ModSc with an emphasis on speech and dialect variation (1984a). This is one of a number of brief descriptions of the language which he has provided in various places. A feature of the (1984a) article is a diaphonic comparison, with lexical exemplification, of the vowel systems of Scots and 'Anglo-English'.

The status of Scots is the subject of a number of articles in the 1970s and early 1980s when there was a great deal of debate about this, and serious talk of linguistic revival in the context of European minority languages. AJA's influence was a moderating one, for instance in McClure ed. (1980), but he was the last person to pour cold water on any enthusiasm for Scots. In (1981b), he discusses the status of Scots, using concepts drawn from the sociology of language, and particularly from Stewart (1966). Stewart defines a standard language (these are the ones perceived as 'real' languages in practice) as having the properties of standardization, historicity (in effect, being the depository of a culture), vitality (i.e. not a dead language) and autonomy. The theme of autonomy is taken up in this volume by John Kirk, who concludes, on the basis of syntactic data, that Scots is heteronomous with other varieties within English. Another aspect of the minority status of Scots is the subject of Hans Meier's article: the very limited extent to which Scots has been exported beyond the boundaries of this country. Derrick McClure's article, on the other hand, takes a positive view, and gives a critical evaluation of some poetic translations by Douglas Young, part of Young's conscious attempt to augment Scots language and culture.

Beyond the peculiarly Scottish minority language debate, Aitken has been sensitive to the wider currents of sociolinguistic thinking, and their influence on educational attitudes in Britain. Recent thinking tends to promote an awareness and tolerance of working-class speech. In most parts of the English-speaking world this is synonymous with non-standard dialect (or creole). But the situation in Scots is more complicated, and Aitken (1982) helps to tease out these complications by describing an idealized, literary middle-class norm of Scots ('Good Scots') as opposed to 'Bad Scots', actual Scots speech (largely working-class, as elsewhere) especially urban varieties. This hypothetical attitudinal distinction is given some empirical confirmation by Sandred (1983). My own article (Macafee, in this volume) is concerned with urban Scots and working-class life. The article by David Daiches testifies to the emotional significance and the richness of especially childhood associations which the language has for Lowlanders of all classes.

Tolerance and optimism about the language are the main themes of Aitken (1976), which is addressed explicitly to those concerned with secondary education in Scotland. Richard Bailey, in this volume, brings an outsider's view to bear on the Scottish situation, and again is optimistic, on the basis of our own history and with encouragement from the rest of the world, about the educational and sociolinguistic choices available to the Scottish people.

The foregoing illustrates, I hope, the range and importance of Aitken's work and influence, before we even consider lexicography. Jack Aitken has been associated in a planning or consultative capacity with a large number of major dictionary projects, including the other period dictionaries, which with DOST are part of William Craigie's original vision. He has written and spoken about lexicography on many occasions. Following as he does in a line of great Scottish lexicographers, he is certainly entitled to take English dictionaries to task, as he does in a forthcoming article for 'the extinction of Scotland in popular dictionaries of English'. His own influence ensures that some are better than others in this respect.

The major work of Jack Aitken's career has, of course, been his part in DOST. Some of the methods, strengths and weaknesses of DOST are discussed elsewhere in this volume, especially in the 'Re-editing of GIF' by others of the DOST team, and in the Appendix to Robinson's article, where she lists constraints on research possibilities that CSD inherits from the parent dictionaries. David Murison's article provides a historical context and shows the inheritance of earlier Scottish lexicography which DOST (and SND) supersede, but also to some extent incorporate.

DOST and the other period dictionaries are in a sense supplements to the OED, covering individual chronological periods and national varieties in much greater detail. The project was publicly proposed in 1919 by William Craigie. As Aitken writes (1964b: 131), each of the period dictionaries

> it is important first as the completest record of its own period, Each is also important as an indispensable unit in this grand scheme to survey in detail the whole history of English and Scots.

Aitken nevertheless emphasizes the importance of OED, and likewise EDD, as *Scots* dictionaries, and deplores the continued use of Jamieson as an authority. Twenty years later, DOST and SND, which obviously *are* Scots dictionaries are still overlooked in quarters where they should be natural sources, for instance the recent edition of Partridge's *Dictionary of Slang and Unconventional English*, revised by Beale (1984) has still only got as far as EDD for its references to Scots.

The first publisher of DOST was the University of Chicago Press, with Oxford University Press as printers. The Dictionary operated on a shoe-string from the start and its publication was probably seen as an act of generosity for a worthy cause, and certainly depended on the willingness of individuals within the Press to champion the continued financing of publication from year to year. Craigie was already familiar with the cleft stick that Aitken writes of (1981c: 46)

> between the need to maintain what he considers adequate academic standards and his paymasters' concern for speed and economy.

There were already in the early 1950s complaints from the publishers about the cost of editorial alterations at a late stage in production — the pursuit of perfection up to (and, the complainers held, beyond) the last moment.

From 1950, the University of Chicago Press and the University of Edinburgh had an arrangement whereby the University contributed towards editorial costs. The Carnegie Trust made intermittent contributions, as it continues to do, and other sources of public funds have also been important. The seeking of funds for DOST and SND together became the business, from 1952, of a Joint Council of the four (later six) Scottish Universities, chaired from the outset until recently by Angus McIntosh, with the universities themselves making a financial contribution. At this point, the two Dictionaries were brought together in Edinburgh, taking up a key position

> in the survey of Scottish language and traditions in which they complement the work of Edinburgh University's School of Scottish Studies and the same University's Linguistic Survey of Scotland. (Aitken, 1964b: 131)

One might add also the close informal links between DOST and the National Museums of Scotland.

In comparison with similar national projects in other countries (including Third World countries), 'many of which have been or are being directly and generously maintained by the state on the same footing as the national museums' (Aitken, 1964b: 139), DOST is 'right at the bottom of the league' (1981c: 45).

Nevertheless, when he became the senior editor of DOST in the 1950s, Aitken took the calculated risk of instituting a second reading programme to ensure a) that DOST would really add enough to the OED to justify its existence, and b) that it would be the best dictionary practicable. This programme approximately doubled the list of works excerpted for the dictionary. In his (1980a) article, he characterizes the corpus of the Dictionary as an open, expanding one. The bulk of the citations for the most common words are drawn from the original 'basic' corpus. This is biased towards verse and literary prose (reflecting their availability in published editions) at the expense of representativeness. The second reading programme attempted to remedy this and was, as expected, highly productive of less common items. But as Aitken writes (1980a), the corpus of OSc is sufficiently large that saturation point (beyond which no new items or uses are to be found) would never be reached in any feasible programme of excerption. The corpus is 'expanding' in the sense that excerption continued after publication had begun. There will accordingly be a considerable supplement especially to the earlier letters of the alphabet, but Aitken anticipates that the unevenness will prove permanent, as excerptors are always less attentive to items falling under letters already published.

The early 1980s, with radical right-wing governments in both the USA and the UK brought financial crisis. The University of Chicago Press withdrew in 1982. Their commitment had certainly continued far beyond what they at first envisaged — in 1931 they expected the project to take ten years. Twenty-two years later, 14 parts had been published and the original estimate of 25 parts was clearly ludicrous. By 1981, 29 fascicles (up to the middle of P) were in print. In the crisis the next two parts were lost in a financial limbo, and the proofs were deposited in the National Library of Scotland. Jack Aitken and James Stevenson in desperation drew up a tragi-comic plan to drop standards drastically and to depend for the sense analysis on OED, which would certainly have speeded up the work considerably. But speed is hardly the point, and R W Burchfield was presumably speaking tongue-in-cheek when he said, in the discussion following Aitken's (1980a) paper

> I wonder if we ought not all return to the general concept of the treatment of literary use rather than branch out indefinitely into sciences, governmental use, private papers, and so forth, and then we might not seem to outsiders to be the slowest performers in Christendom (p 52).

Yes, Aitken agreed, DOST could have continued so limited and would have gone much faster, 'but it would have *said* a lot less'.

The situation was saved by the timely and far-sighted intervention of Aberdeen University Press, championed by their managing director (Publishing), Colin MacLean, who took on a rationalized package of DOST, SND and the new CSD.

Like the OED before it, DOST depends on the work of its amateur and voluntary excerptors:

> Their sole reward had been the interest of the work and the satisfaction of carrying out a patriotic task (Aitken, 1964b: 138).

The excerptors were given detailed instructions on what to look out for, described in Aitken (1980a). But since they could not know what was already in the collection, they were working blind. The task demands

> much knowledge of the language . . . a feeling for the likely distributional range and frequency of incidence of particular forms and usages at different points in the corpus (Aitken, 1971b: 6).

There were difficult textual problems especially when excerption was done from MS, which not infrequently remained problems into the editorial stage (1977b). Published editions presented problems of their own, particularly the normalization of spelling and abbreviations. Since it was impossible to check all sources in MS, DOST retains, for instance, the ⟨j⟩ of modern editors, although many items entered in the *J* section of the Dictionary would have been spelled in fact with ⟨i⟩.

Computer methods came too late to be of great help to DOST. Excerption by computer is most suitable for the most copiously excerpted texts, and therefore of considerably less advantage to a dictionary as far advanced as DOST, which had already established its basic corpus for the most common items. The nature of OSc with its high proportion of homographs also makes mechanical sampling methods particularly subject to error (Aitken, 1971b). Aitken nevertheless thought it worthwhile to set up in the 1960s, with the help of Paul Bratley and later of Neil Hamilton-Smith, the Older Scots Textual Archive, a computer-readable archive of over one million words of OSc literature. The flexible concordance programmes devised for this allow DOST to utilize it in various ways, but its value goes much beyond its lexicographical role. In general, AJA's work in the application of computers to research in the humanities was in the forefront of such work. He played a prominent part in organizing the meeting on computers and literary studies whose proceedings appeared in Aitken *et al.* eds (1973). In a sense the Textual Archive is a continuation by other means of the publishing activities of the Scottish Text Society, of which AJA is a long-serving member. An archive of this kind is an invaluable resource for all kinds of research, and new uses for it will no doubt continue to emerge as the use of computers becomes more routine in the Arts. In this volume, Arne Zettersten describes one such use which is becoming increasingly common, computer-assisted language learning.

The actual work of editing DOST is described in some detail in Aitken (1973a and 1973b). The former also gives a shortened version of the DOST internal guidelines. DOST is remarkable for the detail of its organization, for instance where particular senses are associated with characteristic collocations, as well as with chronological or regional divisions. Since the period dictionaries have a well-recognized relationship to OED, their emphasis is rather different from the latter, and from the dictionaries with which most people are familiar. There is no need to define words in senses already recorded as StE. The first sense of *mone*, for instance, is simply 'the moon'. It is left to OED to tell us that this is 'the satellite of the earth'. Aitken himself has described the definitions as merely 'finding-aids or sign-posts' to the ordering of the citations (1973b: 259). It is the latter which are deployed to elucidate the history of the word.

DOST is remarkable also for the amount of 'secondary research' undertaken by the editors to provide accurate descriptions of technical and specialized vocabulary. Many of the historical researchers who will use DOST in the future will probably be unaware of the extent to which the path to their new insights has already been cleared by the editors of DOST. A staggering amount of knowledge not in itself lexicographical is immanent in the Dictionary. The article by Iseabail Macleod in this volume illustrates the role which the Dictionary can play in the study of any aspect of Scottish life in the past — particular sources, which may or may not themselves have been read for DOST — are provided with a context based on the vast corpus of the Dictionary. In turn, addenda and corrections to the dictionary record may be suggested. The articles by Alexander Fenton and by Margaret Mackay show the kind of ethnological picture which a full understanding of terminology entails, available for ModSc in the field, but for OSc only in DOST.

No-one is in a better position than the DOST editors, past and present, to appreciate what DOST is and what it contains, so I will simply quote here from a description of the dictionary by Aitken and Stevenson from 1981, when they had to justify their existence to publishers (and regrettably even to the Scottish universities):

> The work . . . is a major resource for scholars of Older Scots language, literature and history in a variety of specialisms, and for editors of literary and record texts in that language. Since it defines and illustrates every meaning of every word found in the surviving records of Older Scots (down to 1600) and every Scots meaning of every word for the century following that, the Dictionary touches every facet of medieval and late medieval Scottish life and society. Its great strength is its wealth of illustration (in the form of quotations) of every word and meaning it discusses, with the result that it provides detailed and at the same time first-hand information of a sort that no encyclopedia of medieval Scots society could hope to match, even if such a work existed (which it does not). . . . . . .
>
>   As well as throwing light on the history of things and ideas through its information about the words which named them in earlier Scotland, the Dictionary is of course at the same time the first authority on the national and local vernacular language of late medieval Scotland. Such matters as the history of the forms of words (pronunciation and spellings, changes in meanings, innovation and obsolescence, the special vocabularies and word-forms peculiar

to particular local Scots dialects in earlier times, and the favouring of words and forms in particular 'registers' of Middle Scots writing — all of these are fully treated in the Dictionary.

(circulated in 1981)

The importance and value of DOST can hardly be exaggerated. It is a repository of historical material and as such will be subject to new interrogations and new interpretations by each generation of users. Aitken's (1964b) comparison of the dictionary to a national museum is very apposite. In the modern world, with the past disappearing from us at an accelerating rate, we particularly feel the need to secure our knowledge of what we have been.

> History can only be written about the present and the future. When we analyse historical situations . . . we are speaking to the metaphysical questions, where are we? We are writing of the present. When we analyse the instantaneous historical situation in which we find ourselves, we are making guesses about the likely trajectory of social life. We are thus speaking to the metaphysical question, where will we be? and where would we like to be? We are then writing of the future. (Wallerstein, 1984: 3)

But despite the pace of change, the past continues, in ways of which we are hardly aware, to shape what we are and what we do, from the most personal level up to the national and international. The securing of the past is especially important in a country like Scotland, a nation without being a state, whose unity exists mainly in a shared historical identity and through the institutions of civil society, like museums and universities. Jack Aitken's life work — long may it continue — has been a monumental 'patriotic task'.

We offer this volume of essays as a mark of the respect and love that the academic community has for a great scholar, and out of the admiration and inspiration that such a dedicated career fires in those of us who are privileged to benefit from it.

LEXICOGRAPHY

TWO

Scottish Lexicography

David Murison

In England one of the first dictionaries was a bilingual one, a glossary of Latin words with English equivalents, amounting to about 12,000 entries, the *Promptorium Parvulorum*, *c*.1440; so too in Scotland the first recorded glossary was a Latin-Scots one, a list of some 600 entries appended to the 1595 Latin Grammar of Andrew Duncan, rector of the Grammar School of Dundee (Skeat, 1874). Two years later we have the first specialist dictionary in Scots, Sir John Skene's *De Verborum Significatione*, 'the Expositione of the Terms and Difficill Wordes, conteined in the Foure Buikes of Regiam Majestatem', valuable in dealing with the earlier obscurer period of Scots law and its old Gaelic vocabulary, like *can*, *colpindach*, *cro*, *ochiern*, *toschoderach*.

By the early seventeenth century interest in 'difficill wordes' had given impetus to the first tentative efforts in English lexicography in the works of Cawdrey, Bulloker, Cockeram, and Blount. The civil strife of that century proved more inimical to lexicography in Scotland though not entirely to the lexicography of Scots. For in England three leading 'Saxonists', Lisle, Dugdale and Junius, all glossed or discussed Scots words, for which their chief source of information was Douglas's *Eneados*. Recognizing the common ancestor of English and Scots to be Anglo-Saxon (OE), they held that Scots had preserved Anglo-Saxon words and forms better than English and was therefore a quarry for their own work. Interest in dialect also dates from this time with John Ray's *Collection of English words* (1674), northern and southern, and of course Scots words are to be found in plenty among the northern group.

But it was in the first decade of the eighteenth century that the Union furore led to an outburst of literary activity in the republication of old Scottish poetry by James Watson and Allan Ramsay, and among this was the full-dress edition of Douglas's *Eneados* by Thomas Ruddiman in 1710. To the text Ruddiman added 'a Large Glossary explaining the difficult words, which may serve for a dictionary to the old Scottish Language', containing in round figures some 3000 entries, some simply text references but many fairly full articles on particular words, and giving information about the contemporary

17

and regional currency of the word gathered from correspondents in various localities. Ruddiman thus understood the place of field-work in lexicography and one of his speculations that the development of / f / out of / ʍ / in North-east Scots shows that the / f / must have been bilabial [Φ] as in Gaelic, is a plausible explanation of the sound-change. He does not seem to have known OE himself and though particularly interested in etymology he depends mainly on the derivations of the English scholar Skinner of the *Etymologicum Linguae Anglicanae* (1671). He had also consulted a manuscript glossary of Douglas prepared by Junius, now in the Bodleian, but he does not hesitate to correct Junius or Skinner where he thinks they are wrong, and in not a few cases his emendations are justified, e.g. *anon* from OE *on ān* and *wale*, to choose, from ON *val*. So already amid blunders and guesswork we can see the beginnings of more scientific etymology, if etymology even today can be said to be quite scientific.

For the rest of the century lexicography in Scotland went hand in hand with literature, mainly as glossaries prepared by Scottish poets for their own works, the pioneer in this being Allan Ramsay (1721, 1728). His glossary is not large (about 750 words); there are perceptive observations on the Scots vowel system; it owes a good deal to Ruddiman; there are no etymologies, and as one might expect of Ramsay, the definitions are a bit slapdash, with adjectives for instance defined as nouns. But the glossary is important not only as the forerunner of more of its kind, but also because the spelling provided a model for Scots poets widely followed in the eighteenth century and far on into the nineteenth. The main object seems to have been to spell identically with, or as near as possible to the English spelling, e.g. ⟨gh⟩ rather than ⟨ch⟩ in *bright*, *night*, ⟨-ed⟩ for ⟨-it⟩ in past participles, ⟨oo⟩ representing / ø: / as well as / u: / as in *good*, *soon*, *poor*, ⟨ou⟩ and ⟨u⟩ for / u: /, while ⟨ow⟩ is sometimes the simple vowel / u: / and sometimes the diphthong / ʌu /. The effects of this mixter-maxter of Scots and English in the minds of people accustomed to associate language with its printed form can be heard to this day in the unhappy attempts of performers to sing a Scots song or recite a Scots poem; and it adds to the complications of Scottish lexicography in multiplying spellings and cross-references. Burns also appended a glossary to his Kilmarnock edition which contains judicious comments on verbal forms and succinct and accurate and sometimes humorous definitions (see Murison in Low, 1975: 62, 3).

The high water mark of eighteenth century English lexicography was Johnson's classic work in 1755, where the great innovation, derived from Latin dictionaries and the Italian Della Crusca, was the illustrative quotation from approved authors as models of acceptable usage. Johnson's method was to read as many books as possible, underline the appropriate words and hand them to his amanuenses, of whom five were Scots, to be copied on slips and arranged alphabetically. Johnson then wrote the definitions, decided spellings and added etymologies, for which he relied heavily on Junius. He did not attempt utter completeness and indeed rejected a number of words as being in bad usage or otherwise unacceptable. His purpose was prescriptive, to set a standard of correctness in diction and orthography. Besides his novelties of method his improvements lay in his greater exactness in definition and in a more logical semantic analysis. Incidentally he recommended the compilation of a Scots dictionary to Boswell, who however had not the powers of application to achieve it, and another generation was to pass before the task was taken in hand.

Scottish lexicography received another impetus from a different and unexpected source, the sensitiveness of Scots about speaking a 'provincial' kind of English and using pronunciations and locutions that would not pass muster in London society. This led to the publication of lists of Scotticisms by the philosophers Hume (1752) and Beattie (1779, 1787) and the economist, Sir John Sinclair (1782), and the organization of elocution classes under Thomas Sheridan and others. It is noteworthy how Scotsmen set themselves up as authorities on English. Only two years after Johnson's dictionary appeared, James Buchanan produced his dictionary of English pronunciation (1757) and in 1787 James Elphinston in his *Propriety Ascertained in her Picture* discussed idiom and usage as well, with many asides on Scots in the bygoing. Meanwhile there was at least one effort at research into Scots phonetics by Sylvester Douglas, Lord Glenbervie, in a work still in manuscript in the National Library of Scotland, *A Treatise on the Provincial Dialect of Scotland*, *c*.1770, and Douglas, who claimed kin with the translator of the *Eneados*, projected an edition of it, which however never materialized.

The general effect of all this was at least to make the Scots conscious of their historic speech, and coming on top of it all the poetry of Burns gave the Scots tongue a restricted but powerful new lease of life and made the need for a Scottish dictionary inevitable. In 1802 there was circulated by the Rev. John Jamieson, a Secession minister in Edinburgh, a prospectus of a Scottish Dictionary which he was then preparing. In his previous charge in Forfar he had met the professor of antiquities at Copenhagen, Grim Thorkelin, an Icelander, who had been struck by similarities between Scots words and Scandinavian, from which he deduced close affinities, and who succeeded in arguing Jamieson out of his previously held view that Scots was simply a corrupt form of English. The cleric, impressed by this new-found dignity of Scots as a Norse tongue, set about making a collection of Scots words from printed and oral sources and after twenty years' work felt ready to appeal for help in its publication. Meanwhile there appeared in 1807 the first part of a work of much promise, *A Dictionary of the Ancient Language of Scotland, with the etymons in Anglo-Saxon, Gothic, Danish, Swedish, Islandic, Belgic, Irish, British, Gaelic, Latin and French*, by Robert Allan, Surgeon in Edinburgh. Allan in a brief preface explains that he was using a large word-collection of his father's and that he intended to write a discursus on the Scots language. The basis of the work is the contemporary Scots of the eighteenth century; there is little evidence that he delved into OSc. He seldom quotes sources, but his definitions are good. He clearly understood the origin of Scots to be in OE and his etymologies (in which he took a special interest) are remarkably on the mark, considering the elementary state of English philology at the time. Unfortunately he got no further with his dictionary than the first fascicule and the letter B, and the field was left clear next year for Jamieson to publish his two-volume work and a long introductory essay on the origin of the Scots tongue on the lines of Thorkelin's ideas. The reverend Doctor was writing in the thick of a controversy about the origin of the Picts, whether they were Celtic as was asserted by the redoubtable antiquary, George Chalmers, or Scandinavian according to the less well-founded John Pinkerton. Jamieson weighed in heavily on the side of Pinkerton with much misplaced learning, coming a cropper especially on the slippery slope of place-names; so that his excursus is now merely a curiosity.

About the *Dictionary* itself, the first and most obvious feature is the debt owed in method and treatment to the later editions of Johnson. There is the same accuracy in definition, the same strict analysis of meaning, the same abundance of illustration by means of quotations more fully documented and precisely referenced than in Johnson. It is in the etymologies that Jamieson spreads himself, not merely in the pure linguistics of the case (which of course with his basic Scandinavian assumptions what he called Suevo-Gothic — are very much a matter of hit or miss — and it is surprising how often he hits) but also in his treatment of the word from the points of view of history, sociology and folklore, e.g. his articles on *Beltane* and *Hogmanay*. Jamieson gave his readers full value for their money. It is in these disquisitions that much of the interest of the work lies.

The first edition won immediate and wide popularity. Scott and Hogg amongst others wrote in with new words and additional information and commentary which Jamieson kept amassing, till in 1825 he was able to publish two more volumes containing the supplementary material, generally referred to, though incorrectly, as the second edition. His correspondents acted as local authorities for the various dialect areas, Aberdeenshire for instance is well covered, and Jamieson made full use of the first Scottish dialect dictionary, John MacTaggart's eccentric *Gallovidian Encyclopedia* of 1824. The weakness of Jamieson are fairly obvious now: he had to depend on faulty texts for his early sources; he misread or misunderstood things in manuscript; his etymologies are vitiated by his preconceptions about the origin of Scots and the inadequacies of the dictionaries then available to him; his notice of pronunciation is almost negligible; he failed to tackle the admittedly thorny problem of spelling; and he was guileless enough to allow some jokers from Ayrshire to hoax him with bogus words. Yet despite all these strictures Jamieson's dictionary is a massive personal achievement which provided and still provides a solid foundation on which all later dictionaries were to build.

Its aims of course went beyond the purely lexical and fall into the category of the encyclopedic. Its success encouraged others to compile pocket dictionaries, some little else than plunderings of Jamieson, like 'Cleishbotham' (1851), others independent compilations like Picken (1818) which grew out of a glossary to his own poems (1788), or Brown (1845)[1] or specialist dictionaries like that of Motherby, who published in 1828 in Königsberg a Scots-German pocket dictionary to the writers of the eighteenth century and the Waverley Novels, or, much later, the first technical dictionary of Scots, James Barrowman's *Glossary of Scottish Mining Terms* (1886). Jamieson (with later revisions by Longmuir and Donaldson) remained the standard work. In the 1860s Scottish lexicography turned to the dialects, Edmondston for Orkney and Shetland and Gregor for Banffshire, both in 1866 and both glossaries rather than dictionaries. These were published by the then recently formed Philological Society of England which did a further service to Scottish philology by printing in 1873 a work on the *Dialect of the Southern Counties of Scotland* by J A H Murray, important alike for its subject and its author. The work is in fact the first real scientific account of the history of Scots and it remains the classic study of the subject.

It was to Murray that the Philological Society six years later entrusted the editorship of the *New English Dictionary* (the OED). Partly because Scots sheds a good deal of light on the history of Northern English, partly because its literature has contributed classics and not a few locutions to the English language, and partly no doubt because Murray was a Scotsman, the OED deals with a pretty large number of Scots words, including much pre-1700 vocabulary. More modern Scots (and English) dialect forms were ruled out as not having been completely collected, and as having a mass of variant phonetic forms and spellings and therefore requiring a different lexicographical layout from that adopted in OED for the literary language. This was provided by Joseph Wright when he put together the English Dialect Society's published and unpublished material in the EDD (1900–6). Unfortunately there were available to Wright only the two Scottish county glossaries already mentioned, but he was able to enlist much help from Scottish correspondents, particularly Alexander Warrack, who excerpted a large amount of post-1700 Scottish literature for him and who later extracted the Scottish content of EDD for Chamber's *Scots Dialect Dictionary* of 1911. Wright's work however is purely dialectal in vocabulary, geographical distribution and not historical development being his chief concern. His information for contemporary usage in the various dialect areas of Scotland is patchy and he only occasionally gives etymologies. Already in July 1884 in the *Scottish Review* a writer had pointed out that what was needed was a Scots dictionary on the lines of OED, giving local pronunciations, investigating etymology, attempting uniformity in spelling and treating the words historically.

In 1907 from a suggestion of William Craigie to collect Scots words, ballads, legends and traditions, a decision was made by the Scottish Branch of the English Association to start on words and William Grant was put in charge. Grant's particular interest was in phonetics and for twenty years he collected material up and down Scotland much as A J Ellis had done for the English Dialect Society a couple of generations earlier. The gist of this is contained in the Introduction to the SND where the differentiae of the Scottish dialects are set forth. The full history of these has still to be written but they can be traced at least as far back as 1500. The end of the seventeenth century saw the demise of Scots as a national language and its disintegration into a series of dialects, with, however, a residue of the old literary canon still surviving. The year 1700 then can be taken as marking a watershed in the history of Scots.

Craigie, who had been active in editing Middle Scots works for the Scottish Text Society as well as in the production of OED proposed in 1919 a series of period dictionaries of English, which would also include the classical period of Scots on which he himself had been working and the modern period (post-1700) as Grant's preserve. And so out of these considerations DOST and SND were born in 1929. The editors were by then elderly men hoping no doubt to see their tasks complete in their lifetime and unwilling to delay the start any longer. Problems of completeness of material, recruitment of staff, and adequacy of funding were subordinated to the need to push on, but they surfaced in an acute form after the war and the subsequent horrendous rise in costs. After eight years' swithering the Scottish Universities were persuaded to take over a large share of the burden financially: Grant died in 1946 and the present writer was appointed in his place. Craigie relinquished his interest in DOST to Edinburgh University and Jack Aitken succeeded him in 1955. Aitken (1981) has dealt very fully with the methods and problems of his dictionary and much of what he has to say applies *mutatis mutandis* to SND. Both the new editors were conscious that there were many sources of Scots vocabulary untapped, and reading programmes had to be recommenced to fill the gaps in regional, chronological and topical coverage, DOST in the seventeenth and SND in the eighteenth centuries, to substantiate continuity of usage. Legal terminology for instance had to be gone into much more fully. In both dictionaries lists of sources doubled, DOST to over 1300, SND to 6000, and in consequence the numbers of slips rose dramatically, in DOST to 1.5 million, in SND, which excludes usages common to Scots and English, to half a million. Under Aitken DOST expanded to contain eight to ten times the Scots material of OED, with a profusion of quotations, closer analysis in definition, (see e.g. *Pull, v.*), and full etymological exposition. Add to this historical or other notes on many words and DOST becomes an encyclopedia of medieval and Stewart Scotland, carrying on the traditions and merits of OED to a yet higher degree of excellence.

Of course a price has to be paid for all this in time and money: financing bodies chafe under increasing costs and demand economies in accord with the present political climate, and as Aitken points out, he and his colleagues have been faced with an agonizing dilemma between the highest academic standards and the lowest financial outlays. It is no consolation that Murray was plagued in the same way by the Oxford University Press in his time.

SND attempts to perform the same function for the modern record of Scots. *Suae naturae* it is of a more popular construction, dealing with a period of the literature which is much better known; it contains thousands of words still in use of at least familiar and sentimentally regarded: it illustrates many topics of general interest, e.g. folklore, proverbs, food and drink, games, local festivals and customs, and it includes words of general English currency which have some peculiarly Scottish application. Pronunciations are marked and information provided about the present currency and locale of any given word or phrase in the tradition of Ruddiman, Jamieson and Wright, thanks in no small measure to the work of Sir James Wilson and the Zürich school of Anglists under the late Eugen Dieth as well as to many patient voluntary informants organised by the *Dictionary* itself. SND has added nearly forty per cent more words to Wright, many more phrases and about one third again of quotations. As a rough measure of the growth of Scottish lexicography in more than a century and a half one may compare the length of an article in Jamieson with the same article in DOST and SND. Good examples are *ken*, *kirk*, *lay*, *lift*, *loun*, *lug*, *mak*, *meal*, *mill*, *muir*, *multure*, *na*, *peat*, *penny*, *pleuch*, and *quean*, where SND has articles varying from twice to ten times the length of Jamieson, and DOST, generally speaking, in even larger proportions.

One may say quite dispassionately that between them the two dictionaries represent the most substantial academic achievement of any Arts Faculty in the Scottish Universities in this century, costing only a fraction in manpower and money of similar enterprises abroad. It would be utterly deplorable if DOST were now to be curtailed by ill-considered cheese-paring. It is certain that it will never be done again and never need to be done again, if it can be finished in our generation with all the thoroughness that it has shown up to now. And for this the editors, and particularly the scholar who is being honoured in this volume, deserve unstinted praise and encouragement.

One thing the Dictionaries have done is to stimulate an interest in Scots, not only in academic research, which has proliferated in quantity and excelled in quality in the last twenty years, but also through their skilful abridgement, the CSD under Mairi Robinson. And we can add a brilliant bonus in the Scots New Testament of W L Lorimer, who was one of the most outstanding correspondents of SND. Between them they have given the Scottish nation a worthy monument to a worthy inheritance.

NOTE

1   T Brown, *A Dictionary of the Scottish Language* 'comprehending all the words in common use in the writings of Scott, Burns, Wilson, Ramsay and other popular Scottish authors.' Wilson was the Wilson of *Tales of the Borders*.

THREE

A Re-editing of GIF

The staff of DOST[1]

Jack Aitken's association with the *Dictionary of the Older Scottish Tongue* dates from the autumn of 1948, when he was engaged as an editorial assistant by Sir William Craigie. Over the next few years, until Craigie's retirement, he worked on the latter part of G, and the whole of H and I. In 1955 Aitken took over the editorship of DOST, and since then he has worked on J, K, L, M, N, O, P, Q, all of Sa and part of Se.

Not surprisingly, his thirty-eight year stint on DOST — including twenty-seven years in which he was administrative head — saw major changes in the editorial policy of the Dictionary. A comparison of the earlier volumes, particularly One and Two, with the most recent ones, will bear this out. From its early days as a useful but by no means exhaustive supplement to the early Scots material in OED, DOST has expanded to become a major authority on, and source-book for, the Scots language as recorded in manuscript and print until the beginning of the eighteenth century.

The last point requires some amplification. William Grant, first editor of the *Scottish National Dictionary* (SND), defined that dictionary's contents as follows:

> (1) Scottish words in existence since *c.*1700 (*a*) in Scottish literature, (*b*) in public records, (*c*) in glossaries and in dictionaries, (*d*) in private collections, (*e*) in special dialect treatises, and (2) Scottish words gathered from the mouth of dialect speakers by competent observers. (SND, Vol. 1, xlv)

The SND, in other words, was designed to handle what was left of modern Scots when that component which is also English was subtracted from it. On the sister dictionary, William Craigie had a radically different approach:

> The full vocabulary of the language throughout this older period is included, because any attempt to limit it to words or senses entirely or specially Scottish would (in the lack of complete dictionaries of Middle and Early Modern English) constantly render selection difficult or arbitrary, and would also fail to exhibit fully the relationship between the languages of Scotland and England during the period when they were most distinct from each other.
>
> (DOST, Vol. 1, Preface)

This view of OSc was shared by Jack Aitken, who has always regarded as 'Scots' the totality of the language as found in texts of Scottish provenance in the period covered by DOST. Indeed, experience was to show that many, perhaps most, items from the 'common core' had rather different semantic and/or distributional patterns in Scots and English: a fact which was to reinforce his view of Scots as a fully-fledged language rather than merely a dialectal variant (or variants) of English.

A few years ago Jack Aitken summed up the aims of DOST as follows:

> They are to provide a dictionary entry for every recorded Older Scots word, and each such entry is to display, as far as the existing evidence allows, all of the word's ramifications of form, meaning and collocation, at the same time indicating how these are distributed in time, in place and in *genre*. This is to be accomplished primarily through the arrangement and presentation of a generous selection of quotations from the original sources, and secondarily by editorial notes and comments pointing out features of the word's form, use or distribution which might not be immediately evident.
>
> (1981c: 33)

As early as 1952 he had set in motion a new reading programme, with more than fifty new volunteer excerptors, designed to make good what he perceived to be deficiencies in the existing material available for editing:

> But when I came along as the young Turk I detected gaps in the regional and topical coverage of the corpus and with the help of a newly enlisted corps of voluntary excerptors set about putting this right, adding both printed and MS. works, including, for example, the Fourth Marquess of Bute's publications of western Scots records, various local records in MS., and manuscript account-books of, among others, skippers and coal-mine managers. My ambition at that time was to have examined all reliable modern printed works containing a substantial body of Older Scots text plus enough manuscript material to complete the geographical and topical spread for at least part of the period. . . . In addition to the texts themselves, the contents of something over 120 published and a few unpublished glossaries, indexes, philological treatises and editorial commentaries are incorporated in the collections, as well as, from the later 1960's, the computer concordance.
>
> (1981c: 34)

The fruits of this exhaustive new reading programme are there for all to see from Volume Three onwards; and it is inconceivable that, to take a very obvious example, an article like LORD — with its 34 senses and numerous sub-senses covering almost 17 pages of Volume Three — could have been written on the basis of the limited corpus of material assembled under Craigie's direction. Nor would DOST perhaps have been so likely to attract tributes such as that paid to it by the late James Kinsley, who called it 'assuredly the greatest single contribution to early Scottish studies this century' (1979: vii).

We come now to the main purpose of this article. It seemed to the present editorial staff a good idea to take an article from an early (pre-Aitken) volume of DOST, and to re-edit it in the light of later editorial practice. The 'word' chosen was the common verb *give*, which by virtue of its ubiquitousness in all manner of literary and non-literary texts, as well as its membership of the lexical 'common core' shared by Scots and English, was felt to be particularly suitable for the purpose. The existing material in Volume Two was copied on to dictionary slips, and in addition each volume of DOST was scanned for any further idiomatic examples which had been missed in the first editing. The re-editing of *give* which followed was an enlightening experience for all of us, for, to an even greater degree than we had anticipated, it highlighted the deficiences of, and potential for error in, the earlier method.

One innovation should be mentioned at the outset. Whereas in Volume Two no fewer than five separate articles are devoted to the various phonemic variants of *give* in OSc, in the present article these have all been gathered under one heading. The original articles were:

> **Gef, Geff,** *v.* Var. of *geif*, GEFE *v.*
> **Gefe, Geif, Geyf,** *v.* Var. of GEVE *v.*
> **Geve, Gewe,** *v.*
> **Gif, Gyf,** *v.*
> **Give, Gyve,** *v.* Var. of GEVE *v.*, GIF *v.*

The theoretical justification for this means of proceeding is that the 'word' has more than one phonological source: e.g. different strands may come from different OE or OF dialects, falling together at some point in the history of the word. OED has little or no difficulty with this as the modern word usually provides the obvious headword for an OED entry. However, things are not quite so obvious when it comes to a period dictionary whose beginning and ending dates are both in the relatively remote past. Furthermore, one of the most striking aspects of the early stages of the language is precisely this phonological variety. It is not too surprising, then, that Craigie was led up what now seems to us something of a blind alley in displaying phonological variety, very much, as it turns out, to the detriment of an equally interesting and characteristic (if less immediately obvious) semantic variety. Thus over the years the balance has been adjusted. Furthermore, the very interest in Scots that Jack Aitken has helped generate has led more recent editors to realise that a less academic approach might be more suitable for the modern dictionary user. The truth of this is demonstrated by the remarkable success of the *Concise Scots Dictionary*, which revealed a hitherto undreamt-of potential market for dictionaries of Scots among the general reading public: most of whom will have little interest in the intricacies of historical philology. As Jack Aitken himself once wrote of DOST:

> I believe we are more given than most dictionaries to separating as distinct entries phonemic variants or heteromorphs . . . in which Older Scots happens to have been extremely prolific. But we have no rigid rule about this and each case is handled on its own merits.
>
> (1973a: 5)

Where recent editions of OSc texts have supplanted ones used by Craigie, we have quoted from the newer editions. Examples of this are Barbour's *Brus*, where we now prefer the Stevenson and McDiarmid edition to that of Skeat, and the poems of Dunbar and Henryson, which we now quote from the O.U.P. editions by Kinsley and Fox respectively. Similarly, we have added quotations from texts which have only recently become available: e.g. William Lamb's *Ane Resonyng of ane Scottis and Inglis merchand betwix Rowand and Lionis* (LAMB *Resonyng*). Our hope is that these innovations will make this article more interesting and useful for the reader, over and above the complimentary purpose for which it is intended. Forms of reference, abbreviations, etc. have also been revised in many cases since Volume Two was published.

Two important points remain to be made: the second following naturally from the first. In recent years the various procedures followed in editing, and in checking edited copy for accuracy, have been modified to promote speed in processing material, precision in checking and cooperation at all levels in the preparation of copy. At one time it was possible for edited copy to be filed away in a drawer for several years, while material, imprisoned by the cumbrous inheritance of 'sending-on', was released a batch at a time. Now 'sending-on' forms a part of the editing process, with the result that edited copy, after being laid aside for some six months, can be revised and updated with the addition of minimal fresh material. The resulting copy is produced by the original editor when the shape of his original article is still relatively fresh in his mind. This copy is 'reviewed' by another editor, whose comments and suggestions are checked and, if necessary, implemented by the original editor.

In the next stage, the press-preparer examines each quotation to see how accurately or otherwise it has been copied onto the dictionary slip, and checks such features as the form of reference, page- and/or line-number and date. Spelling-forms or 'variants' are checked in two directions: those in the headword list being checked against those in the article, and vice versa. A further check ensures that the ordering of variants in the headword section is followed in the paragraphing of the article. The chronological order of the quotations is also checked at this stage.

Later stages include the keying of copy onto disk, the keying-in of editorial alterations, the checking of print-out, etc., but we have probably said enough to indicate that the potential for error has been greatly reduced since Craigie's day. In the event, the present re-editing revealed numerous inaccuracies in the line-numbering, page-numbering and dates of the earlier (Volume Two) articles. Forms given in the headword sections were missing from the articles. Quotations given in excessively truncated form (in the interests of saving space) often turned out, once the contexts had been checked, to have been assigned to the wrong senses. These and other errors have been silently corrected, as a comparison with the earlier volume will show.

These comments are not intended as an attack on Craigie, whose achievement, performed with little outside help, remains an impressive one. What they do reflect are the advantages following upon the formation of the Scottish Dictionaries Joint Council (now the Joint Council for the Dictionary of the Older Scottish Tongue), and assured financial assistance from the Scottish universities. This made possible a larger and more settled editorial staff who were able to develop expertise in lexicography, and to bring a variety of minds to bear on every aspect of the work of editing a historical dictionary. More hands and more time were essential ingredients of the post-Craigie method of editing DOST which has evolved over the last 25 years, for most of which Jack Aitken was editor. The expertise will we hope continue, and even develop. What cannot be replaced is the wealth of Jack's knowledge of all aspects of Scots life and language in the period under study — so intimate that at times we felt as if we had a resident Middle Scot on the staff.

One of the main features of our present method — as should be obvious by now — is the stress laid on teamwork. We have moved away from the authoritarian figure of the omniscient editor with his staff of subordinates towards a more flexible system in which, as colleagues and fellow-professionals, we work together to do our collective best for the Dictionary. It is in this spirit of friendship and teamwork that we dedicate this article to Jack Aitken, our colleague and friend.

NOTE

1   The DOST team presently consists of: Marace Dareau (editor), Eileen Finlayson, Marjorie McNeill, Lorna Pike (editorial assistants), Harry Watson (editor). Dr J A C Stevenson (editor, now retired), also contributed to this article.

Gif, Gef, Give, Geve, *v.* Also: **gife, giff(e, gyf(e, gyff; gefe, geff, geif(f, geyf(f; giw(e, gyve, gywe; gewe, geiv(e, geiwe; (geiffyn).** P.t. **gaf, gave, gaif; gef, geve,** etc., also **geawe** and **ga.** P.p. **gif(f)-, gyf(f)in, giv-, gyvin(e,** etc. [ME *gif(e, giff(e, gyfe, gyffe, geve,* etc., earlier *gifa(n, gefa(n, give(n,* etc., ME and e.m.E. *give* (Cursor M.), *gyve* (Manning), *give* (1485), etc., OE *giefan (geaf, géafon, giefen),* ON *gefa.*] To give, in various senses. Cf. also DOUNGEVING *vbl. n.,* FORGEVE *v.,* FURTHGIF *v.,* GAIN-GEVYNG *n.,* OURGIVE *v.,* OURGIVING *vbl. n.,* OUTGIF *v.* and OUTGIV(E)ING *vbl. n.*

I. 1. *tr.* To give, without obligation, as a gift; to grant, donate. Also, *specif.,* to give alms.

(1) *pres.* Aske me quhat thu wil. . . Gyf me Iohn the baptist hed in desch; *Leg. S.* xxxvi 519. Quhat-euir it wes thu thocht In weding fore to gif to me To gyfe to poure men I leife thé; *Ib.* xliv 69, 70. Tyll hyme [*sc.* a king] fallis mekle thinge That may nocht les his stat to gyfe; *Ratis R.* 1022. Of quhilk gudis He gyfis habundaunce to wys men; *Hay II 79/37.* Kepe thame fra giftis to gif or craff; *Gud Wyf & D.* 111. We sall be bundyn . . Sum part off gold to gyff you; *Wall.* VIII 899. Sum giffis [*O.U.P.* gevis] money, sum giffis meit; DUNB. *Maitl. F.* 290/12.

(*b*) Syluir and gold he gert on to him geyff; *Wall.* I 447. I sal 3ou geiffyn ilk man as efferis; DOUG. v vi 39.

(*c*) To the quhilkis [*sc.* kings, etc.] to geve grete giftis is thing tynt; *Hay I 300/32.* Quhasumeuer sall geve moneyis to ony sojer, or chift the billet vpone ane nichtbour; 1648 *Peebles B. Rec.* I 383.

p.t. The endentur till him gaf he; BARB. I 565. Syk hansell to that folk gaiff he; *Ib.* V 120. Aneothir chesybill he gave alsua; WYNT. IX 598. To a man . . that gafe the king a hors; 1448 *Treas. Acc.* I 93. Thare he gafe grete giftis . . to thame; *Hay II 93/28.*

(*b*) Thare sik hansell gaue he me That I am takin; *Alex.* II 4668. The byschape . . gave twa lang coddis off welwete; WYNT. IX 591. Barrell heryng and wattir thai him gawe; *Wall.* II 171. Ane garmond he me gaue; DOUG. VIII iii 167.

p.p. Tyl hafe granttyt and gyfin tyl the aldirmen . . of Elgyne . . al the wol [etc.]; *Chart. T. Dunbar.* The defesance . . sal be qwit of it selfe and be giffin to thame freli; 1399 *Holyrood Chart.* 113. As ony pensioun or annuale is giffyn grantit or confermyt; 1431 *Reg. Great S.* 45/2. To haif . . gifin and grantit . . my haill insycht [etc.]; 1589 *Coll. Aberd. & B.* 355. Four eir ringis . . gifin . . to my Lady Haringtouns vemen; 1603 *Montgomery Mem.* 248.

(*b*) Dauid Kyng . . of Scotland . . has gyvin to the religious men the Abbot and the Conuent of Meuros . . all the custume of all thair wollys; 1389 *Facs. Nat. MSS* II xlvii.

(*c*) Gyf a knycht . . had gevyn a coursour to the provost of Paris unaskit; *Hay I 139/18.* A gowne . . gevin to the hereald of Inglande; 1474 *Treas. Acc.* I 27. Geving; 1542 *Reg. Cupar A.* II 19.

(*d*) Haf I nocht ryches gewine thé? *Leg. S.* xxxiv 255. That [pension] thay haif gewin her fyve yeiris; 1606 *Peebles Gleanings*

25. He reserwit . . the dowarreis gewing for the mareage of the eldest sonis; *Chron. Kings* 51.
(*e*) A sartan som . . qwylk he had geyfyng hym . . to kyp; 1456 *Peebles B. Rec.* I 118.
(*f*) Gyf that to Salyus the fyrst reward beys geyf; DOUG. v vi 106.
(2) That kynge . . Gef almus to thame; *Leg. S.* v 654. Thu . . nocht gyffis thaim of thi gud; *Ib.* xvi 315. Tendys or monay That wes gywyn in offerande; WYNT. v 1797. I . . gyffis and grayntis in pure and perpetuale almus . . fourty punde of annuale rent 3erly; 1429 *Reg. Episc. Brechin.* I 42. It that ladyis wynnis vnlefully . . thai may lefully geve in almous; IRLAND *Asl. MS* 34/3. The almes . . sall be gevin to honest decait personis and not to commond beggaris; 1574 *Aberd. Eccl. Rec.* 19.

b. To transfer (property, lands, etc.) to the possession of another; also, to transfer the possession of lands, etc. to another.

Freq., *to grant and gif*, and *to gif charter and possessioun* (see CHARTER *n.* 1 b and POSSESSIO(U)N(E *n.* 1 d).

(1) *pres.* Gyff; 1404 *Maxwell Mem.* I 146 (see ANALY *v.*). It is lachfull . . till ilke burges to geyff or sell his lande; *Acts* I 24/2. The forsayd Alan sall geff . . fourty marcis worth of land; 1438 *Montgomery Mem.* 29. George Dowglace . . gewis and infeftis till ws the saidis landis; 1509 *Douglas Chart.* 189. Gefand to thame xl merkis worth of land; 1515 *Reg. Privy S.* I 407/1. To the qwhilk lorde I geiwe and leiffis all the landis that I possessit; 1525 *Misc. Bann. C.* III 107.

p.t. He gaf all Cummerland till his apperand aire; *Asl. MS* I 256/12.

p.p. Quhen he herd . . at his landis . . War gevyn to the Clyffurd; BARB. I 317. Thre housis that gewine ware To vphauld Sancte Laurens altere; *Leg. S.* xxii 633. The forsaid wode sall neuir be giffin na sald; 1388 *Antiq. Aberd. & B.* III 294. The land grantit and gewin to him; c1400 *Newbattle Chart.* (Reg. H.). Me tyl haf gyffin and granttyt . . tyl Alexander of Ochterlowny . . the landis of Grenforde; 1402 *Reg. Panmure* II 184. Gifyn; 1412 *Melville Chart.* 18. Gyffyng; 1456 *Liber Aberbr.* II 89. Gifen; 1485 *Antiq. Aberd. & B.* III 32. The ix penneland of Saba is sa fre gyffin and cheyngytt . . to the said Jhone Irwyngis fadyr and mother that [etc.]; 1509 *Rec. Earld. Orkney* 82. [To] suffir . . al Lyby land Be geif in dowry to thi son; DOUG. iv iii 28. Tuay acris of outfeild land . . to be gevin to our forester; 1550 *Reg. Cupar A.* II 73.

(2) The sayde erll haffis gyffyn . . sesyng and possessioune; 1392 *Lennox Mun.* 45. At 3e ger be geffin . . sesyng to the said Herbert; 1421 *Montgomery Mem.* 23. To the quhilk [lands] I the forsaid Johne has gefin heritable possession to . . myn eme; 1440 *Cart. S. Nich. Aberd.* I 11. The forsaid bal3ae . . hes gewin . . possession of the sayd 3ard; 1531 *Prot. Bk. M. Fleming* 13b. Ane of the baillies . . to give ane actuall possessioun to the said David W. . . be delyverance of ane penny and the knok of the foiryet of the said

Sanct-Thomas-land; 1587 (1600) *Reg. Great S.* 360/2.

c. To confer a right or privilege, or entrust a duty (*to* another); to give power or authority, freq. *to do* something.

(1) The patronage of the said kyrke . . to be gyffin at his lyking; 1405 *Maxwell Mem.* I 145. That I . . has sawld and gyffyne tyll a nobyle man . . all the richt and the clame that I haf; 1420 *Antiq. Aberd. & B.* IV 384. The forsaid lord has . . giffin to the forsaid Michel, the keping of hys Castell of Louchmabane; 1420 (1430) *Reg. Great S.* 30/1. That the forsaid seruice sal be gyfyn to the mast abyl chaplan [*supra* The seruice of Sant James alter . . the qwhylk alter had nocht seruice to wphald a chaplan]; 1476 *Peebles B. Rec.* I 181. The baillerie gewis sufficient authoritie of the apprehensioun of ony suspect of pykerie; 1598 *Crim. Trials* II 43.

(2) He . . gawe hym large and full powere To do that lykand tyll hym were; WYNT. II 377. Giffande and grantande to . . Schir Robert . . oure ful and playne poware . . al oure said landis to sett [*pr.* sets], oure malis to raisse [etc.]; 1439 *Edinb. Chart.* 64. 1508 *Reg. Privy S.* I 233/2. St. Paull ordinat Timothe and Tite geueand thame pouer and command to ordour wthiris; WIN3ET I 99/13. Gewand . . hir full power to hym to intromit and dispone thairupone; 1578 *Prot. Bk. J. Scott* 55. The saidis commissioneris . . gewis powir and commissioun to the saidis brughis [etc.]; 1601 *Conv. Burghs* II 109.

d. To give a material symbol or token of a non-material award, honour or privilege.

The crowne wes gyvyn for wyctory In auld tyme; WYNT. IV Prol. 13. O Prince, think quhi thi crown was giffin thé til; *Regim. Princ.* 43 (Marchm.). Thou the ceptour gevis me in hand Of all this realme; DOUG. I ii 44. The armys that 3e bair in 3our scheildis and in 3our seylis [etc.] . . var gyuyn to 3our predecessours . . for ane takyn of nobilnes; *Compl.* 148/4.

e. *absol.*

Til [= while] men . . has fre will To gyfe, or to hald thame still; *Leg. S.* vi 360. To . . hald it as heretage, . . nocht gevand na restorand agayn; HAY II 31/16. He that gevis atour his power . . heryis himself; *Ib.* 81/30. The first is . . that thow geve blythlye and frely; IRLAND *Asl. MS* 33/13. Ane fule . . Cryis ay, Gif me, in to a drene; DUNB. (O.U.P.) 206/7. Sum gevis to thame can flattir and fen3ie; *Ib.* 209/42.

2. To bequeath.

Alexander Iruyne . . gaff, grantit, and assignit . . to Dauid Iruyne . . ale and hale his gudis; 1493 *Antiq. Aberd. & B.* III 301. To the quhilk lorde I geiwe and leiffis . . my schipe callit the Carvell; 1506 *Orkney & Shetl. Rec.* 248, etc. Gyf it wer ane saltwat or sic other thynge as his wyf had ado with, to gewe to hir; 1565 *Hist. Carnegies* 51. He desyrit that he swld gewe the lands of Etthie to his sonne; *Ib.* The rest of my haill geir I gyff to the lard of Calder; 1585 *Thanes of Cawdor* 187. Tua coilhors quhairof one blind givine to the coilman; 1644 *Edinb. Test.* LXI 2.

3. Of God or Christ: To confer (a gift, privilege, mark of favour or disfavour, etc.) on (*to*) a person.

To thé I gyff the keys of hewyne; *Leg. S.* i 16. To borne-blynd thu giffis sycht; *Ib.* xi 26. *Ib.* xxvii 1358, etc. God gif to thé ane blissed chance; DUNB. (O.U.P.) 69/5. God giff thé ane ewil deid; GAU 13/10. Lord, giff me faith; *Ib.* 76/7. That heuinlye Muse . . The quhilk gaif sapience to King Salomone; LYND. *Mon.* 249. 1560 *Acts* II 527/1. The keyis of heuin will I gif vnto thé; *G. Ball.* 7. God gife thé grace aganis this gude new 3eir; SCOTT i 56.

b. To impart (to someone) the means *to do* something. Also const. *how* and noun clause.

(1) He thame gafe Playne powar our the laffe To bynd and lois . . Al syne; *Leg. S.* Prol. 134. God off swete will gyve hym gras To govern . . his land; WYNT. IX 1118. He sais God gewys to the wysman wyt & visdome to gouerne hyme weill in this warld; *Wisd. Sol.* (S.T.S.) 158. IRLAND *Asl. MS* 66/25. The quhilk [*sc.* God] hes geuin ws lybertie Tyll eait of euery fruct [etc.]; LYND. *Mon.* 913.

(2) He [*sc.* Christ] . . gevand doctrine and exampill to princis [etc.] . . how . . thai suld gouerne thame; IRLAND *Mir.* I 6/10.

c. In the interjection *God gif,* God grant that, would that.

Now God gyff grace that I may swa Tret it; BARB. I 34. All Karrik cryis, 'God gif this dowsy be drownd'; DUNB. *Flyt.* 158. God gif 3e war Johne Thomsounis man; *Ib.* (O.U.P.) 96/4. God gif I wer wedo now; *Maitl. F.* 244/8.

d. *passive.* Granted or imposed directly or indirectly through God's agency.

To bind and lous . . Plane poware is gewin thé thare-till; *Leg. S.* i 18. We . . cummys . . For to preche Goddis word As is gefyne vs in til hurd; *Ib.* xv 76. I am content to rassayff the mast wylld deid that may be geyn me; 1544 *Bk. Carlaverock* II 29. Quhow the Jowis by the solenniteis of thai dayis gefin tham afore in the Scriptur, institute [etc.]; WIN3ET I 28/30. Sancts . . to quhome is gewine . . to liwe maist familiar withe Christ; KING *Cat.* 33.

e. With Nature or Fortune as subject.

Nature . . for3et to gyf thame faith or lawte; MYLL *Spect.* 276/24. The dyuers falls that Fortune geuis to men; JAMES VI *Ess.* 42.

II. 4. To hand over, deliver (an object) (*to* another).

I wil that thu Drinke the venome I sal thé gyfe; *Leg. S.* v 329. Quhat amowis thé The kyrtil fore to gyf to me; *Ib.* 362. All forfautis excedand viij s. . . . salbe geyffin to this gylde; *Acts* I 90*/2. He beand redy to geve the sacrament, thai strike on him; HAY I 202/30. Sum me the cop giffis; DUNB. *Tua Mar. W.* 484. Alisoune . . sal mak & gefe to the said Dauid . . ane sufficient lettir of bail3ery; 1519 *Fife Sheriff Ct.* 147. To ane boy send . . to gif thame billis desyring thame to cum fordwart; 1548 *Treas. Acc.* IX

181. Richart Myllar . . requiryt Jhone Ondirwod officer geyf he gayf the copy of . . [the] byll to Adame Myllar; 1562 *Prestwick B. Rec.* 66. Quhen cautioun is found thair is no warrand thairof gevin to the pairtie arreistar bot onlie a tikkett; 1617 *Acts* IV 547/1. [He] gave the elements [*sc.* of Communion] with his awin hand to al the people; 1619 *Fife Synod* 89. Not to gife them [*sc.* the moneys] til the treaty be ueale aduanced; 1650 *Blairs P.* 27.

5. To furnish or supply what is needful or appropriate (also, *to do* something).

For *to gif* (*the*) *maist penny*, see PENNY *n.* 3 b.

(1) Martha . . gafe til thame al that afferyt; *Leg. S.* xvi 78. He bande [his beasts] wp and gaff thaim haye; WYNT. IV 2687 (C). This wolf . . gevand thame souke with hir pappis; BELL. *Livy* I 18/12. Withoute respect tyll ony wycht, Suld kyngs geue euery man thare rycht; LAUDER *Off. Kings* 18. The haill profeit . . to be geivine to the marriage of hir said twa dochteris; 1562 *Will A. Betoun* 226. Quha giffis thame seruice to pay xl s. as unlay; 1581 *St. A. Baxter Bks.* 29. Sho gifs hir horse both brydle, chak and vand; J. STEWART 17/87. To gif . . to the bankets ky, oxin, scheip [etc.]; 1594 *Conv. Burghs* I 430. Equitie in things arbitrall giuis euerie ane that quhilke is meittest for him; JAMES VI *Basil. Doron* 148/4. Gif the millar beis not abill to gif tham sufficient service they to be free of anie multeris or knevschip; 1633 *Misc. Spald. C.* V 220. [The fuel] salbe . . giwin into the said bairnes chalmerer into the colledge; 1637 *Ib.* 226. To geive the ministers thair denner at Mr. Patrik Gillespies entrie; 1648 *Glasgow B. Rec.* II 128.

(2) To gywe hyr wemen tow to spyn; WYNT. V 5049. To geve yow corage for to do in sik maner [etc.]; HAY I 3/34. Giffin to Rolland Robysone to ryde to the Bordour xl s.; 1496 *Treas. Acc.* 281. The feyndis gaif thame hait leid to laip; DUNB. (O.U.P.) 153/101. The quenes majestie hes send for sum baggage to be gewyn to the kyng; *c*1567 *Melville Corr.* 232. That same flesche hie geawe ws to eatte; 1580 HAY in *Cath. Tr.* (S.T.S.) 68/35. Luif ȝoung is paintit lyk ane prettie boy . . Thay [*sc.* painters] giwe him vings hich vith the vind to brall; J. STEWART 156/11.

b. To confer or impose (a name) on (*to, till*) a person.

For thi that name wes gevyn hym tille; WYNT. V 1418. The name thairof beand gevin to him in write; 1486 *Bk. Carlaverock* II 447.

c. To attribute (to a thing) a certain identity, quality or value; to realise or interpret (one thing in terms of another).

We geve it [*sc.* the letter A] alwaies ane sound, beath befoer and behind the consonant; HUME *Orthog.* 8.

6. To give a pledge; to hand over or surrender (something of value) *in plege of* (debts, etc.).

See also PLEG(E *n.* for further examples.

(1) Personis . . quhilkis wil be bund to . . gif sufficient plegis and

band thairupoun; 1516-17 *Reg. Privy S.* I 449/1.

(2) Ane meyr of myne quhilk I gef hyme in plege of xxx s.; 1558 *Inverness Rec.* I 21.

7. To hand over, to entrust (a person or persons) *to* (*till*) another, for a specific purpose. Also, const. *infin.*

E.g. a woman, in marriage; children, in tutelage; soldiers, for waging war, etc.

(1) Men and armys till him gaff he; BARB. II 164. I trow that lang quhile na lady Wes gevyn till hous sa richely; *Ib.* XX 102. Thire two sonnes . . War gevin in tutory . . To King Teuteus; *Troy-bk.* II 1624. To hym a servand woman . . Was geyf; DOUG. V v 74. Ane greit armie King Robert . . In gyding syne to James of Douglas gawe; STEWART 50515. Kyng Henry . . gaif Joanna his sistir to Kyng Alexander our kyng in mariage; LAMB *Resonyng* 107/8. *Ib.* 121/5. [To] execut his office . . to the comfort of the floke gewin in his cwir; 1570 *Reg. Episc. Brechin.* II 307. The brichtest thing . . That euer creat bein The lustiest & leill The gayest and best gein; ARBUTHNOT *Maitl. Q.* 87/20.

(2) His dowchtyr . . He gave hym . . to be hys wywe; WYNT. III 529. Geuand the saulis . . To blynd pastouris . . to keip; LYND. *Trag. Card.* 349. That God . . had geuin the king and the preiste to be despysit; WINƷET I 31/14. Being a poore fellow and gevin be the landislordis to be a threscher in a barne; 1613 *Denmylne MSS* in *Highland P.* III 134.

III. 8. To pay (money, etc.) in settlement of a due or obligation, for services rendered, or as a tax, tribute, fine, reimbursement, etc.

pres. (*a*) [Their cottars] sal gif (L. *prestabunt*) [the sixteenth] fat (L. *vas*) [of every] kynd o [grain growing on the said land]; *a*1350 *Facs. Nat. MSS* II xix. And anyd for hys rawnssownyng For to gyff . . hym tylle Schyppys and wyttaylle; WYNT. III 525. *Acts* I 369/2. For the quhilk he sall gyf the belman twa d.; 1469 *Ayr Friars Pr. Chart.* 52. The personis abonewritin . . gifis and disponis to . . Colyne and his airis thair calpis; 1549-50 *Breadalbane Doc.* No. 71. Ane free man . . sall gif . . of tuentie bolles ane firlot (as knawship); SKENE *Reg. Maj.* II 3. My cowsine . . sal be ready to . . gif them pay; 1642 *Fam. Rose* 330.

(*b*) Clerkys . . litill had to gyve . . The great prelatys . . war better bodyn to pay; WYNT. VII 2690. To gife and to pay . . a hundreth pundis of vswale money of Scotland; 1456 *Reg. Dunferm.* 340. Tha sal gyfe to ws . . sex bollis of quhet; 1473 *Reg. Cupar A.* I 172. This angle noble . . Vnto your lordschip I will gife To cause you to renew my tackis; 1584 SEMPILL *Sat. P.* xlv 450.

(*c*) Quha-sa-euir gef hir maste Suld haf his wil of hir . . as men that chafere sellis . . , quha-sa wald mast hir gefe [etc.]; *Leg. S.* xxxiv 49. That . . men of kirk gevis tributis . . of thair gudis to the king; HAY I 237/9. Gef; 1482 *Bamff Chart.* 32. Quhair ƷE can spye ane man to geue Ʒow mair [*sc.* rent], Ʒe schute thame furth;

LAUDER *Minor P.* i 530. Thow promesit that all suld be weill, gewand thé hir draff for peyment; 1597 *Misc. Spald. C.* I 91. They haif na power to geve the teyndis thairof; 1608 *Peebles Gleanings* 31.

(*d*) He sal geyf viii s.; *Acts* I 28/2. Geifand a penny . . in name of blanch ferm; 1500 *Buccleuch Mun.* II 102.

p.t. That brede He gawe the batwartis hym to lede; WYNT. VI 1992. The golde that he . . geff for the charteris; 1438 *Misc. Spald. C.* V 392. The balye gaf v s. to James Gybson for the hos bycgyn; 1457 *Peebles B. Rec.* I 123. John Beyn grantit . . that he gef ane arill penne to Androu Mylln; 1546 *Elgin Rec.* I 88.

p.p. Al thar gudis suld be . . gefine as eschete; *Leg. S.* xxxviii 11. The balyais . . has gewyn of the myller of the som of his x lib. befor wrytyn ij markis; 1457 *Peebles B. Rec.* I 123. Geyfyng; *Ib.* The saidis Roberte and Jonet . . has geffynne and grantit . . [24s. 4d.] of anwell rente of thar land; 1485 *Liber Coll. Glasg.* 195. Giffin . . to the masonis at Mowtrayis toure . . ix s.; 1501 *Treas. Acc.* II 103. William . . desyrit bakwart of the said sovme mair nor he aucht till haif geving; 1556 *Peebles B. Rec.* I 236. Geiffin for conwoyinge of the pressoneris to Blaknes, xlix l.; 1567-8 *Bk. Old Edinb. C.* VI 83. Gyffen at command of the beal3ies to the peyper; 1588-9 *Dundee Treas. Acc.* In land mail of 1 fdg. terrae . . gewen in excambion to Magnus Loutit; 1595 *Orkney Rentals* II 44. Giuein; 1602 *Elphinstone Chart.* 165. Gewine to Pattrik Pattersone for the depursmentis he hade depursit in Selkirk . . vj li. xiiij s.; 1623-4 *Peebles B. Rec.* I 412. Wald 3e not have gewin hir ane amends of me? 1626 *Kinghorn Kirk S.* 30.

9. To give up, relinquish, surrender.

I . . giffis bot a lytil wra, A vyd merkat thare-for I ta; *Leg. S.* xliii 495. Gif he will nocht gif the ox that he tuk to hyr bot haldis him the space of the moneth the borows ar haldyn at the terme forsaid; *Acts* I 386/2.

10. To *gif sute and presence*, to attend court as a feudal obligation.

For further examples see PRESENCE *n.* 1.

All [of them] amerciat for not giffin suite and presence to this Heid Court; 1597 *Misc. Spald. C.* II 135.

IV. 11. a. *reflex.* To dedicate (oneself) *to* some end. **b.** *passive.* (*To be*) *gifin to* (a cause, goal, etc.), to be dedicated to, given over to. **c.** With following infin.: To be dedicated to doing something. **d.** *To be gifin fra* (something), to be debarred or excluded from.

Cf. EVILL-GEVIN *adj.*

a. Thow suld . . thé fra lustys to wertu gywe; WYNT. IV 1928. I gif me to the feynd all fre; DUNB. (O.U.P.) 167/28. Quha will nocht haill to Christ him giue; *G. Ball.* 31.

b. Fra the tyme of his 3outhede That he to God al gevine vas; *Leg. S.* xviii 31. A man all gyvyne to wykkytnes; WYNT. V 5704.

Thay ar gevin sa plenly to oppressioun; HENR. *Prayer* 60. 3oure playis . . to quhais sicht sal the pepill be maist ernistfully gevin; BELL. *Livy* I 193/3. Albeit it chance . . that he . . be gevin to pastyme; WIN3ET I 6/14. All haill thair hartis to covatice ar gewin; MAITLAND *Maitl. F.* 312/5.

(*b*) Partlie for gean [= gain] wharto he was gein; MELVILL 117.

c. I should more largely notefie it now How much t'augment thy greatnes I am ge'ine; GARDEN *Garden* 5.

d. Men . . That war fra delitis gevyne, Scho couth restore agane in deid; *Troy-bk.* I 450.

V. 12. To seek physical contact with, or use physical force against (another); to manipulate (a thing) vigorously. **a.** To deal a blow or blows (etc.); to inflict a weal by means of a blow. Also *absol.*

To give (someone) *his paikis,* see PAIKIS *n. pl.*

Thai . . with axys sic duschys gave That [etc.]; BARB. XIII 147. To Schyr Colyne sic dusche he gewe [*C.* gave]; *Ib.* XVI 130. Gyfand hyme mony dintis sare; *Leg. S.* xxvi 692. Quyncyane [Bad] gef hire buffetis; *Ib.* xlii 122. The enforce of Grece he saw Geuand and takand mony rout; *Alex.* I 2455. He gaue ane braid with his brand to the beirne by; *Rauf C.* 858. For twa blais giffin to Androw Flemingis wyfe; 1602 *Shetland Sheriff Ct.* 16. For dinging and striking Issobell Thomson . . in the armes and heid, thairby geweing hir many bla strakis in both the armes; 1642 *Aberd. B. Rec.* III 292. The saids serjants . . gave him many . . sever stroaks with great keans; 1686 *Reg. Privy C.* 3 Ser. XIII 88.

absol. With the swerd awkwart he him gawe Wndyr the hat; *Wall.* I 407. I sall do ane cursit deid, and gif you with ane quhynger; 1536 *Antiq. Aberd. & B.* III 402.

b. To direct gunfire at (someone).

Sum of the luiftenant's men . . did geive them a woille of shoat; 1615 *Denmylne MSS* in *Highland P.* III 185.

c. *To gif battall,* or (*a*) *felde,* to offer to fight ((*to*) someone) in battle.

Mod[rat] . . gaif a feild till his vnkle; MYLL *Spect.* 294/4. As he to geif batale all redy war; DOUG. IX ii 44. The feild quhare was the batell gevin; *Boece* 72. Ay da be da [*pr.* ba] puttand thame in beleue To gif battell; STEWART 6623.

d. Of horsemen: *To gif a charge* (*upon* someone), to make a mounted attack upon.

Thair was gevin upone thame ane charge be sum horsmen; KNOX II 59.

e. To inflict, mete out (a military defeat).

For *to gif* (someone) *pay,* to mete out punishment, see PAY *n.* 1.

The day after the defait was gevin thame be me lord of Mortone; BANN. *Memor.* 138.

f. *To gif deforcement* (*to*), to offer violence to, or otherwise hinder (an official), with the intention of diverting from duty.

It is statute . . that non . . giffe deforcement neither to the barroun officer nor bourlawmen; 1665 *Stitchill Baron Ct.* 35.

g. *To gif* (ingredients) *a play* (in a pan), see PLAY *n.* 1 c.

13. *To gif* (someone) *a kiss.*

Athir of the saide parteis has takyn and gewyn wtherlie the kys of pece; 1476 *Thanes of Cawdor* 61. My gentill jo, gif me a kis; *Bann. MS* 264b/52.

14. To show, display, present to the view or for inspection.

a. *To gif a sign*, to make a sign or gesture.

Zeno . . for to gif more proofe of it this sing . . did giwe, Was opning wpp his hand and palme and falding than his niwe; FOWLER I 117/137. That he gif thame ane sing to cum fordwart, quhilk was be haldin vp of his nepkyn vpoun his wand end; 1609 *Crim. Trials* III 46.

b. *To gif the* (*thair*) *bak* (*bakkis*), to turn one's back (to the enemy). See BAK *n.*[1] 3.

c. *To geve* (*one's*) (*the*) *muster*(*is*, to present oneself, or troops under one's command. See MUSTER *n.* 1 b (2).

d. Of an apprentice: To submit (a test piece) for assessment.

The samyn prenteis . . gevand his assay quhen it pleissis him; 1573 *Bk. Old Edinb. C.* VI 60.

e. To display in ordered sequence; to list.

My bukes als thay ar gevin in roll in the cathalog; 1584 *Edinb. Test.* XIV 70b.

f. In a more abstract sense: To set (an example) (*to*) (*til*) others).

Til gyf ensampil vthyre til; *Leg. S.* xxxvii 149. To geve otheris ensample in tyme tocum, he suld be punyst; HAY I 87/35. [Christ] gevand doctrine and exampill to princis [etc.]; IRLAND *Mir.* I 6/10.

15. To issue or deliver a writ or other legal document.

Quytclaimis to giw and generally all and sundry wthair thingis to do in the redeiming of my forsaid landis; 1474 *Antiq. Aberd. & B.* III 528. It salbe leissum to onie uther notary to gef writ tharupon; 1594 *Paisley B. Rec.* 160.

b. *passive.* In legal documents: Put for L. *datum* given, i.e., issued.

Dowyn and gyffyn the yer and the day . . befor nemmyt; 1394 *Liber Aberbr.* II 43. Gefyn wnder our signet at Pertht the sewynt day of July; 1460 *Ayr Chart.* 35. Gevin vnder oure priue seile at . . Edinburgh; 1507 *Edinb. Chart.* 192.

c. To intimate or proclaim (information).

See also KNAWLAG(E *n.* 4 b (1) for further examples.

Providit allwais that the said Edward . . sall gif knaulege of his plesur and electione . . in takin or refusin of the said mariage; 1482 *Edinb. Chart.* 147. Acteon . . in . . ane hart translatit . . Backwert he blent to giue thame [*sc.* his hounds] knawledgeing; DOUG. *Pal. Hon.* 326. That ane declaratour be gevin be my Lord Governour . . thairupoun; 1550 *Reg. Privy C.* I 103. This day beand assignit to him to eik to his former defences gevein in against the libell of removing [etc.]; 1606 *Melrose Reg. Rec.* I 17. Notaris sall gif na testymonie of the merchandice coft; BISSET II 230/10. The day befor the expayering of the 8 gevene in your majesties last proclamatione; 1639 *Hamilton P.* (Camden Soc.) 80. He . . sall giw noties to the cuntrie people; 1653 *Aberd. Sheriff Ct.* III 61.

d. To impart (advice) *to (til, unto)* (another) (also, about *(to)* a subject). Also, *to gif (another)* . . *to counsel.*

(1) He sal gif tham the best counsale that he may; 1454-5 *Edinb. Chart.* 80. Thi consel gef hym tyl; *Bernardus* 201. I giue ȝour counsale to the feynd of hell; LYND. *Answ. Flyting* 43. All thay [that] geuis consultatioun . . salbe haldin pertakeris of this act; 1570 *Sat. P.* xiii 157. They sall giwe wnto thame thair . . upricht counsall; 1623 *Aberd. B. Rec.* II 388.

(2) Tak him . . As I had gevyn thar-to na reid; BARB. II 122.

(3) Deucalyon dyde all hale As Pyrra gawe hym to consalle; WYNT. II 508.

e. To give a reason, proof or opinion.

To gyf a resone for al thingis that God has maid; *Wisd. Sol.* (S.T.S.) 21. Saturne gaue his sentence; HENR. *Test. Cress.* 151. FOWLER I 117/137 (see 14 a above).

f. To give (someone) an order to obey, or a regulation to observe. Also, *to gif (someone) in commanding that* (etc.).

(1) Ane angell . . gawe byddyng ay Pasce to mak apon Sownday; WYNT. V 1511. It is ordanit that na baxtar brek the pais that is giffin or salbe giffin hym the baillies; 1433 *Aberd. B. Rec.* I 390. This exemptioun to endure . . quhil he geyf uther command in the contrare; 1508 *Reg. Privy S.* I 258/2. Giffand . . to our said baillyes . . expres mandament [etc.]; 1559 *Coll. Aberd. & B.* 313. To mak princes iniunctiounis geif; 1573 DAVIDSON *Sat. P.* xlii 833. Gewing him charges to obey; 1584 SEMPILL *Sat. P.* xlv 1066.

(2) The king That thaim had gevyn in commanding . . that [etc.]; BARB. IX 450.

g. To declare or pronounce (judgement, a sentence). Also const. *of* the penalty. Also, *to gif for dome.*

For further examples in this sense see DECRETE *n.*, DOME *n.* 1 b, JUGEMENT *n.* 3 and SENTENCE *n.* 3.

I gif for dome [etc.]; 1410 *Reg. Episc. Brechin.* I 31. Sentens gywyn but fowrme off lawe; WYNT. V 3851. And that I geif for dome; 1478 *Acta Aud.* 66/2. Thai . . geff na dome tharapoun; 1492

Acta Conc. I 250/1. According to sentence . . Geuin and pronouncit than be that awful juge; ROLLAND *Seven S.* 10709.

h. *To gif the (ane, a) ley to*, to accuse (another) of lying (see LEY *n.*[4] 2).

i. To grant permission (*assent, consent, lefe*, etc.). In various collocations, and variously const.

For further examples see ASSENT *n.*, CONSENT *n.*, LEFE *n.*[2], LEVE *n.* and LICENCE *n.*

(1) WYNT. V 1001 (see ASSENT *n.*). Throw his tressoun the king gaif his essent; *Bk. Chess* 905.

(2) Quhy has thu . . gyfine thi consent? *Leg. S.* xxvi 440. The said Erle of Mar hase gifin his . . ful consent that [etc.]; 1405 *Antiq. Aberd. & B.* III 200. Gyff thai wald gyff consent thare-till; WYNT. VI 944. The king . . has giffyn consent thar till; *Wall.* VIII 1136.

(3) The Grekes . . wald scantly gif thaim leve; *Troy-bk.* II 1633. He gawe consent and lewe thare-tille; WYNT. V 710. Quhen he gawe thame lewe to say All that [etc.]; *Ib.* 2935. Schire Johne . . hes gewyn and grantyt . . full leue . . to make a myllyn dam; 1427 *Melville Chart.* 245. Giff of casse I or my ayris . . gevis ony leiffe . . to mak ony drauchtis of the said Magdelan burn; 1466 *Reg. Dunferm.* 356. No tennant . . sall presume to sell any peittes . . without leaw askit and gewen; 1670 *Urie Baron Ct.* 91.

(4) Gevand him licence and benevolence to gif presentatioun . . to the vicarage of Cluny; 1516-17 *Reg. Privy S.* I 451/2. The legence gevin to vnfremen to saill with merchandeise; 1518 *Aberd. B. Rec.* I 94.

(5) Set tyll this I gawe my wylle; WYNT. I Prol. 33.

j. *To gif* (one's) (*bodily*) *athe* (*athis*), to swear an oath or oaths. *To gif* (*bodily, gude*, etc.) *faith*, to make a declaration of good faith or loyalty. *To gif* ((*to*) someone) *manrent*, to swear to be another's 'man' or supporter.

For further examples see ATHE *n.*, FAITH *n.* 4 and OTHE *n.*

(1) Twychande the haly ewangellis, we gaf bodily hathe; 1392 *Lennox Mun.* 49. Ader of the said parteis . . has gyffyn bodely ath; 1432 *Lamont P.* 14. Aythyr has geffyn othyr thair bodyly ath; 1438 *Montgomery Mem.* 30. All the lordis . . gaf bodely aithis to kepe that respit; *Asl. MS* I 240/6. The said Jonat . . geif hir greit aitht; 1556 *Stirling B. Rec.* I 67. The superintendent requirit the sayd Joanna to geyf hyr ayth of calumpne; 1565 *St. A. Kirk S.* 235. John Howstoune . . gef his aith of fidelitie; 1607 *Glasgow B. Rec.* I 270. [The jailer] hes gevin his grit aith of fidelitie thairintill; 1632 *Peebles B. Rec.* I 372.

(2) This fredome to kepe . . aythire of the partis has gewin gude faith; 1427 *Melville Chart.* 245. The sayd lordis hafe gefyn bodyly fayth; 1478 *Lennox Mun.* 116.

(3) To thaim [*sc.* nobles] was gevin hie honour manrent and seruice of thar subiectis; *Porteous Noblenes* 174/4 (Asl.). To geff the forsaid Sir Johne . . our calp, kenkennoll and our manrent

acontrare all man at lewis; 1519 *Thanes of Cawdor* 130.

k. *To gif compt* (*accompt*) (*of* or *in* something), to give an account or explanation.

He . . aw to geve compt to the hiest juge of thair . . mysdedis; HAY I 243/33. Of the quhilk reparation the principal sal geif coumpt 3eirly; BUCH. *Wr.* 7. Anent the service-book and book of canones, wherin our greatest Prelate gewis ane accompt to the B. of Canterburry; 1637 BAILLIE I 429.

VI. 16. To express (something) by verbal means, either orally or in writing; to communicate feelings, opinions, or information, issue orders or judgements, etc.

a. To utter, or give vent to one's feelings by (a cry, groan, etc.).

Al the prestis gef a 3ell; *Leg. S.* vi 659. Ilk baroun and freehaldare that . . geve voce with the said dome is . . in amerciament; 1478 *Acta Aud.* 66/2. The nychtbouris . . sal incontinent geve the cry and tak the sade trespassour; 1498 *Acta Conc.* II 101. Scho gaiue fiue or six lytle groanes; 1619 *Misc. Abbotsf. C.* 83.

b. To address a remark, greeting, etc. to (another).

For *to gif* (*another*) *answer*, see ANSWER *n.*

For *to gif* (*another*) *a meting,* ? to return his greeting, see MET-ING *vbl. n.*[1] 1 c.

A cumpany of the most honest . . geve thair salutationis at hir chalmer wyndo; KNOX II 270. The response whiche his wyffis wyttches had gevin; *Ib.* 357. The haill inquest findis Thomas Dikisoun in the wraing for giffin Rolland Scot . . ingurius wordis; 1567 *Peebles B. Rec.* I 304.

VII. 17. In various phrases denoting attitudes of mind, or behaviour, towards (persons or things). Variously const.

a. *To gif* (*audience, cure, diligence, kepe, laubour*(*s,* etc.).

For further examples see these and other words functioning as the obj. of *gif.*

To his raifand word he gaue na rewaird; *Rauf C.* 650. Pietie . . This Bissines hes sene and gave gud keip; *K. Hart* 363. Quhat honour . . is to a king to . . geve his lauboure and study to wissdome; IRLAND *Mir.* I 8/12. I 3ow beseik to gevin aduertens; DOUG. III Prol. 30. *Ib.* XIII Prol. 124. Caratake . . gaif his cure that his pepill in . . gude maneris suld be instructit; *Boece* 124. Swa thir twa my companionis geif attendance to heir 3ow reasown in the mater; LAMB *Resonyng* 13/18. The Empreour to sic wordis gaue audience; ROLLAND *Seven S.* 1321. Quhen Antichrist wald thé blind That thow suld geue him na eir; *G. Ball.* 159.

b. *To gif* (*credence, faith, trust*) *to* (*till*) (a person or thing).

Thocht na fath to me 3e gefe; *Leg. S.* xxiii 393. Thane thai . . Gaf full credence thar-to; *Troy-bk.* II 1888. I thé besek . . To the berer ye . . gyff credance; *Wall.* VIII 1650. That this lady suld . . gif ferme credens and faithe thar till; IRLAND *Mir.* I 136/4. Papirius . . ga . . na trast to the fals goddis; ABELL 14b. Gif na credens to comune clatteraris; MAITLAND *Maitl. F.* 446/43.

c. *To gif (honour, obedience, respect,* etc.) (*to* a person or thing).

Mare reuerens is gewine always To vekyt men; *Leg. S.* X 72. Na man . . may tak honour away quhare it is anys gevin; HAY II 37/28. Saturne gaue his sentence Quhilk gaue to Cupide litill reuerence; HENR. *Test. Cress.* 152. Reput nocht hym frende quhilk in thi face Gyffis gret lowynge; *Bernardus* 194. Two pur men quhom to I gaif reuerens; *Bk. Chess* 1934. Vnto thy celsitude I gif gloir, honour, laud and reuerence; LYND. *Sat.* 500. To that gret God gyfe pryse and glore; Id. *Mon.* 1869. I grant that I haif faultit sore To stok and stane geuand his glore; *G. Ball.* 61. Give they shall give readie and reall obedience efter they are sentenced; 1640-59 *Mouswald Kirk S.* 1 July.

d. *To gif silence,* to be quiet, to cease talking.

[He] wald giff no silense but rais up . . braiging and minassing the said Alex. Hervie [etc.]; 1616 *Inverurie* 201.

VIII. 18. To bestow a (non-material) benefit or favour, esp. of a charitable nature.

For *to gif licht,* to confer spiritual illumination, see LICHT *n.*[1] 5 d.

The byschapys off Scotland . . Gaw hym mynystratyown Confirmatyown and blyssyn hale; WYNT. VII 1488. The Pape gaf his benesoun and blissit thaim all; *Howlat* 243 (A). Gyf thaim . . quhen thow may sum confortinge; *Consail Wys Man* 362. Sic pardoune as we haiff In oys to gyff; *Wall.* VI 138. At hellis ʒettis he gaf hyme na succour; DUNB. (S.T.S.) lxxxvi 29. War . . grace him gevin als oft for frawd; *Ib.* (O.U.P.) 108/38. To gif the wedow and fatherles confort; 1570 *Sat. P.* X 366. Thei meane not heirby that ony impunitie suld be gevin to sic; 1572 Bann. *Memor.* 239. The lyk dischearge to be gevin be him to the tennentes of that quhiche is deu be theme; 1614 *Denmylne MSS* in *Highland P.* III 168.

19. With non-personal subject.

a. To produce, supply, furnish (a particular effect).

Fredome all solace to man giffis; BARB. I 227. Idilnes giffis novrysingis To vicis; *Leg. S.* Prol. 2. Oyl . . for seknes sere Gaf hop and but; *Ib.* xxvi 579.

b. To emit, give off (sound or light).

Bassynetis burnyst brycht That gave agayne the sone gret lycht; BARB. XI 470. His hippis gaff mony hoddous cry; DUNB. (O.U.P.) 100/18. Venus . . in the mornyng . . Gyffis ane grit lycht; *Compl.* 53/32. On the morn as Phebus gave the light; *Clar.* V 2560.

c. In the phrase *My (his,* etc.) *hart* (once, *curage*) *giffis me* (etc.) *to do* (something), my heart (feelings, emotions) prompt(s) me. Also (once) with impers. construction.

(1) Myne hart giffis me na mar to be With 30w duelland; BARB. XIX 97. Off kynd his hart gaffe hym . . To mak him serwys; WYNT. III 738. My curage has gevin me to mak sum newing [etc.]; HAY I 3/30.

(2) Sen it giuis me in my hart; LYND. *Meldrum* 353.

d. *impers.* To prompt, incite, inspire (someone *to* something).

Quhen I behald . . thi gret bewte . . it gyffis me to gret consolatioun & blythnes in my hart; MYLL *Spect.* 273/5.

e. Of a commodity: To fetch (a certain price). Of a shop: To yield (a certain sum in takings).

(1) The avale and price of the said gold as it gevis in Flanderis; 1480 *Acta Conc.* I 76/1. The avale of the said salmonde as salmonde gevis now in Aberdene; 1485 *Ib.* *109/1. The meill gaif xij shillingis the peck; *Diurn. Occurr.* 306. At this tyme . . the boll of quhyt gave viij markis; PITSC. II 317/7. [At] the dairest pryces that the . . burdis sall happin to gif in this contrey at the tyme; 1582 *Prot. Bk. J. Scott* 138. They could not haue moneyes for any thinge . . for wictuall heir geives noe pryse; *c*1627 *Bk. Carlaverock* II 608.

(2) The westmost . . chope, giffand x s. [a] yeir; 1554 *Edinb. Old Acc.* II 20.

20. To allow, concede, yield (*to* another) (a non-material thing). Also with clause object.

For further examples see CHOSE *n.* and PLACE *n.* 1 b, 12.

[They] . . gaif thaim entre thare in haist; *Troy-bk.* II 3105. A consul . . wald hald him at the portis, and nocht geve him entree; HAY I 60/34. Few of thaim wald geif place to othir; BELL. *Boece* I 96. We dessyirrit them to dail and gif ws wr chois; 1552 *Corr. M. Lorraine* 358. — And, geifand at that same pece land had pertenit to Ingland, suld 30ur kyng haue mouit so haistie crewell weir for ane thing of so sobir valour . . ? LAMB *Resonyng* 47/9.

b. *To gif* (*to* someone) *the credit for* (*of*) (something).

Cf. CREDIT *n.* 1.

Lykeas it pleasit thair worships . . to geue the credit of the selling thairof to the supplicant; 1645 *Aberd. B. Rec.* IV 49.

21. With adv. complement. **a.** *To gif agane*, to return, restore. Also, *to gif back agane*.

(1) Gyfand thaim [*sc.* worldly goods] to hyme gladly agane; *Cr. Deyng* (S.T.S.) 191. Henry . . sal restore, deliuer and gif agane to Johne . . vj nolt; 1474 *Acta Aud.* 31/1. Thomas sal restore and geif again . . the sade sovme; 1482 *Ib.* 101/2. To caus tua servandis of his gif agane certane geir tane fra twa A[l]manis; 1549 *Treas. Acc.* IX 327.

(2) That his mother . . would . . giff back my tikitt agane; 1640 *Red Bk. Grandtully* II 39.

b. *To gif away.*

Sancte George . . his knychtly clething . . gef away; *Leg. S.* xxxiii 386.

c. *To gif doun* (money), ? to pay out; ? to renounce.
I . . leue my said smyddie graith to . . my sone he defalkand &
gevand doun ten merkis of his portioun thairfore; 1584 *Edinb.
Test.* XIV 176b.

d. *To gif furth,* to announce, proclaim, set out.
The said personis sal . . gyfe furth thar delyuerance ande decret
on the morn nyxt after . . Ascensioun Day; 1472 *Lennox Mun.* 92.

e. *To gif in,* to hand over (to some authority) an
official document, esp. a list of names. Also (once) to
report (a person).
For further examples see DITTAY *n.* 1.
(1) Entres of courtis of all termes bigain . . to mak be gevin in;
1484 *Exch. R.* IX 605. That nane of ʒow . . gife in dittay or accuse
the said Adam; 1510 *Reg. Privy S.* I 315/1. Anent the supplicatioun gevin in be Thomas Richartsoun; 1540 *Edinb. Chart.* 210.
Ane rentale gevin in be the Erle of Argile; 1563 *Reg. Cupar A.* II
274. Jonnet Cwnighame gaiff in ane dittay of thift vpon James
Vylʒe & Jonnet Vylʒe; 1574-5 *Prestwick B. Rec.* 74. The persones
mentionat in ane doket gewine in to the dene of gild; 1580 *Dundee
Shipping L.* 198. His former defences gevein in against the libell of
removing; 1606 *Melrose Reg. Rec.* I 17. The articles underwrittin,
proponit and gewin in ʒisternicht to the magistratts of this burghe;
1640 Spalding I 276 n. . . be the collectouris of Abirdene as at the
(2) He is gevin in . . be the collectouris of Abirdene as at the
horne; 1574 *Reg. Privy C.* II 346.

f. *To gif our* (*over*), to resign, give up (an office,
right, etc., lands, etc.); to surrender (a castle, etc.); to
renounce, deny (an allegiance, etc., to reject, with-
draw support or allegiance from (a person). Also
absol. or *intr.*
(1) That . . he . . suld incontinent discharge and gif our the
saide office to the saide Malcolm; 1466 *Acta Aud.* 5/1. Andro
renunsit & gafe oure al tak of the said landis; 1467 *Ib.* 8/1. I . . sal
freli giff oure . . & resigne al richt & clame [etc.]; 1469 *Charter*
(Reg. H.) No. 416. The said Jonet . . had gevin our the samyn
[terce]; 1483 *Acta Conc.* II cxxxiii. As he gef owr the office of
bailʒery; 1489 *Acta Aud.* 121/2. The said Duncane sal gife me oure
the said landis; 1498-9 *Highland P.* II 197. [The] provest . . hes
frelie gevin over . . the bigging that he hes maid; 1516 (c1580)
Edinb. B. Rec. I 159. This lord . . thocht he wald nocht . . gif ower
the admerallschipe; PITSC. I 257/13.
(2) Archebald of Dunbar . . cowardlie gaf it [*sc.* Hailes Castle]
owr to the master of Douglas; *Asl. MS* I 219/9. He cryit and said,
Gif ouir the hous; LYND. *Meldrum* 1110. Down [*sc.* Doune Castle]
was geuin ouir, for feir of weir assay; 1571 *Sat. P.* xxvi 43. I . .
smellit that he wald neuir geiv over that hous to be torterit; 1614
Melrose P. 182.
(3) Ane abbot past and gaif our this liegance; *Wall.* I 77. He . .
Of all sik thingis gaue our the cure and charge; DOUG. VII ix 127.
Thy will obey sall I And giffis owr the caus perpetualy; *Ib.* XII xiii
66. This sall he do . . Or I science and cunning sall gif ouir; ROL-

LAND *Seven S.* 313.

(4) The saidis . . hes ranunsyt, left & gewin our thair cheyff, the lard McGregour; 1552 *Breadalbane Doc.* No. 84.

(5) *absol.* or *intr.* His hors gaiff our and mycht no forthir ga; *Wall.* v 904.

g. *To gif out*, to publish, make known (an official decree); to hand out, distribute (something) *to* persons.

(1) The said deliuerance to be gevin out betuix this and the last day of the Justice Are of Lanark; 1493 *Acta Conc.* I 316/2. Befoir definitive be givin out; 1578 *Conv. Burghs* I 59. Lettiris of captioun [are] gevin out aganis ws; 1625 *Bk. Carlaverock* II 71.

(2) Being hansell Monday I gave my wife to give out to people who expected handsel 4 dollars; 1670-5 LAUDER *Jrnl.* 244.

h. *To gif up*, to resign (a right, etc.); to surrender (a castle, or oneself); to present, hand over (a document, etc.); to report (a person or thing). Also, *to gif up the gaist* (also, (one's) *braith*), to die.

(1) In-till that tretys wp thai gaff . . all the clame that thai mycht haff In-till Scotland; BARB. XX 47. Esaw . . Gawe wpe alle hale hys herytage; WYNT. II 208.

(2) The saide Wilham . . sall frely delyuer and gyf up the Castell of Drumlanryge; 1429 *15th Rep. Hist. MSS* App. VIII 10. A man that gevis him self up cowartly in the handis of his fais; HAY II 81/35.

(3) To summond ane assis to gif up dittay; 1553 *Treas. Acc.* X 199. The testament datiwe . . eiked and giwen wp to Ludovick Grant; 1677 *Grant Chart.* 354.

(4) The schirefys . . sal do thair besines til arreste the personis sua gifyn vp be enquerre or complaynt; 1398 *Acts* I 211/2. Gif ony thing be eschapit my rememberance, that he gif vp the samin; 1584 *Edinb. Test.* XIII 377b. To giwe vp thair names to the session; 1605 *Aberd. Eccl. Rec.* 44. To convene the haill persones . . gevin vpe in roll; 1633 *Peebles B. Rec.* I 372.

(5) He . . geuis vp the gaist; *G. Ball.* 30. His last wordis befoir he gef wp his braitht; 1596-7 *Misc. Spald. C.* I 88.

The original DOST entries follow.

Gef, Geff, *v.* P.t. **gef, geff.** P.p. **geffin, -yn(e, -ynne.** [Var. of *geif,* GEFE *v.* The short vowel is difficult to account for.] *tr.* To give, in various senses.

(a) Quyncyane bad gef hire buffetis; *Leg. S.* xlii. 121. The forsayd Alan sall geff..fourty marcis worth off land; 1438 *Montgomery Mem.* 29. Wrang iugment thow geffys; *Bernardus* 93, Thi consel gef hym tyl; *Ib.* 201. Alexander Ramsay sal gef thame othir twenti markis; 1482 *Bamff Chart.* 32. To geff the forsaid Sir Johne..our manrent; 1519 *Thanes of Cawder* 130. It sall be leisum to ony uther notary to gef writ tharupon; 1594 *Paisley B. Rec.* 160.

(b) That kynge..Gef almus to thame; *Leg. S.* v. 654. Al the prestis gef a ʒell; *Ib.* vi. 659. The golde that he..geff for the charteris; 1438 *Misc. Spald. C.* V. 392. As he gef owr the office of bailʒery; 1489 *Acta Aud.* 121/2. Thai..geff na dome thairapoun; 1492 *Acta Conc.* 250/1. John Beyn grantit..that he gef ane arill penne to Androu Mylln; 1546 *Elgin Rec.* I. 88. [He] geff hir many bauch and bla straiks; 1593 *Edinb. B. Rec.* V. 85. His last wordis, befoir he gef wp his braith; 1596 *Misc. Spald. C.* I. 88. John Howstoun..gef his aith of fidelitie; 1604 *Glasgow B. Rec.* I. 240.

(c) Haf I nocht geffyne thé The space of a nycht; *Leg. S.* iii. 556. At ʒe ger be geffin..sesyng to the said Herbert; 1421 *Montgom. Mem.* 23. Aythyr has geffyn othyr thair bodyly ath; 1438 *Ib.* 30. The saidis Roberte and Jonet..has geffynne and grantit [etc.]; 1485 *Liber Coll. Glasg.* 195. I..the said Charlys..has geffin mye bodele aith herapon; 1545 *Montgom. Mem.* 139. We depone our decret &..ordanis..dwyme [to be] geffin thair apoun; 1564 *Prestwick B. Rec.* 68.

Gef, Geff, *conj.* [Cf. prec. and GEFE *conj.*] If. — Geff it happynnis that the said Sir Wylyam Gybson..decessis; 1478 *Peebles B. Rec.* 183. Gef at it sall happin the yeirly annuell.. to be unpait; 1491 *Ayr Friars Pr. Chart.* 62. Geff hapinnis.. that we ma act to wex, trubill, or unquiet the said reuerend fader; 1506 *Charter* (Reg. H.) No. 93. I wat nocht geff he hes schewin tham in the court or nocht; 1554 *Corr. M. Lorraine* 392. Gef ony victuell beis wat or stolling; 1572 *Lanark B. Rec.* 65.

Gefe, Geif, Geyf, *v.* Also: **geife, geiff, geyff.** P.t. **gafe, gaif, gaiff, gayf(f, geif.** P.p. **gefin(e, -yn(e, geifin, geiffin, geyffine, geyfyng.** [Var. of GEVE *v.* with normal Sc. use of *f* for *v.* The inf. *geiffyn* and p.p. *geif, geyf* used by Douglas are by analogy from southern Eng.] *tr.* and *intr.* To give, in various senses.

(a) Thocht na fath to me ʒe gefe, Ma fal to thame ʒe wil be-lif; *Leg. S.* xxiii. 394. Quha-sa wald mast hir gefe Of erand suld ereste eschewe; *Ib.* xxxiv. 50. Gefand to thame xl merkis worth of land; 1515 *Reg. Privy S.* I. 407/1. Alisoune..sal mak & gefe to the said Dauid..ane sufficient lettir of bailʒery; 1519 *Fife Sheriff Ct.* 147. Gif ony maner of persoun gefis arlis.. on ony maner of fische; 1540 *Acts Jas. V* (1566) c. 78.

(b) It is lachfull..till ilke burges to geyff or sell his lande; *Acts* I. 24/2. He sall geyf viii s.; *Ib.* 28/2. The sayd Jonet sal geyf hym..xl s.; 1457 *Peebles B. Rec.* 118. Syluir and gold he gert on 'to him geyff; *Wall.* I. 447. This exemptioun to

endure. .quhil he geyf uther command in the contrare; 1508
Reg. Privy C. I. 258/2. The Superintendent requirit the sayd
Joanna to geyf hyr ayth of calumpne; 1565 *St. A. Kirk S.* 235.
(c) That I geif for dome; 1478 *Acta Aud.* 66/2. Thomas sal
restore and geif again. .the sade sovme; 1482 *Ib.* 101/2.
Geifand a penny. .in name of blanch ferm; 1500 *Buccleuch
Mun.* II. 102. We. .sall geiff him or thaim our leill & trew
consall; 1506 *Charter* (Reg. H.) No. 693. I sal ʒou geiffyn ilk
man as efferis; DOUG. V. vi. 39. As he to geif batale all redy
war; *Ib.* IX. ii. 46. Few of thaim wald geif place to othir;
BELL. *Boece* I. 96. Of the quhilk reparation the principal sal
geif coumpt yeirly; BUCH. *Wr.* 7. To mak princes iniunctiounis geif; 1573 *Sat. P.* xlii. 833.
   (b) He thame gafe Playne powar our the laffe; *Leg. S.* Prol.
137. Thare he gafe grete giftis. .to thame; HAY II. 93/28.
Andro renunsit and gafe oure al tak of the said landis; 1467
Acta Aud. 8/1. To a man. .that gafe the King a hors; 1488
Treas. Acc. I. 93.
   (b) Ane abbot past, and gaif our this legiance; *Wall.* I. 77.
His hors gaiff our, and mycht no forther ga; *Ib.* v. 904. Throw
his tressoun the king gaif his essent; *Bk. Chess* 905. This ilk
schaddo. .gaif the bak and fled; DOUG. X. xi. 106. The quhilk
gaif sapience to king Salomone; LYND. *Mon.* 249. The meill
gaif xii shillingis the peck; *Diurn. Occurr.* 306. I. .gaif him. .
better counsellis; 1614 *Lett. Eccl. Affairs* I. 320.
   (c) The said Jonat. .geif hir greit aitht; 1556 *Stirling B. Rec.*
I. 67.
   (c) To preche goddis word as is gefyne vs; *Leg. S.* xv. 76.
Al thar gudis suld be. .gefine as eschete; *Ib.* xxxviii. 11. The
forsaid Johne has gefin heritable possession; 1440 *Cart. S.
Nich. Aberd.* I. 11. Gefyn wnder our signet at Pertht; 1460
Ayr Charters 35. The sayd lordis hafe gefyn bodyly fayth;
1478 *Lennox Mun.* 116. By the solemniteis. .gefin tham afore
in the Scriptur; WINʒET I. 28/30.
   (b) All forfautis excedand viij s.. .salbe geyffin to this gylde;
Acts I. 90/2. A sartan som. .qwylk he had geyfyng hym. .to
kyp; 1456 *Peebles B. Rec.* 118. To hym a servand woman. .
Was geyf; DOUG. V. v. 74. *Ib.* vi. 105.
   (c) The quhilkis twa merkis of land. .I haue geifin our and
resignit; 1506 *Glasgow Dioc. Reg.* II. 161. [To] suffir. .al Lyby
land Be geif in dowry to thi son; DOUG. IV. iii. 28. Geiffin for
conwoyinge of the pressoneris to Blaknes, xlix l.; 1567–8
Bk. Old Edinb. C. VI. 83.

Geve, Gewe, *v.* Also: **geiv(e, geiwe.** P.t. **gave, gaive,
gawe, gewe, geawe, geve, gev.** P.p. **gevin(e, -yn(e, -yng,
gewin(e, -yn(e, -en, geivin, geyn, gein, ge'ine.** [ME. *geve*
(14th c.), ON. *gefa* (*gaf, gáfu, gefenn*). Cf. GIVE *v.* and
GIF *v.*] To give, in various senses.
   1. *tr.* To give, hand over (something *to* a person).
   (a) That. .men of kirk gevis tributis. .of thair gudis to the
king; HAY I. 237/9. To the quhilkis to geve grete giftis is
thing tynt; *Ib.* 300/31. It that ladyis wynnis vnlefully. .thai
may lefully geve in almous; IRLAND *Asl. MS.* I. 34/3. Thou
the ceptour gevis me in hand Of all this realme; DOUG. I. ii. 44.
Quhair ʒe can spye ane man to geue ʒow mair, ʒe schute
thame furth; LAUDER *Minor P.* i. 530. [The Council] geves

to Jhonn Hog,..ten pund to be gevin to the barbouris for
curing him; 1594 *Edinb. B. Rec.* V. 124. They haif na power
to geve the teyndis thairof; 1608 *Peebles Gleanings* 31. Quhasumeuer sall geve moneyis to ony sojer; 1648 *Peebles B. Rec.*
383.
absol. To..hald it as heritage.., nocht gevand na restorand
agayn; HAY II. 31/16. He that gevis atour his power..heryis
himself; *Ib.* 81/31. The first is..that thow geve blythlye and
frely; IRLAND *Asl. MS.* I. 33/13. Sum gevis to thame can
flattir and fenзie; DUNB. xvi. 42.
(*b*) George Dowglace,..gewis and infeftis till ws the saidis
landis; 1509 *Douglas Chart.* 189. Except gyf it wer..sic oder
thynge..to gew to hir; 1565 *Hist. Carnegie* 51. Thow promesit
that all suld be weill, gewand thé hir draff for peyment; 1596
Misc. Spald. C. I. 91. The prouest, baillies, and counsall..
gewis and grauntis to the said Andro the samen yeirlie stipend;
1636 *Aberd. B. Rec.* III. 97.
(*c*) To the quilk lorde I geiwe..my schipe callit the Carvell;
1506 *Orkn. & Shetl. Rec.* 248. To the qwhilk lorde I geiwe and
leiffis all the landis that I possessit; 1525 *Misc. Bann. C.* III.
107. I geive зow heir ane ring of gold royall; *Clar.* I. 1044.
To geive the ministers thair denner at Mr Patrik Gillespies
entrie; 1648 *Glasgow B. Rec.* II. 128.
(**b**) He gewe fyrst..Teyndis, as the Bybyll sayis; WYNT. II.
161. That bred He gawe the batwartis; *Ib.* VI. 1991. The
byschape..gave twa lang coddis of welwete; *Ib.* IX. 591.
Barrell heryng and wattir thai him gawe; *Wall.* II. 171. Ane
greit armie king Robert..In gyding syne to James of Douglas
gawe; STEWART 50515. The dewellis gawe thame hat leid to
lape; (Dunb.) *Maitl. F.* xvi./101. That same flesche he geawe
ws to eatte; 1580 *Cath. Tr.* 68/35.
(**c**) Quhen he herd..at his landis..War gevyn to Clifford;
BARB. I. 317. This wes grauntit and gevyn thare, And to this
wes gevyn mare; WYNT. VIII. 7105. Gif a knycht..had gevyn
a coursour to the provost of Paris unaskit; HAY I. 139/18. A
gowne..the quhilk was gevin to the hereald of Inglande at the
passing of the ambaxat; 1474 *Treas. Acc.* I. 27. Gevin vnder
oure priue sele at..Edinburgh; 1507 *Edinb. Chart.* 192. Tuay
acris of outfeild land..to be gevin to our forester; 1550 *Reg.
Cupar A.* II. 73. The haill profeit..to be geivine to the
marriage of hir said twa dochteris; 1562 *Will Agnes Betoun*
226. The almes..sall be gevin to honest decait personis and
not to commond beggaris; 1574 *Aberd. Eccl. Rec.* 19. Quhen
cautioun is found thair is no warrand thairof gevin to the
arreistar bot onlie a tikkett; 1617 *Acts* IV. 547/1. Gevin to
Collein Campbell for half a yeares craig maill; 1656 *Mun.
Univ. Glasg.* III. 497.
(*b*) Thre housis that gewine ware To vphauld sancte Laurens
altere; *Leg. S.* xxii. 633. Haf I nocht ryches gewine thé; *Ib.*
xxxiv. 257. The land grantit and gewin to him; *c.* 1400 *Newbattle Chart.* (Reg. H.). The balyais..has gewyn to the myller
ij markis; 1457 *Peebles B. Rec.* 123. The xx crownis that was
gewin to my lord of Angus; 1488 *Lanark B. Rec.* 4. Nota that
Andro Pereys land [is] gewin him for keiping of ouir cwnigair
and parkis; 1542 *Reg. Cupar A.* II. 183. The quenes Majestie
hes send for sum baggage to be gewyn to the kyng; *c* 1567
Melville Corr. 232. In land mail of 1 fdg. terrae..gewen in

excambion to Magnus Loutit; 1595 *Orkney Rentals* ii. 44. That [pension] thay haif gewin her fyve yeiris; 1606 *Peebles Gleanings* 25. Gewine to Pattrik Pattersone for the depursmentis he hade depursit in Selkirk, vi li. xiiij s.; 1623–4 *Peebles B. Rec.* 412.

(*c*) For certane sowmis of money geving to ws be our louitt Alexander Jaksone; 1542 *Reg. Cupar A.* II. 19. William.. desyrit bakwart of the said sovme mair nor he aucht till haif geving; 1557 *Peebles B. Rec.* 236. He reserwit..the dowarreis gewing for the mareage of the eldest sonis; *Chron. Kings* 51.

2. To give, grant, or bestow (a benefit, power, privilege, etc.) to or upon a person.

(**a**) To geve yow corage to do in sik maner; HAY I. 3/35. A consul..wald hald him at the portis, and nocht geve him entree; *Ib.* 60/34. Giff of casse I or my ayris..gevis ony leiffe ..to mak ony drauchtis of the said Magdelan burn; 1466 *Reg. Dunferm.* 356. Gevand him power balʒe courtis..to set [etc.]; 1508 *Reg. Privy S.* I. 234/1. Gevand him licence and benevolence to gif presentatioun..to the vicarage of Cluny; 1517 *Ib.* 451/2. Sen God geuis vs libertie..frelie to think; WINʒET I. 9/10. Geueand thaim pouer..to ordour wthiris; *Ib.* 99/13. Withoute respect tyll ony wicht, Suld kyngs geue euery man thare rycht; LAUDER *Off. Kings* 17. I grant that I haif faultit sore, To stok and stane geuand his glore; *G. Ball.* 61. Than ioy and myrth thow sall me geue; *Ib.* 123. Lykeas it pleasit thair worships..to geue the credit of the selling thairof to the supplicant; 1645 *Aberd. B. Rec.* IV. 49.

(*b*) He sais god gewys to the wysman wyt and wisdome; *Wisd. Sol.* 490. Thar is a makar of al thinge..That gewys to mankynd wyt & skill; *Ratis R.* 29. Gewand..hir full power to hym to intromit and dispone thairupone; 1578 *Prot. Bk. J. Scott* 55. The baillerie gewis sufficient authoritie of the apprehensioun of ony suspect of pykerie; 1598 *Crim. Trials* II. 43. The saidis commissioneris..gewis powir and commissioun to the saidis brughis [etc.]; 1601 *Conv. Burghs* II. 109.

(**b**) He..gawe hym large and full powere To do that lykand tyll hym were; WYNT. ii. 377. Quhen he gawe thame lewe to say All that [etc.]; *Ib.* v. 2935.

(**c**) We haue geuyn and grauntit..al rycht..and possessioun ..to the said landis; 1447 *Edinb. Chart.* 68. Na man..may tak honour away quhare it is anys gevin; HAY II. 37/28. My v wittis of nature that God..has gevyne me to vse wele in his seruice; IRLAND *Asl. MS.* I. 66/25. The lecence gevin to vnfremen to saill with merchandeise; 1515 *Aberd. B. Rec.* I. 94. The quhilk has geuin us lybertie Till eait of euery fruct [etc.]; LYND. *Mon.* 914. Thei meane not heirby that ony impunitie suld be gevin to sic; 1572 BANN. *Memor.* 239. The lyk dischearge [is] to be gevin by him to the tennentes; 1614 *Highland P.* III. 168.

(*b*) To bind and lous..Plane poware is gewin thé til; *Leg. S.* i. 18. Foure prewilege hym gewyn wes; *Ib.* v. 4. Schire Johne ..hes gewyn and grantyt..full leue..to make a myllyn dame; 1427 *Melville Chart.* 245. The forsaid balʒae..hes gewin.. possession of the sayd ʒard; 1531 *Prot. Bk. M. Fleming* 13 b. Sancts..to quhome is gewine..to liwe maist familiar withe Christ; KING *Cat.* 33. No tennant..sall presume to sell any peittes..without leaw askit and gewen; 1670 *Urie Baron Ct.* 91.

3. To give, in secondary senses varying according to the object governed by the verb.
(1) Tak him..As I had gevyn thar-to na reid;BARB. II. 122. The king Had gevin thame in commandyng That [etc.]; *Ib.* IX. 445. Deucalyon dyde all hale As Pyrra gawe hym to consalle; WYNT. II. 307. Ane angell..gawe bydding ay Pasce to mak apon Sownday; *Ib.* v. 1512. Ilk baroun and freehaldare that..geve voce with the said dome is..in amerciament; 1478 *Acta Aud.* 66/2. Quha geuis ʒow this counsell; ROLLAND *Seven S.* 2251. The response which his wyffis wyttches had gevin; KNOX II. 357. All thay [that] geuis consultatioun,..salbe haldin pertakeris of this act; 1570 *Sat. P.* xiii. 159. Gewing him charges to obey; 1583 *Ib.* xlv. 1066. This day beand assignit to him to eik to his former defences gevein; 1606 *Melrose Reg. Rec.* I. 17.
(2) To schir Colyne sic dusche he gave [*E.* gewe]; BARB. XVI. 130. The enforce of Grece he saw Geuand and takand mony rout; *Alex.* I. 2454. With the sweird awkwart he him gawe Wndyr the hat; *Wall.* I. 407. He gaue ane braid with his brand to the beirne by; *Rauf C.* 858. I am content to rassayff the mast wylld deid that may be geyn me; 1544 *Bk. Carlaverock* II. 29. Thair was gevin upone thame ane charge be sum horsmen; KONX II. 59. The day after the defait was gevin thame; BANN. *Memor.* 138. The dyuers falls, that Fortune geuis to men; JAMES VI *Ess.* 42. Sum of the luiftenants men..did geive them a woille of shoat; 1615 *Highland P.* III. 185. Geweing hir many bla strakis; 1642 *Aberd. B. Rec.* I. 292.
(3) Set tyll this I gawe my wylle; WYNT. I. 31. To that sone he gawe assent; *Ib.* v. 1001. The byschapys..Gawe hym.. blyssyn hale; *Ib.* VII. 1489. He aw to geve compt to the hiest juge of thair..mysdedis; HAY I. 243/33. The prince suld.. understand all the mater before..he geve his consent; *Ib.* 285/30. To..geve his laubour and study to wisdome; IRLAND *Mir.* I. 8/12. I ʒow beseik to gevin advertens; DOUG. III. Prol. 28. Of tyme nor ressoun gevis he na cuyr; *Ib.* XI. Prol. 42. Gevand his mind..to serche the verite of thir..dowtis; BELL. *Boece* I. p. xlii. The Empreour to sic wordis gaue audience; ROLLAND *Seven S.* 41/2. Quhen Antichrist wald thé blind, That thow suld geue him na eir; *G. Ball.* 159. Wherin our greatest Prelate gewis ane accompt to the B. of Canterburry; 1637 BAILLIE I. App. 429.
(4) Fra the tyme of his ʒouthede That he to God al gevine vas; *Leg. S.* xviii. 31. Men that eilde hade ourdrevyne, That war fra delitis gevyne; *Troy-bk.* I. 450. My curage has gevin me to mak sum newing [etc.]; HAY I. 3/30. Thay ar gevin sa planly to oppressioun; HENR. III. 164/60. ʒoure playis..to quhais sicht sal the pepill be maist ernistfully gevin; BELL. *Livy* I. 193/3. Albeit it chance..that he..be gevin to pastyme; WINʒET I. 6/13. All haill thair hartis to covatice aʳ gewin; *Maitl. F.* xcix. 5. The gayest and best gein; *Maitl. Q.* xxxv 20. Partlie for gean [=gain], wharto he was gein; MELVILL 117. I should more largely notefie it now How much t' augment thy greatnes I am ge'ine; GARDYNE *Garden* 5.
(5) This fredome to kepe..aythire of the partis has gewin gude faith; 1427 *Melville Chart.* 245. 1456 (see FAITH *n.* 4 (2).) [They haue] gewyn thar bodely athis; 1472 *Lennox Mun.* 92. A cumpany of the most honest..geve thair salutationis at hir

chalmer wyndo; KNOX II. 270. [They] being sworne..gawe
their aythis in maner following; 1617 *Aberd. B. Rec.* II. 353.
[The jailor] hes gevin his grit aith of fidelitie thairintill; 1632
Peebles B. Rec. 372.
(6) *c* 1456 (see DOME *n.* 1 b). The deliuerance and sentence
gevin..be the grete assise in Aberdene; 1479 *Acta Conc.* 21/1.
The saidis lordis haid gevin a decrett contrare him; 1490 *Acta
Aud.* 139/2. That ane declaratour be gevin be my Lord
Governour..thairupoun; 1550 *Reg. Privy C.* I. 103. According
to sentence..Geuin and pronouncit be that awful juge; ROL-
LAND *Seven S.* 10709. The day befor the expayering of the 8
gevene in your Ma^{tis} last proclamatione; 1639 *Hamilton P.* 80.
(7) The avale and price of the said gold as it gevis in Flanderis;
1480 *Acta Conc.* 76/1. The avale of the said salmonde as salmonde gevis now in Aberdene; 1485 *Ib.* *109/1. At this tyme..
the boll of quhyt gave viij markis; PITSC II. 317/7. They could
not haue moneyes for any thinge..for wictuall heir geives noe
pryse; *c* 1627 *Bk. Carlaverock* II. 608.

b. In miscellaneous uses. (See also BAK *n.*¹ 3 a.)
For thi that name wes gevyn hym tille; WYNT. v. 1420. To
geve otheris exempil in tyme to cum, he suld be punyst; HAY
I. 88/1. He beand redy to geve the sacrament, thai strike on
him; *Ib.* 202/30. Gevand doctrine and exampill to princis;
IRLAND *Mir.* I. 6/10. The nychtbouris..sal incontinent geve
the cry and tak the sade trespassour; 1498 *Acta Conc.* II. 102.
This wolf..gevand thame souke with hir pappis; BELL. *Livy*
I. 18/12. The feild quhare the batell was gevin; *Boece* II. viii.
72. The place quhare the feild was gevyn; *Ib.* v. ii. 166 b. On
the morn as Phebus gave the light; *Clar.* v. 2560. The samyn
prenteis..gevand his assay quhen it pleissis him; 1573 *Bk. Old
Edinb. C.* VI. 60. We geve it alwaies ane sound beath befoer
and behind the consonant; HUME *Orthog.* 8. Scho gaiue fiue
or six lytle groanes; 1619 *Misc. Abbotsford C.* 83. Wald 3e not
have gewin hir ane amends of me? 1626 *Kinghorn Kirk S.* 30.

c. With complementary additions.
I trow that lang quhill no lády To hous wes gevin so richly;
BARB. xx. 102. Thir two sonnes..War gevin in tutory..To
king Teuteus; *Troy-bk.* II. 1624. The name thairof beand gevin
to him in write; 1486 *Bk. Carlaverock* II. 447. His grace quite
clamys and dischargis him thairof and gevis thaim quyte be
thir lettrez; 1508 *Reg. Privy S.* I. 259/2. Geuand the saulis..
To blynd pastouris..to keip; LYND. *Trag. Card.* 350. That
God..had geuin the king and the preiste to be despysit;
WIN3ET I. 31/14. [To] execut his office..to the comfort of the
floke gewin in his cwir; 1570 *Reg. Episc. Brechin* II. 307. My
bukes als thay ar gevin in roll in the cathalog; 1584 *Edinb.
Test.* XIV. 70 b. Being a poore man and gevin be the landislordis to be a threscher in a barne; 1613 *Highland P.* III. 134.

4. With adverbs as *doun, furth, in, our, out, up.*
(1) Esaw..Gawe wpe all hale hys herytage; WYNT. II. 207.
A man that gevis him self up cowartly in the handis of his fais;
HAY II. 81/35. He..geuis vp the gaist; *G. Ball.* 30. To convene
the haill persones..gevin up in roll; 1635 *Peebles B Rec.* 372.
(2) The said Jonet..had gevin our the samyn [terce]; 1483
Acta Conc. II. p. cxxxiii. He..Of all sik thingis gaue our the
cure and charge; DOUG. VII. ix. 127. [The] provest..hes frelie

gevin over..the bigging that he hes maid; 1516 *Edinb. B.
Rec.* I. 159. The saidis..hes ranunsyt, left, & gewin our thair
cheyff, the lard McGregour; 1552 *Breadalbane Coll.* (Reg. H.)
No. 84. Down was geuin ouir, for feir of weir assay; 1571 *Sat.
P.* xxvi. 43. I..smellit that he wald neuir geiv over that hous
to be torterit; 1614 *Melrose P.* 182.

(3) Entres of courtis of all termes bigain..to mak be gevin
in; 1484 *Exch. R.* IX. 605. Anent the supplicatioun gevin in
be Thomas Richartsoun; 1540 *Edinb. Chart.* 210. Ane rentale
gevin in be the erle of Argile; 1563 *Reg. Cupar A.* II. 274. He
is gevin in..be the collectouris of Abirdene as at the horn;
1574 *Reg. Privy C.* II. 346. The persones mentionat in ane
doket gewine in to the dene of gild; 1580 *Dundee Shipping L.*
198. His former defences gevein in against the libell of removing; 1606 *Melrose Reg. Rec.* I. 17. The articles underwrittin, proponit and gewin in 3isternicht to the magistratts
of this burghe; 1640 SPALDING I. 276.

(4) The said deliuerance to be gevin out betuix this and the
last day of the Justice are of Lanark; 1493 *Acta Conc.* 316/2.
Lettiris of captioun [are] gevin out aganis ws; 1625 *Bk.
Carlaverock* II. 71. — The..frierlandis..gevin furthe of the
landis of the said burgh; 1632 *Lanark B. Rec.* 326.

(5) I..leue my said smyddie graith to..my sone, he defalkand
& gevand doun ten merkis of his portioun thairfore; 1584
Edinb. Test. XIV. 176 b.

Gif, Gyf, *v.* Also: giff, gyff, gife, gyfe. P.t. gaf, gaff,
gaffe. P.p. gifin, -yne, -en, (gif), giffin, -yn(e, -en,
giffne ; gyfin(e, gyffin(e, -yn(e, -yng, -en. [ME. *gyf,
gyfe, gyffe, gif, gife, giffe*, early *gifen* (*c* 1200), OSw.
giva (Sw. *gifva*), ODa. *givæ* (Đan. *give*), varying in
vowel from ON. *gefa*, GEFE, GEVE. The double *f* is
most frequent in disyllabic forms as *giffis, gyffis, giffin,
gyffyn,* etc.] To give, in various senses.

1. *tr.* With some material thing as object.

(a) Homines prestabunt [*gl.* sal gif], etc.; *a* 1350 *Facs. Nat.
MSS.* II. 14. I sall gif hym my chartyre; *c* 1380 *Charter*
(Reg. H.). It that thu gifis..Thu gifis for thu ma nocht away
ber it; *Leg. S.* xliv. 75. Gifand till him..the remane therof gif
ocht be attour; *Acts* I. 369/2. Kepe thaim fra giftis to gif or
craff; *Gud Wyf & D.* 111. Thai..said thai wald nocht gif him
the hous; *Asl. MS.* I. 217/30. I gif me to the feynd all fre;
DUNB. xxxiv. 28. [To] gif fra thame all armour and sic geir;
STEWART 38285. The personis abonewritin..gifis and disponis
to..Colyne and his airis thair calpis; 1549–50 *Breadalbane P.*
No. 71. The keyis of heuin will I gif vnto the; *G. Ball.* 7. To
gif..to the bankets ky, oxin, scheip [etc.]; 1594 *Conv. Burghs*
I. 430. My cowsine..sal be ready to..gif them pay; 1642
Fam. Rose 330.

absol. Ane fule,..Cryis ay, Gif me, in to a drene; DUNB. xv. 7.

(*b*) Quhill God..thi ful far crowne Thé giff in hewine; *Leg. S.*
xxvii. 1358. I..giffis bot a lytill wra; *Ib.* xliii. 495. We sal
noght..giff, sel, na analy..the said land; 1444 *Chart. St. Giles*
70. The avale of the said landis that thai now giff; 1493 *Acta
Conc.* 269/2. Sum me the cop giffis; DUNB. *Tua Mar. W.* 484.
Sum giffis money, sum giffis meit; (Dunb.) *Maitl. F.* xci. 12.

(c) Quhat amowis thé The kyrtill for to gyf to me; *Leg. S.*
v. 362. Gyf me Iohn the baptist hed in desch; *Ib.* xxxvi. 519.
He is obliged to gyf.. ten pund; 1418 *Liber Melros* 503. Gyfand
thaim [*sc.* wardly gudis] to hyme gladly agane; *Cr. Deyng* 182.
Of quhilk gudis he gyfis habundaunce to wys men; HAY II.
79/37. For the quhilk he sall gyf the belman twa d.; 1469 *Ayr
Friars Pr. Chart.* 52.

(d) To thé I gyff the keys of hewyne; *Leg. S.* i. 16. Thu..
nocht gyffis thaim of thi gud; *Ib.* xvi. 315. For to gyff..hym
tylle Schyppys and wyttaylle; WYNT. III. 525. I..gyffis and
grantis.. fourty pundis of annuale rent; 1429 *Reg. Episc.
Brechin* I. 42. We sall be bundyn.. Sum part off gold to gyff
you; *Wall.* VIII. 899. Gyffand yerly tharfor.. sex schillingis;
1488 *Dunferm. B. Rec.* 2. My lord governour gyffis the samyn
..to the said Andro; 1515 *Reg. Privy S.* I. 408/2. The rest of
my haill geir I gyff to the lard of Calder; 1585 *Thanes of
Cawdor* 187.

(e) I wil that thu drinke the venome I sal thé gyfe; *Leg. S.*
v. 329. Til [=while] men.. has fre will To gyfe, or to hald
them still; *Ib.* vi. 358. To gife and to pay.. a hundreth pundis
of vswale money of Scotland; 1456 *Reg. Dunfermline* 340. Tha
sal gyfe to ws.. sex bollis of quhet; 1473 *Reg. Cupar A.* I. 172.
This angel noble.. Vnto 3our lordschip I will gife; 1583 *Sat. P.*
xlv. 449. Not to gife them [*sc.* the moneys] til the treaty be
weale advanced; 1650 *Blairs P.* 27.

(b) The endentur till him gaf he; BARB. I. 565. Men and
armys till him gaff he; *Ib.* II. 163. Martha.. gaf til thame al
that afferyt; *Leg. S.* xvi. 78. He bande [thaim] wp and gaff
thaim haye; Wynt. IV. 2687 (C). Ane other chesabil he gaff
alsswa; *Ib.* IX. 598. The balye gaf v s. to James Gybson; 1457
Peebles B. Rec. 123. Alexander Iruyne.. gaff, grantit, and
assignit.. to Dauid Iruyne.. ale and hale his gudis; 1493
Antiq. Aberd. & B. III. 301. He gaf all Cummerland till his
apperand aire; *Asl. MS.* I. 256/13. Jhone Ondirwod denyit
at [he] gaf yt that day; 1562 *Prestwick B. Rec.* 66.

(c) The forsaid wode sall neuer be giffin na sald; 1388 *Antiq.
Aberd. & B.* III. 294. Til haue gifyn.. al my landis; 1412
Melville Chart. 18. Till hald.. als frely.. and in pese as ony
pensioun or annuale is giffyn; 143ɪ *Reg. Great S.* 45/2. O
Prince, think quhi thi crown was giffin thé til; *Liber Plusc.* 393.
Alexander Irvin.. has gifen.. to me.. the landis of Ful3emond;
1485 *Antiq. Aberd. & B.* III. 32. Giffin to Rolland Robysone
to ryde to the Bordour; 1496 *Treas. Acc.* I. 281. Giffen.. to
the masonis at Mowtrayis toure.., ix s.; 1501 *Ib.* II. 103. To
reskew the landis.. Carentius had giffin thame befoir; STEWART
17864. To haif.. gifin and grantit.. my haill insycht [etc.];
1589 *Coll. Aberd. & B.* 355. Four eir ringis.. gifin.. to my
Lady Haringtouns vemen; 1603 *Montgomery Mem.* 248.

(b) Tha landys fornemmit troch hym gyffyn; 1389 *Wemyss
Chart.* 24. The sayde Erll haffis gyffyn.. sesyng and possessioune; 1392 *Lennox Mun.* 45. Tyl hafe granttyt and gyfin
tyl the aldirmen.. of Elgyne.. al the wol [etc.]; 1393 *Charter
Thos. Dunbar* (Reg. H.). Tyl haf gyffin and granttyt [etc.];
1402 *Reg. Panmure* II. 184. That I.. has sawld and gyffyne tyll
a nobyle man [etc.]; 1420 *Antiq. Aberd. & B.* IV. 384. The
saide lord.. has gyffyng.. to the hous of Aberbrothoc.. tua
pecis of land; 1456 *Liber Aberbr.* 89. With outheris possessionis

gyfyn to the sayd abbay; 1459 *Acts* XII. 26/1. Gyffyne for
castyne of the erd fra the schip, iij s. viij d.; 1494 *Treas. Acc.*
I. 249. The ix penneland of Saba is fre gyffin and cheyngytt..
to the said Jhone Irwyngis fader; 1509 *Rec. Earld. Orkney* 82.
Quhilk land was gyffine to hyme..in arff; 1562 *Ib.* 114.
Gyffen at command of the bealȝies to the peyper; 1588–9
Dundee Acc. MS.
(*c*) To suffir..all Libie land Be gyf in drowry to thi son;
DOUG. IV. iii. 28 (Sm.).

2. With non-material or abstract object.
(*a*) The Grekes..wald scantly gif thaim leve; *Troy-bk.* II.
1632. I gif for dome [etc.]; 1410 *Reg. Episc. Brechin* I. 31.
He sal gif tham the best counsale that he may gif; 1455 *Edinb.
Chart.* 80. Thai..walde nocht gif a full and determit sentence
in the said mater; 1491 *Acta Conc.* 173/2. Personis..quhilkis
wil be bund to..gif sufficient plegis and band thairupoun;
1517 *Reg. Privy S.* I. 449/1. We dessyirrit them to dail and
gif ws wr chois; 1552 *Corr. M. Lorraine* 358. To gif the wedow
and fatherles comfort; 1570 *Sat. P.* x. 365. Gif na credens to
comune clatteraris; *Maitl. F.* clxxx. 43. The judge sould gif his
sentence siteand in judgement; SKENE *Reg. Maj.* II. 122 b.
(*b*) Fredome all solace to man giffis; BARB. I. 227. Idilnes
giffis novrysingis To vicis; *Leg. S.* Prol. 2. To borne blynd
thu giffis sycht; *Ib.* xi. 26. Giffande and grantande to..schir
Robert..oure ful and playne poware [etc.]; 1439 *Edinb. Chart.*
64. It giffis to me gret consolatioun..in my hart; *Asl. MS.*
I. 273/5. God giff thé ane ewil deid; GAU 13/10. Lord, giff
me faith; *Ib.* 76/6. Giffand..to our said baillyes..expres
mandament [etc.]; 1559 *Coll. Aberd. & B.* 314. Quha giffis
thame seruice to pay xl s. as unlay; 1581 *St. A. Baxter Bks.* 29.
All [of them] amerciat for not giffin suite and presence to this
Heid Court; 1597 *Misc. Spald. C.* II. 135. Ye sall giff ane
perticular assign[a]sion off ten chaders victuall,..to Mester
Gorg Greme; 1604 *Misc. Hist. Soc.* II. 246. It is statute..that
non..giffe deforcement neither to the barroun officer nor
bourlawmen; 1665 *Stitchill Baron C.* 35.
(*c*) I sall gyf gud leif hym till To pas frely; *Leg. S.* i. 134.
Til gyf ensampil vthyre til; *Ib.* xxxvii. 150. To resayue this
cause..and thairof to gyf iugement; 1385 *Red Bk. Grandtully*
I. 138*. To gyf a resone for al thingis that God has maid;
Wisd. Sol. 360. Gyf thaim..quhen thow may sum com-
fortinge; *Consail Wys Man* 362. Nature..forȝet to gyf thame
faith or lawte; *Asl. MS.* I. 276/24.
(*d*) Now God gyff grace that I may swa Tret it; BARB. I. 34.
Reput nocht hym frende quhilk in thi face Gyffis gret lowynge;
Bernardus 194. Sic pardoune as we haiff In oys to gyff; *Wall.*
VI. 138. I thé beseik..To the berer ye..gyff credance; *Ib.* VIII.
1650. Venus..in the mornyng..Gyffis ane grit lycht; *Compl.*
53/32. Ȝe can nocht faill To gyff ane desolate man counsaill;
LYND. *Mon.* 321. Our will is..that ȝe gyff dome of baneschment
aganes the said James; 1590 *Digest Justiciary Proc.* M. 12.
(*e*) Tyll hyme fall[is] mekle thinge That may nocht les his
stat to gyfe; *Ratis R.* 1022. [Thai] sal..gyfe furth thar
delyuerance; 1472 *Lennox Mun.* 92. That nane of ȝow..gife
in dittay or accuse the said Adam; 1510 *Reg. Privy S.* I. 315/1.
[We] sal gife thame our..trew and best counsail; 1527 *Antiq.*

Aberd. & B. III. 307. To that gret God gyfe pryse and glore; LYND. *Mon.* 1869. God gife thé grace aganis this gude new ʒeir; SCOTT i. 55.

(**b**) God gaff thame sic mycht; *Leg. S.* Prol. 112. Oyle..for seknes sere Gaf hop and but; *Ib.* xxvi. 579. Twychande the haly ewangellis, we gaf bodily hathe; 1392 *Lennox Mun.* 49. Thane thai..Gaf full credence thar-to; *Troy-bk.* II. 1888. The Pape gaf his benesoun; *Howlat* 243. All the lordis..gaf bodely aithis to kepe that respit; *Asl. MS.* I. 240/6. At hellis ʒettis he gaf hyme na succour; DUNB. lxxxvi. 29.

(**c**) The curt..assignet thareto Tewisday..to caus his dome ..to be giffyn; 1385 *3rd Rep. Hist. MSS.* 410/2. The defesance ..sal be qwit of it selfe and be giffin to thame freli; 1399 *Holyrood Chart.* 113. The said Erle of Mar hase gifin his..ful consent that [etc.]; 1405 *Antiq. Aberd. & B.* III. 200. The forsaid lord has..giffin to the forsaid Michel, the keping of hys Castell of Louchmabane; 1420 (1430) *Reg. Great S.* 30/1. Quhen dome is giffin, and na remede set ford; *Liber Plusc.* 399. The king..has giffyn consent thar till; *Wall.* VIII. 1136. The coppe of ane sentence arbitrall gifin..apon the said hors; 1540 *Elgin Rec.* I. 54. War..grace him giffin als oft for frawd; (Dunb.) *Maitl. F.* x. 37.

(*b*) Quhy has thu..gyfine thi consent? *Leg. S.* xxv. 440. He.. has thé gyfine lyf and aynde; *Ib.* xxviii. 188. Down and gyffyn the yer and the day..befor nemmyt; 1394 *Liber Aberbr.* 43. The patronage of the said kyrke..to be gyffin at his lyking; 1405 *Maxwell Mem.* I. 145. Ader of the said parteis..has gyffyn bodely ath; 1432 *Lamont P.* 14. That the forsaid seruice sal be gyfyn to the mast abyl chaplan; 1476 *Peebles B. Rec.* 181. The doym that ye has gyffyn is ewyl; 1488 *Dunferm. B. Rec.* 5. Thomas Howeson said..that thair is ane fals sentens gyffin aganis him; 1526 *Carnwath Barony Ct.* 56. The..sentence and arbytrall decret..to be gyffyne; 1529 *Lennox Mun.* 232. The sayd Thom is jugit in amerciament and dome gyfin thairapon; 1556 *Inverness B. Rec.* I. 2.

3. With the adverbs *again, back, our* (=over), *up.*

(1) In-till that tretys wp thai gaff..all the clame that thai mycht haff In-till Scotland; BARB. xx. 48. The schirefys..sal do thair besines til arreste the personis sua gifyn vp be enquerre or complaynt; 1398 *Acts* I. 211/2. The saide Wilham ..sall frely delyuer and gyf up the Castell of Drumlanryge; 1429 *15th Rep. Hist. MSS. Comm.* App. VIII. 10. To summond ane assis to gif up dittay; 1553 *Treas. Acc.* X. 199. Gif ony thing be eschapit my rememberance, that he gif vp the samin; 1584 *Edinb. Test.* XIII. 377 b.

(2) That..he..suld incontinent discharge and gif our the saide office to the saide Malcolm; 1466 *Acta Aud.* 5/1. I..sal freli giff oure..& resigne al richt & clame [etc.]; 1469 *Charter* (Reg. H.) No. 416. The said Duncane..sal gife me oure the said landis; 1499 *Highland P.* II. 197. Archebald of Dunbar tuke the castell of Halis..and syne cowardlie gaf it owr to the master of Douglas; *Asl. MS.* I. 219/9. Thy will obey sall I And giffis owr the caus perpetualy; DOUG. XII. xiii. 66. He cryit and said: Gif ouir the hous; LYND. *Meldrum* 1110. This sall he do..Or I science and cunning sall gif ouir; ROLLAND *Seven S.* 313. This lord thocht that he wald nocht..gif ower the admerallschipe; PITSC. I. 257/13.

(3) Henry..sal restore, deliuer and gif agane to Johne..vj
nolt; 1474 *Acta Aud.* 31/1. To caus tua seruandis of his gif
agane certane geir tane fra tua A(l)manis; 1549 *Treas. Acc.*
IX. 327. That his mother..would..giff back my tikitt agane;
1640 *Red Bk. Grandtully* II. 39.
4. In various idiomatic uses.
Basnetis weill burnyst bricht That gaf agane the sonne gret
licht; BARB. XI. 462. Thai with axis sic duschis gaff; *Ib.* XIII.
147. Thai..gaf the bak but mair abaid; *Ib.* XVIII. 323. Myne
hert giffis me no mor to be With 30w dwelland; *Ib.* XIX. 97.
Gyfand hyme mony dintis sare; *Leg. S.* xxvi. 692. Of kynd
his hart gaffe hym..To mak him serwys; WYNT. III. 738. It is
ordanit that na baxtar brek the pais that is giffin or salbe
giffin hym be the baillies; 1433 *Aberd. B. Rec.* I. 390. His
hippis gaff mony hoddous cry; DUNB. liii. 18. Ay da be da
puttand thame in beleue To gif battell; STEWART 6622. I sall
do ane cursit deid, and gif you with ane quhynger; 1536 *Antiq.
Aberd. & B.* III. 402. The westmost..chope, giffand x s. [a]
3eir; 1554 *Edinb. Old Acc.* II. 20. The haill inquest findis
Thomas Dikisoun in the wraing for giffin Rolland Scot ingurius
wordis; 1567 *Peebles B. Rec.* 304. [At] the dairest pryces that
the..burdis sall happin to gif in this contrey at the tyme;
1582 *Prot. Bk. J. Scott* 138. Sho gifs hir horse both brydle,
chak and vand; J. STEWART 17/87. For twa blais giffin to
Andrew Flemingis wif; 1602 *Shetland Sheriff Ct.* 16.

b. *God gif*, God grant that, would that.
All Karrik cryis, God gif this dowsy be drownd; DUNB. *Flyt.*
158. God gif 3e war Johne Thomsounis man; Id. lxii. 4. God
gif I wer wedo now; *Maitl. F.* lxxx. 8.

Give, Gyve, *v.* Also: **giw(e, gywe. P.p. givin, -ine,
-ein, gyvyn(e, -in ; giwin, -en, gywyn, -in.** [ME. *give,
gyve,* var. of GEVE *v.,* GIF *v.* In later use prob. adopted
from English.] *tr.* To give, in various senses.
(**a**) That thai..litill had to gyve; WYNT. VII. 2690. God gyve
him gras To govern..his land; *Ib.* IX. 1118. I giue 3our
counsale to the feynd of hell; LYND. *Answ. King* 43. Sen it
giuis me in my hart; Id. *Meldrum* 353. Quha will nocht haill
to Christ him giue; G. *Ball.* 31. Giueand him consall to have
devoirit his sone; PITSC. I. 220/11.
(**b**) Thow suld..thé fra lustys to wertu gywe; WYNT. IV. 1928.
To gywe hyr wemen tow to spyn; *Ib.* v. 5049. [Power]
quytclaimis to giw; 1474 *Antiq. Aberd. & B.* III. 527. It sall
nocht be lesum..to giwe nor to mak ony akkaring..of the
said land bot to the said prowest; 1531 *Reg. Soltre* 104.
Thay giwe him vings hich vith the vind to brall; J. STEWART
156/11. Who..this sing and show did giwe; FOWLER I.
117/137. To giwe vp thair names to the session; 1605 *Aberd.
Eccl. Rec.* 44. They sall giwe wnto thame thair..upricht
counsall; 1623 *Aberd. B. Rec.* II. 388. He..sall giw noties to
the cuntrie people; 1653 *Aberd. Sheriff Ct.* III. 61.
(**c**) For qwhy that..Dauid kyng qwhilom of Scotland..has
gyvin [etc.]; 1389 *Facs. Nat. MSS.* II. 47. The crowne wes
gyvyn for wyctory In auld tyme; WYNT. IV. Prol. 13. A man
all gyvyne to wykkytnes; *Ib.* v. 5704. Efter the fulfilling of
mariage and joynt feftment gyvin; 1428 *Antiq. Aberd. & B.*
III. 460. The armys..var gyuyn to 3our predecessours be

the prince; *Compl.* 148/4. Befoir definitive be givin out; 1578 *Conv. Burghs* I. 59. To pay silvir for the victuall I sould haif giuein him fearneyeir; 1602 *Elphinstone Chart.* 165. Tua coilhors, quhairof one blind, givine to the coilman; 1644 *Edinb. Test.* LXI. 2.

(*b*) Tendys or monay That wes gywyn in offerande; WYNT. v. 1757. Sentens gywyn but fowrme off lawe; *Ib.* 3851. Twa chalderis wittell.., gywin to him; 1566 *Melville Chart.* 115. [The fuel] salbe..giwin into the said bairnes chalmerer into the college; 1637 *Misc. Spald. C.* V. 226. The testament datiwe..eiked and giwen wp to Ludovick Grant; 1677 *Grant Chart.* 354.

FOUR

The Concise Scots Dictionary as a Tool for Linguistic Research

Mairi Robinson

INTRODUCTION

The publication of the *Concise Scots Dictionary* (CSD) in 1985 did not exhaust the potential of the material assembled for the dictionary. This paper explores the possibility of research projects using the CSD which were not specifically envisaged when it was being planned and compiled, and attempts to stand back from CSD and evaluate it from this point of view.

CSD will clearly be of use as a first point of investigation in many research enquiries. It very conveniently provides, within a single volume, information on a whole range of matters relating to Scotland, not only in the sphere of language but also in the areas of culture and history. At the same time CSD always provides references to the fuller information in the parent dictionaries should that be required. My purpose here, however, is to look into CSD's potential as a more penetrating linguistic research tool in itself. *Prima facie* there are two very good reasons why it is worth investigating this. Firstly, CSD was produced in electronic form and is available for computer-assisted analysis. This makes possible a previously unattainable degree of speed and thoroughness for research inquiries. Furthermore, it is the only complete Scots dictionary available at the moment in electronic form.[1] Secondly, the size and scope of the data collection on which CSD is based might perhaps allow a more broadly based analysis of Scots than has hitherto been possible for scholars.

CSD is an extremely detailed and information-rich dictionary of its type. However, it is a condensation and selection,[2] based mainly on three major works, themselves based on even larger bodies of data. These too are only a small proportion of the total information extant on the Scots language.[3] The questions to be investigated here are: granted all these preselections, which if any of CSD's data is sufficiently rigorous to be used for research purposes?

And for research into what? I propose to look now at various possible areas of research and see how far CSD can be useful in investigating them.

1. Lexis

1.1 Lexical items in CSD are arranged alphabetically according to first headword, with homographs of different etymological origin treated as separate entries, e.g.

fa^1
fa^2

Derivatives, compounds and phrases may occur either in paragraphs of their own towards the end of the entry, or within the main part-of-speech sections, the latter if they are the chief illustration of the meaning given, e.g.

pliskie *n* 1 a practical joke, *chf* play someone a ~ play a (dirty) trick on someone.

For many derivative items, the headword is likely to be replaced by '~', which must be remembered when setting up a computer search.

1.2 The wordlist in CSD is based on those of SND, DOST and OED. Some features of the wordlists of the parent works and the effects of these on CSD are discussed in the Appendix. The parent wordlists were condensed by means of the exclusion criteria described in CSD Introduction pp. xvii to xx (and see Note 2). Further condensation was achieved by combining several parent dictionary entries into a single entry in CSD. The policies of the parent works and of CSD in relation to how much was put into a single word-article were very different. These are summarised in the table below.

MATERIAL TREATED AS SEPARATE ARTICLES IN SND, DOST, OED, CSD

	SND before D	SND after D	DOST	OED	CSD
PARTS OF SPEECH	Y	N	Y	Y	N
PHONEMIC VARIANTS	Y	N	Y	N	N
ORTHOGRAPHIC VARIANTS	Y	N	N	N	N
DERIVS	Y	N	Y	%	N
COMPOUNDS	Y	N	Y	N	N
PHRASES	N	N	N	N	N

Key
Y = all or most of such material is treated in a separate article
% = a significant proportion of such material is treated in a separate article
N = none or very little of such material is treated in a separate article

From this it can be seen that DOST in particular normally separates different parts of speech into individual entries, as does OED. DOST also frequently separates phonemic variants into distinct word-articles, while usually keeping orthographic variants within one article (Aitken, 1980: 56).

SND, from D onwards at least, is more likely to have all material from the same etymological source in the same article, including different parts of speech as well as both orthographic and phonemic variants. But A to C in SND regularly separates both parts of speech and variants, whether phonemic or orthographic, into several articles.

Derivatives are almost always given as separate entries in DOST and early SND, while OED usually subsumes minor derivatives but keeps separate those which have many examples of use. SND from D onwards usually subsumes all derivatives under the base word. Compounds are usually subsumed in DOST, OED and SND from D onwards, but kept separate in early SND. Phrases are usually subsumed in all three parent works.

CSD's policy, on the other hand, is to subsume within a single entry everything with the same etymological origin. This is interpreted broadly, to include separate parts of speech; all variants, whether orthographic or phonemic; and all types of derivative material, i.e. derivatives proper, compounds and phrases. Its policy, therefore, is most similar to SND's, but it goes still further in subsuming phonemic variants. This is probably the main reason for the apparent smallness of the CSD wordlist as compared with the parent works, especially DOST and OED.[4]

For example, in a short section of C where SND has 17 main entries, nine of these appear in CSD but only five of them as main entries in the same alphabetical position; one appears as an alternative headword in this same section, and three as sub-entries outside this section. In a section of M where DOST has 16 main entries, only ten of these appear in CSD, and four of them are sub-entries.[5]

1.3 CSD also notes two kinds of example of the beginnings of lexicalization, where new meanings develop unilaterally within a single part of a verb or noun paradigm. The first type of lexicalization occurs when a past participle is found in meanings not shared by the finite verb, e.g.

fecht *v* **2** *vt*, *chf in ptp* harassed, worn out.

Secondly, and usually with a slighter shift in meaning, is the specialized use of the plural of nouns, e.g.

fungible *n*, *chf in pl* consumable goods;
fee *n* **2** *also in pl* a servant's wages.

1.4 Summary of research possibilities.
Some kinds of research which could usefully be carried out on the CSD wordlist would be counting individual headwords or headwords plus

derivatives, either on their own, to discover the overall size of the Scots vocabulary; or in association with one or more of the following:

a) date of first and/or last use (see 8.1), to assess the growth and decline of the Scots vocabulary;
b) length of period of use (see 8.1), to assess for instance how much of the vocabulary was ephemeral;
c) etymology (see 9), to assess the proportion of vocabulary coming from the different sources and perhaps also (in association with a)) at different dates;
d) semantic field (see 2), to assess which semantic fields are strong in Scots;
e) dialect distribution (see 7.2), to assess the relative strengths of different dialects.

2. Semantics.

CSD's policy on the provision of semantic information is described in CSD Introduction pp. xxix–xxx.

2.1 Division by sense is the primary means of analysis in CSD, as it was in DOST and SND. The ordering of parts of speech and senses in CSD is historical, semantic and logical in that order of preference. In creating a CSD article, all of the parent dictionary entries were considered together. Their definitions and quotations were studied carefully. Sometimes a selection of their definitions could be immediately transferred to CSD; at other times it was felt to be more satisfactory to reallocate the sense divisions, now that the full range of historical evidence could be considered together.

2.2 In addition to the definition itself giving information on the meaning, CSD also frequently provides collocational information of a semantic type outside the definition proper, either by specifying the semantic field of the subject or object of a verb, e.g.

fung *v* 1 *vi*, *esp of a restive horse* kick;
grapple *v* 2 *vt* drag (water) for a corpse;

or of the noun complement of an adjective, e.g.

far . . . **far ben** *of the eyes* dreamy;

or by giving a field-label to the definition as a whole. These, however, are not always derived from the parent dictionaries. The most frequent are 'law' and 'mining' and for these two subjects-areas additional reference works were used as CSD sources (Gibb and Duncan, 1982; Kerr, 1980). In addition, Professor Robert Black was consulted on many points of legal detail, especially in the areas of meaning, currency and pronunciation. A number of other field-labels are also used. Examples in fairly frequent use are:

'Presbyterian Church', 'golf', 'curling'.

2.3 Summary of research possibilities

CSD could therefore be a useful tool in various kinds of computer-based research into semantics, e.g.

- a) searching for specific definitions, which consist either of single or of multiple words;
- b) searching for members of a semantic field, either by using field-labels or by matching definitions;
- c) counting the number of definitions of specific words or covering specific semantic fields, perhaps in association with date-range (see 8) or dialect distribution (see 7.2), in order to assess the length or breadth of use of the words or fields.

3. Orthography

The CSD Introduction illustrates some of the features of the Older Scots spelling system, in particular on p. xiv. For CSD's policy on the selection of headwords, see CSD Introduction p. xx. For its policy on the omission of predictable variants, see Robinson (1985: 118–119) and CSD Introduction pp. xviii–xx.

3.1 Summary of research possibilities

On the whole, CSD would not be a helpful research tool where any kind of specific orthographic detail is required. In particular

- a) Many discrete spelling forms given in the parent dictionaries are omitted from CSD. It is impossible therefore to investigate all spelling variants of any item by means of CSD.
- b) It is impossible to tell from CSD how a word is spelled in the original text.
- c) Such forms as are given in CSD illustrate the commoner, more 'normal' spelling preferences of ModSc and OSc. Less common spellings will very rarely be found in CSD.
- d) It is impossible to tell from CSD how many or which variants occur in Scots but have been omitted from CSD, except in cases where none has, i.e. where there is no '&c'.

However, in the absence of any other computer-readable source, CSD may be useful for a limited overview of the data in certain areas. For example, a *representative* spelling is provided where relevant for

- a) ModSc versus OSc;
- b) phonological variants;
- c) spellings restricted to specific meanings or date-ranges:

4. Phonology

The phonological entries in CSD, uniquely including reconstructions for obsolete words, were compiled by Jack Aitken. A fairly full description of CSD practice in this area is provided in CSD Introduction §5, and, from a rather different viewpoint, in Aitken (1985). Some general features of the Scots sound system are described in CSD Introduction pp. xiii–xiv. I shall not repeat that information here.

4.1 Summary of research possibilities

Clearly CSD cannot be used for primary research on phonology, as each piece of information it provides is based on the observations and analysis of at least one and frequently two or three previous scholars. But its wide coverage could make it very helpful as corroborative evidence for new primary research, or as base material on which to form initial hypotheses. It may therefore be useful to note here the significance of CSD's various conventions and its organization of information.

a) Where no transcription is given, the headwords should be used on their own, in conjunction with the tables in CSD Introduction pp. xxii–xxiii, and xxvi–xxvii.
b) The first transcription is of the most widespread modern pronunciation.
c) Less common widespread variants (if any) are then given, in decreasing order of frequency.
d) Modern localized variants are then given. Where these are labelled 'also', the restricted pronunciation applies in addition to the more general one(s) given under b) and c) or to be inferred from a).
e) Finally, marked '*', reconstructed modern pronunciations based on obsolete spelling forms are given. These are wholly derived from the knowledge and research of Jack Aitken himself.

Two particularly promising areas, then, in which to use CSD as backup for phonological research might be

a) positional phonology, e.g. examining certain consonant clusters, or the difference in development of specific vowels in medial and initial position;
b) diaphonology, e.g. examining the various dialectal reflexes of OE ō in Scots over a broader range of items than has hitherto been possible.

5. Morphology

5.1 Inflexional morphology

The CSD Introduction mentions some general features of inflexion in Scots on pp. xiv–xv.

As usual, the predictable is omited from CSD (see Note 2), the predictable here being either the regular Standard English or the regular Scots pattern. So either English or Scots regular plurals of nouns, past tenses and past participles, present participles and verbal nouns are not normally specified in CSD. In addition the regular non-Standard English conflated past tense and past participle form (e.g. 'he done it') is not normally given either. The numerous examples of regular forms which will be found are there because some other aspect qualifies for inclusion in CSD, and this is therefore given along with the form(s) in which it is found, e.g.

> paint . . . ~it 1 = painted *15–*. 2 *of glass* coloured, 'stained' *e16.3 fig, of words, speeches etc* highly 'coloured' for show or to deceive . . .

All known unpredictable inflexional forms which fulfil the frequency criteria are included in CSD. Where additional predictable inflexional forms exist, but have been omitted, CSD adds 'also'.

5.2 Derivational Morphology

Here the same predictability criteria apply. Thus regular diminutives of nouns, comparatives and superlatives of adjectives, adverbs formed from adjectives, agent nouns in *-er* and abstract nouns in *-ness* are normally omitted, unless the item has to be included because some other aspect is not Standard English. However, CSD does contain a great number of derivatives and compounds. Here there is an additional criterion to be applied before an item is judged worthy of inclusion: that the item must be more than the sum of its parts. This is assessed in the areas of meaning, period of currency and pronunciation.

5.3 Summary of research possibilities

CSD could, therefore, be used to investigate irregular formations, both for inflexions and for derivations. Furthermore, inflexions are always labelled (e.g. *pl* (= plural), *pt* (= past tense)), so that a computerized search for specific inflexions should be possible without any further marking up of the text. Some derived forms are also labelled, e.g. 'comparative', 'superlative', but most are not.

6. Syntax

6.1 The CSD Introduction touches briefly on Scots syntax on p. xv. In the dictionary text, CSD is fairly generous in its syntactical information. For verbs, for example, it gives information on:

    a)   transitivity, for every meaning; (the CSD convention is that specific labels (such as *vt*, *vi*) continue to operate from one sense to the next until cancelled by another label);

b)   where relevant, which adverbs or prepositions are used with each verb, e.g.

   fair *v. of weather* clear (up).

Most phrasal verbs however are listed in the final paragraph of an entry, e.g.

   pey . . . ~**aff** pay for others' drink or entertainment . . . ~**on, alang etc** go quickly, hurry . . . ~**up** do (something) wirh energy.

c)   whether the following sense is restricted to specific constructions. This is always explicitly mentioned in CSD for verbs in

1) passive constructions;
2) negative constructions, e.g.
   fa *v* 5 (3) *chf in negative* not be able to obtain or keep; be unable to afford;
3) impersonal constructions, e.g.
   fa *v* 6 (1) *freq impersonal with indirect object* fall (to one) as a duty or turn; he appropriate, suit.

For nouns, countable and non-countable nouns are differentiated only by their definitions, e.g.

   fussoch *n* 1 the grass that grows in stubble; waste fragments of straw, grass etc. 2 a loose, untidy bundle of something.

It would thus be possible to use CSD to investigate specific known examples of countable or non-countable nouns, but not to search for either class as a whole.

Other parts of speech have their syntactic collections specified, e.g.

   juist *adv* 2 *freq following the word or phrase it modifies* really, quite.

Function words usually have a considerable amount of collocational information to illustrate the syntax, either descriptive of the general context or specifying exact usage. They are also frequently given brief illustrative quotations, e.g.

   wi *prep* 2 by: (1) *after passive verb* by means of, by the action of *la14-*: '*eaten with the mice*'. (2) *now followed by gerund* by reason of, through *la14-*: '*wi being ill be couldna come*'.

6.2 Summary of research possibilities

CSD could therefore be used for a computerized search for

a)   examples of Scots items matching known English items, e.g. specific count nouns; verbs meaning 'belong to', etc;

b)   examples of Scots items where part of the construction in Scots is known, e.g. phrasal verbs using 'aff';

c)   examples of Scots items matching specific types of construction, where neither the English nor the Scots is known, e.g. impersonal verbs.

7. Linguistic Variation

7.1 Stylistic Variation

Unfortunately, literary genre and stylistic register are not always explicitly noted in the parent dictionaries. Such comments as they do have are usually passed on by CSD, plus a few more noted by CSD editors. Examples of labels in both areas are:

a) Literary genre — 'verse', 'ballad';
b) Stylistic register
   1) written Scots — 'literary', 'arch', 'hist';
   2) spoken Scots — 'contemptuous', 'familiar', 'child's word', 'gipsy'.

Sociolinguistic variation was not investigated by SND, nor is it illustrated in CSD, except occasionally with such labels as 'familiar' or 'child's words'.

Since the information on stylistic variation in CSD, as in the parent works, is very far from complete even for the categories which are noted, it cannot be used as a reliable source. It would thus be of very little use as a tool for analysis of registers.

7.2 Dialectal Variation

CSD's information in this area is based mainly on the SND, with significant additional sources for phonology (see 4 above).

The main area of spoken Scots not well covered by the SND data on which CSD is based is modern urban Scots, but there is occasional information on the towns and cities. All of these except Glasgow ('Gsw') and Edinburgh ('Edb') are always written out in full in CSD, e.g. 'Aberdeen', 'Perth' etc., in contradistinction to county names, which are abbreviated, as 'Abd', 'Per' etc. CSD does from time to time supplement the data from SND, but reliable coverage of Scottish urban usage must await further research.

However, SND did have a system for acquiring up-to-date information on modern rural dialect. CSD transmits an outline of this information, combined with the dialectal provenance of the written texts which were used as evidence in the parent works. All current items in CSD, whether meanings, spellings or pronunciations, have their dialectal provenance specified if it is restricted. In cases where the dialectal restriction appears to be recent, CSD notes this, e.g.

laith . . . ~fu 1 reluctant(ly) *18-, now Wgt* . . . 3 disgusting(ly) *19-*, NE Per *Loth*.

Here sense 1 is dialectally restricted only at the present day; whereas sense 3 has apparently always been restricted. Deductions by CSD editors about earlier usage are based on the literary evidence supplied by SND and (occasionally) DOST.

Current items which are unmarked in CSD can be taken to be known over the whole of Scotland, i.e., in SND's terminology, they are 'General Scots'. Obsolete items are only occasionally specified as to dialect in CSD. For one thing, the total evidence for obsolete items in the sources is much less substantial, consisting as it does only of written texts. And written sources alone rarely give sufficiently clear evidence of dialectal restriction to be reliable. But when the evidence was judged to be sufficiently clear, CSD included the information. The majority of OSc dialect labels in CSD are derived from a specific note on provenance in DOST.

CSD could therefore be used, in a computer search, to investigate for example

a)   The relative strengths of the different dialects in ModSc, principally at the lexical and semantic levels;
b)   The relative proportion of localized as against General Scots usage in Modern spoken Scots;
c)   Evidence of dialect in OSc.

8. Synchronic and diachronic features of Scots

Based as it is upon three historical dictionaries, it is not surprising that the historical aspect of Scots vocabulary is extremely well documented in CSD.

8.1 First and last dates of use

Dates of currency are provided for every meaning and spelling, where the evidence in the sources is thought to be reliable. First and last dates of known use are given to the nearest half-century, immediately after the definition or form. An open-ended date means that the item is still current. Where no date is provided this is either because

a)   the information is already provided for the spelling(s), and is the same for the meaning(s), e.g.
     senzie &c *16-e19*, *latterly hist*; **senze &c** *15-e16 n* a synod, deliberative meeting of clergy.

     or the information is provided for the meaning(s), and is the same for the spelling(s), e.g.
     sensement &c, censement &c; sensament &c *n* a decision, judgement *la15−16*.
b)   the evidence in the sources is insufficient to provide reliable dates. Instances of this are almost always senses shared with English (these are marked in CSD by ' ='), for which excerptors (or editors) for the parent dictionaries have failed to supply any or enough Scots examples, though they certainly exist, e.g.
     sequel &c *n* 1 = sequel. 2 . . . .

There is a particular problem about final dates in the twentieth century.

Because SND's first fascicle was published in 1931, final dates for several early letters should strictly be early twentieth century (e20). In general, however, CSD's policy was to count all SND's dates of publication as current, so that normally all SND date-of-publication material will also be given as current in CSD, i.e. with no end-date. Sometimes however CSD editors might have additional evidence suggesting that items were in fact obsolete, and if so the items would be marked as ending in e20. But CSD's resources for checking current usage were not even as extensive as SND's, so that almost certainly there will be some usages which actually did terminate in e20 but which are wrongly marked as still current in CSD, and vice-versa, some which are in fact still current but are wrongly marked in CSD as ending in e20. The safest procedure is probably to regard all items for which there are twentieth century datings as potentially still current, and this in fact has been the policy followed in the phonetics section.

8.2 Summary of research possibilities

Research could therefore be carried out into either synchronic or diachronic features of Scots in time-bands of half-centuries. These should prove to be realistic periods for analysis. Apparent exactness, e.g. by specifying a particular year, is often spurious and can mislead, especially when historical material is being dealt with.

Some appropriate areas to investigate have been suggested under 1 and 2 above.

9. The relationship of Scots with other languages

9.1 CSD gives etymologies for most items for which SND and/or DOST have reasonably certain etymologies. Where the etymology is either unknown, uncertain or highly conjectural, CSD usually makes no comment other than 'unknown', 'uncertain' or 'obscure'. The other main instance where the etymology is omitted is where the '=' convention has been used in the definition. Here it is to be understood that the etymology is the same as that of the Standard English definition.

Where an etymology is given, it is placed at the end of the entry, section or phrase etc. to which it refers, and follows the pattern:

a)   the word's previous history in the British Isles, beginning with the nearest in time and working backwards. Comments such as 'only Sc', 'chf Sc', 'earlier in Sc' refer specifically to the word's history in Scots in relation only to English from Early ME onwards, i.e. since the twelfth century, as this is covered by OED. Thus for example an item described as 'only Sc' may also have occurred in French or Dutch or even OE; but it can be taken not to occur in English of any period since OE, as covered by OED.

b)   the word's antecedents in other languages, again beginning with the nearest in time and working backwards.
c)   any relevant cognate material, beginning with the British Isles and working outwards and back in time. This is only included if it sheds useful light on the Scots.

9.2 Summary of research possibilities

CSD could therefore be used for a computerized search for any specified dialect or period of British English, or for any external source or cognate.

10. Frequency

The absolute frequency of items in Scots itself cannot be estimated from CSD. Even in the parent dictionaries this is not really possible for a reader to estimate, for the reasons given in the Appendix.

But some guidance on *relative* frequency of items in CSD may be gleaned from three directions:

a)   CSD's frequency rules (see CSD Introduction p. xviii);
b)   CSD's distributional information (see 7.2 and 8 above in particular).
c)   how productive the lexical item appears to be, e.g. in polysemy, number of variants or amount of dependent derivative material.

Thus an item given as occurring from the late fourteenth century to the present day is likely to have been more frequent overall than one restricted to half a century, though it may never have been particularly common at any single period. And a modern item either in General Scots or found over many dialect areas is likely to be commoner than one restricted to a single district. On the other hand an item of relatively short duration which nevertheless has many unpredictable variant spellings and/or a number of derivatives and phrases formed from it is likely to have had a lot of use during its short life.

CONCLUSION

Overall, then, the major areas for linguistic research based on CSD would appear to be:

a)   The lexis of Scots, especially additions to it and losses from it over the history of Scots (see 1.4).
b)   Semantics in Scots, especially semantic fields (see 2.3).
c)   Dialectal variation (see 7.2).
d)   Synchronic and diachronic studies, chiefly in a) or b) above (see 8).
e)   Comparative philology, for the relationship of Scots to the other varieties of British English and also to other languages (see 9.1).

NOTES

1   This electronic form only extends to the capture of the text. CSD was not edited using a computerized database format with predefined mutually exclusive fields, but by the traditional method, based partly on the use of a number of predefined rules but also on the editors' lexicographic experience and intuition being applied pragmatically to individual lexical items. CSD cannot therefore immediately be used for computerized access to any category of information. My own current research is concerned to achieve the maximum yield of information from CSD with the minimum additional input of data.

2   In brief, the criteria for the inclusion of items in CSD are: a certain level of frequency of use; difference from Standard English; and absence of predictability. All of these themes will be referred to in this paper without further explanation. For a full discussion of CSD's principles of condensation and selection, see CSD Introduction pp. xvii ff. and Robinson (1985).

3   For a list of the main areas in which the parent dictionaries do not provide exhaustive information on Scots, see the Appendix.

4   Aitken (forthcoming b: Table 2, and see also Note 35) gives the wordlist sizes as:
OED 240,165 main entries;
DOST (estimated total) c.38,000 main entries;
SND c.20,000 main entries (but '50,000 words').
CSD promotional material claims c.25,000 main entries and c.45,000 sub-entries for CSD's wordlist.

5   The C section is the one-and-a-half-page SND section from *cocka-* to *cocke-* the M section the one-and-three-quarter-page DOST section from *mensal* to *menstrel-*.

APPENDIX

The shortcomings of the parent dictionaries as a record of Scots, and the consequences for CSD

a)   The source material used by the parent dictionaries is predominantly written.

b)   The corpus of texts used by the parent dictionaries is only a selection of the total available in Scots; some areas of the language are much better represented than others. For example, for OSc, early verse and literary prose were far better covered than was non-literary prose (Aitken, 1980a: 35).

c)   The collection (i.e. the actual examples selected by the excerptors) is based on excerption densities varying between 0.33 per cent for OED and 50 per cent for some of DOST's texts (Aitken, 1980a: 34, 39).

d)   For ModSc in particular there is also the additional factor of the variable density of the Scots itself in the source texts. Compare for example the density of Aberdeenshire Scots in William P. Milne's *Eppie Elrick* (1955), which has very dense Scots, with George Macdonald's novels (1857–1897), which have relatively thin Scots. See also 7.2.

e)   For middle and low frequency items excerption is likely to be exhaustive; while for the commonest words excerption is selective (see Aitken, 1980a: 34). It is notoriously easier for human excerptors to pick out examples of new or rare words than e.g. of unusual shades of meaning or new applications for common words.

f)   The overall coverage of Scots in DOST and SND varies greatly at different alphabetical points, because of the new reading programmes initiated by each dictionary's second editor.

g)   The need for CSD to use OED instead of DOST for OSc items from Pr- onwards will have resulted in a significant omission from CSD both of whole entries and of additional information about included items, compared with the earlier part of the alphabet. For example, in the first 40 pages of DOST L there are 25 words and important compounds which are not found in OED, and 17 in the first 60 pages of O, including about ten containing 20 or more quotations (Aitken, 1981: 43).

h)   In general, then, CSD's overall coverage is best between D and Z for ModSc, and between J and P for OSc.

OLDER SCOTS

FIVE

A Taxonomy of Older Scots Orthography[1]

Alex Agutter

The orthography of a historical dialect can be studied from different angles. McIntosh (1956) urges that orthography should be studied in its own right as a written form and not just as a visual representation of speech. His paper gives fair warning that some variation is really purely orthographic, and that it is inappropriate to force a phonological explanation on such variation. The present paper accepts this point, but nonetheless sets out to classify the orthography of OSc in terms of its relationship to the phonology, taking note of those orthographic conventions which have no significance in terms of phonological change. My point of departure is Jack Aitken's substantial collection of orthographic data and his appeal for further research in this area (see e.g. Aitken, 1971a).

Orthographic data from earlier periods of the language can be distorted by investigations that are based on premises relevant to modern data. For example, present-day English has a standard orthographic system in which (with very few exceptions) each word form has only a single spelling. This was not always the case. In the Preface to his *Dictionary* (1755), Dr Johnson comments on variant representations of individual words, and describes his principles for selecting one representation per word form. An alternative standard spelling system would be one in which each phoneme has a restricted set of orthographic representations, and any one of the set could be used for any occurrence of the phoneme. The first system allows no alternative in the spelling of a phoneme in a particular word form, so homophones could be reliably distinguished in the orthography e.g. ⟨rough⟩ ≠ ⟨ruff⟩. In the second system, homophones would not be reliably distinguished orthographically e.g. ⟨lean⟩ adj = ⟨lean⟩ vb. OSc seems to have had a more or less standardized orthography, in the sense that, according to our present understanding, few texts give orthographic clues about the provenance of author or scribe; but did it have the first, lexicalized orthographic system, or the second grapheme-phoneme kind of system, or a system which was neither of these? The answer to this question is not immediately apparent.

Aitken (1971) discusses issues relating to OSc orthography, including the possibility of a complete list of the types and tokens of recorded graphemes; an account of the types of variation possible within the standard system; and the relationship between an individual's practice and the system as a whole. My objectives in this paper are more restricted. Using mainly familiar data, I wish to propose a taxonomy of the OSc orthographic system which will classify spellings in terms of their relationship to sound changes. The exposition of this taxonomy throws light on, among other things, the question of what kind of standard spelling system OSc had.

The need for a taxonomy

The researcher into OSc orthography is confronted by a wealth of largely unanalysed data. Such an abundance of data obscures rather than illuminates the issues that are of interest unless it is classified in a systematic way. With the aid of a rigorous classification scheme — a taxonomy — we are less likely to overlook important data or, conversely, to overinterpret data that are of doubtful significance. A taxonomy allows us to construct hypotheses which are scientific in the Popperian sense, about the interpretation of the orthography. These permit, and indeed prompt, the design of specific small-scale studies consistent with a hypothesis, or inconsistent in a way that leads to refutation of the hypothesis and appropriate amendment of the taxonomy. Obviously this kind of progress in understanding cannot be achieved systematically without a taxonomy. The most important point here is that progressive amendment of the initial taxonomy integrates and unifies the outcome of small-scale orthographic studies, which would otherwise be more or less wholly separate from each other, and thus it allows a systematic advance.

THE TAXONOMY

The taxonomy outlined below is designed for interpreting orthographic data in relation to phonological change. It is the simplest one that I can contrive that is consistent with the data considered but is, of course, likely to require modification and elaboration in the light of further studies. The taxonomy which I propose has four major taxa.

Type 1: Basic Spellings

These spellings are found from the beginning of the OSc period and in this sense they are native spellings. They provide no evidence of sound changes within OSc although they may of course provide evidence of earlier sound changes such as / i /-umlaut, palatalization or ME Open Syllable Lengthening. Using the graphemic theory of Hall (1961: 14; see also

Venezky, 1967) graphemes such as ⟨sch⟩ for / ʃ /; and ⟨ch⟩ for / x / are type 1 spellings.

I anticipate that the majority of spelling forms in OSc will prove to be of this type. This taxon includes not only such well known standard OSc spellings as those above; but also spellings shared by OSc and southern ME and Early ModE. For example, ⟨Vce⟩ for / V: /: this is primarily derived from the effects of ME Open Syllable Lengthening, but as this sound change predates the OSc period such spellings have no significance for phonological change within OSc.

Type 1 can also accommodate a large amount of variation e.g. in spelling affixes ⟨browstare/browsteris⟩; ⟨-ioun/-iown/-ion⟩. Such variation in type 1 does not imply phonemic or even necessarily phonetic variation in the language, but merely the absence in OSc (as in other dialects of English) of any single regular representation of unstressed vowels.

Type 2: Additional Spellings

These are spellings which, although not native to OSc, are borrowed from some 'foreign' orthographic system and become conventional in OSc. They are normally used alongside type 1 spellings but, at least theoretically, they could supplant type 1 spellings. Only graphemes borrowed within the OSc period are included as type 2 — earlier loan graphemes are classed as type 1. Obviously there is a grey area between types 1 and 2 where early loans are concerned, and a full study of the chronology of grapheme occurrence would be required to verify allocations. However, as a hypothesis, I propose that e.g. the French compound grapheme (Hall, 1961) ⟨que#⟩ for / k# / and the latter loan southern English graphemes ⟨sh⟩ for / ʃ /, ⟨wh⟩ for ?/ ʍ / (see below) and ⟨oa⟩ for / o: / should be classed as type 2. Some forms which occur rarely in the ESc period, such as ⟨ea⟩ for / ɛ: /, may belong in this category or may be rare members of type 1. Only a thorough analysis of their earliest known occurrences will clarify the assignment of these spellings.

The earliest uses[2] of type 2 graphemes imply an active knowledge of 'foreign' orthography, but their later uses, once they have become conventional in OSc, imply no such knowledge on the part of the writer.

Type 2 might be complicated by the addition of a subclass 2b of spellings which, while not obviously imported, differ from type 1 graphemes in their lexical distribution, frequency or chronology. Probably the least contentious member of this class would be the use of ⟨z⟩ in place of ⟨ʒ⟩ for / j / in printed texts. This change led to later spelling pronunciations e.g. [mɛnziz], but was not itself caused by phonological change but by the socio-economic pressures of printing.

⟨VCC⟩ came to be used for / V / in monosyllables in place of the earlier type 1 ⟨VC⟩. Its source is not external orthographic practice but the type 1

⟨VCC⟩ which was confined to polysyllables. This change can be classed as 2b because its source is not related to phonological change within OSc.

Far more contentious is my classification of ⟨Vi, Vy⟩ for / V: / as type 2b.[3] Although Kohler (1967) gives a number of possible sources for this spelling based on sound changes (monophthongization of / V: / diphthongs; loss of syllabic / I / in inflections following / V: / e.g. in ⟨gais⟩ *goes*, ⟨wais⟩ *woes*) some other possible sources (Kohler, 1967) do not relate to phonological change within OSc (the existence of doublets from separate cognate loan sources e.g. OF *point*, L *punct-*; dialectal OF *glore, gloir*). Moreover, southern English also shows the adoption and spread of digraph spellings for / V: / at this period. In the south, the choice is ⟨Va, Ve⟩ rather than ⟨Vi, Vy⟩, but it suggests that the adoption of a digraph for / V: / was orthographically motivated rather than phonologically motivated. This view is also supported by the fact that ⟨Vi, Vy⟩ became extremely common, if not the most frequent, marker of / V: / in OSc. This contrasts markedly with the rare use of type 3b (see below) and underlies my reluctance to class ⟨Vi, Vy⟩ as back spellings resulting from phonemic mergers.

Type 2 spellings are all additions to the basic set of type 1. 2a might be called external additions, while 2b might be called internal additions. Like type 1, these spellings apparently imply no change in the phonology. However, unlike type 1, all type 2 spellings indicate a change in orthographic practice possibly through the influence of scribal schools, fashion etc. It is an open question whether there is a need for the addition to the taxonomy of sub-class 2b or whether such spellings can best be classified as lexically- or temporally-restricted type 1 spellings.

Type 3: Innovations

These involve the lexical redistribution of type 1 and 2 graphs to represent changes in the OSc phonological system. They have two distinct sub-classes.

3a: Direct

These spellings provide evidence of a sound change specifically occurring in a particular word-form. Spellings of this type would be e.g. ⟨1⟩-less spellings of words which have undergone / 1 /-vocalization e.g. ⟨gowd⟩ *gold*; ⟨v⟩-less forms denoting / v /-deletion e.g. ⟨deil⟩ *devil*; forms such as ⟨ck#⟩ for earlier ⟨ct#⟩ e.g. in *collect, conduct*, ⟨n#⟩ for earlier ⟨nd#⟩ e.g. in *send, hand*, ⟨1#, 11#⟩ for earlier ⟨1f#⟩ *self*, all illustrating consonant cluster reduction.

Any and all instances of the use of type 3a spellings, whether early or late, can be taken as evidence that the writer is familiar for instance with a phonemically / 1 /-less pronunciation of that word, either in his own speech or in that of his contemporaries. These spellings are the ones of crucial importance in determining whether a sound change progresses, not gradually or regularly, but by lexical diffusion through specific items (Wang & Cheng, 1970; see also Toon, 1983; Harris, 1985 ch. 3). One instance of a type 3a spelling cannot be taken to imply that the change occurred in any other word-form at the same time. Numbers of such occurrences can, however, be taken to indicate the lexical diffusion of a change.

Type 3a spellings provide evidence for a synchronic account of the phonology i.e. they relate to the contemporaneous language only, and do not provide information about earlier states of the language.

3b: Indirect

These are also known as reverse, inverse or back spellings. This type indicates the generalization of a sound change resulting in a phonemic merger or coalescence (Penzl, 1957). 3b spellings involve the use of originally type 1 (or 2) graphemes in unexpected distributions. An example would be the use of the ⟨1⟩ grapheme in words which etymologically never had / 1 /, but which contain a vowel phoneme that can (but in such cases doesn't) occur as a result of / 1 /-vocalization. Thus ⟨VI⟩ occurs in ⟨awalk⟩ *awake*; ⟨golk⟩ *gowk*. Other examples include ⟨ev⟩ in words which never had / v / but which contain a vowel phoneme that can occur as a result of / v /-deletion: as ⟨even⟩ for *eyen* (eyes); and ⟨nd#⟩ in words which never had / d# / e.g. ⟨send⟩ for *sen* (since).

In terms of graphemics, what used to be two separate graphemes in type 1 e.g. ⟨a⟩ and ⟨1⟩; or ⟨e⟩ and ⟨v⟩; or ⟨n⟩ and ⟨d⟩; as a result of a sound change, have been reinterpreted as single compound grapheme (Hall, 1961) of type 3b. Hence ⟨al⟩ for / au / → [ɑː, ɔː]; ⟨ev⟩ for / iː /; and ⟨nd#⟩ for / n#/. (Contrast type 1 compound graphemes e.g. ⟨ch⟩ for / x /.)

Type 3b spellings are often thought of as mistakes, for instance erroneously 're'-instating ⟨1⟩ in *awake*, hence ⟨awalk⟩. This view presupposes a lexicalized orthographic system (see above). If the orthography were actually only grapheme-phoneme related (and not grapheme-phoneme-word related) then once a sound change had become general, resulting in a phonemic merger, either type 1 or type 3 (a or b) spellings would be 'correct' for any affected word. For instance, ⟨al⟩ and ⟨au, aw⟩ would be equally acceptable spellings for / au / → [ɑː, ɔː].

If we adopt the hypothesis that OSc had a grapheme-phoneme related orthography, then it follows that after a particular sound change, words containing the affected phonemes would soon have occurred equally frequently with type 1 and type 3 spellings. Although a thorough word-based orthographic study would be required to corroborate or refute this hypothesis, an initial study of the orthographic variants of specific words in DOST suggests to me that type 3 spellings are comparatively rare even after the relevant sound changes. From this it seems that the OSc orthographic system is not solely grapheme-phoneme related: it is partially lexicalized.

If the system were fully lexicalized, type 1 and 2 spellings would continue to be used after a sound change and there would be no type 3 spellings. If, on the other hand, the OSc orthographic system were not lexicalized at all, but were only a grapheme-phoneme related system, then for those sound changes in OSc which result in phonemic mergers, we would expect innumerable instances of a type 1, (2), 3a, 3b pattern of spellings. Relatively few such sequences occur:

/ 1 /-vocalization	type 1	⟨wal⟩ *wall*
	type 3a	⟨wawys⟩ *walls*
	type 3b	⟨walter⟩ *water*
/ v /-delection	type 1	⟨douve⟩ *dove*, ⟨even⟩
	type 3a	⟨dow⟩, ⟨eine⟩ *evening*
	type 3b	⟨ewine, evin⟩ *eyes*

While type 1 spellings obviously occur before type 3a, which occur before type 3b for any particular sound change, in any period after the sound change all three types coexist. Of these spellings, only type 3b provide evidence for a diachronic account of the generalization of sound changes, i.e. they relate current forms to a different, prior, state of the language.

In a parallel fashion to type 2 spellings, the earliest occurrence[2] of a 3b spelling implies familiarity of the writer with the relevant sound change and misinterpretation of a word as having undergone that change. Subsequent uses of the spelling, while still providing evidence of the sound change, do not necessarily imply any more about the writer than that he is familiar with what has become an orthographic convention (Aitken, 1971).

Type 4: Invasions

These involve the lexical redistribution of type 1 and 2 graphs apparently to represent a foreign, usually southern English, phonology. They differ from type 3 spellings in that they do not show the normal progression of an internal phonological change (see below), but apparently an abrupt switch from native to foreign phonology in particular words. Many of these spellings are apparently stylistically marked. Examples of type 4 would be the frequent use in e.g. ⟨quhois⟩ *whose*, ⟨lone⟩ *alone*, ⟨no⟩ *know*, ⟨lork⟩ *lark* of ⟨oi⟩, ⟨o⟩ presumably for southern / o: /, / o /. In these words we would expect type 2 ⟨ai, ay⟩ or type 1 ⟨aCe⟩, ⟨a⟩ for northern post-Great Vowel Shift / e / or [ɑ:, ɔ:] or for / a /.

Where a major difference exists between the native OSc phonology and the invasive form, there is no problem about assigning these spellings to taxon 4. However, it is debatable whether the compound grapheme ⟨wh⟩ used in late

MSc implies a sound any different from that implied by the earlier ⟨quh⟩ i.e. / xw / → / ʍ /. Since the sound was (and is) undergoing a very slow progression in all the dialects of English, from OE / xw / to / w / in present-day southern English, any move from / xw / to / ʍ / may be by parallel development in all English dialects rather than by invasive phonology. Similarly, does the use of ⟨gh⟩ as opposed to type 1 ⟨ch⟩ imply loss of / x / following its loss in the south, or merely the importation of a grapheme? At our present state of knowledge I support the less radical interpretation of these as type 2a spellings, first because underinterpretation is more easily corrected than overinterpretation, and second because ⟨wh⟩, ⟨sh⟩ and ⟨gh⟩ are external graphemes regardless of their phonological import in OSc whereas the other type 4 spellings are all native graphemes in non-native distributions.

My assertion that type 4 spellings do not represent the normal progression of a sound change by gradual spread through geographical space is based on the (rare) occurrence of so-called hypercorrect forms e.g. the overgeneralization of the rule of southern English rounding of OE / a / which gives orthographic forms such as ⟨lork⟩, ⟨bonc⟩. These forms are rare, geographically irregular (unlike the normal progression of sound changes) and lexically very confined.

Type 4 forms therefore seem to be intended to be read with a foreign phonology (hypercorrect forms do occur in phonology as evidenced in modern sociolinguistic research), but they might be interpreted alternatively as purely orthographic markers of foreignness. Since it is only the distribution of the type 4 graphemes which is foreign to OSc, not the graphemes themselves, their use would be a very inefficient marker of orthographic foreignness e.g. ⟨oa⟩ would serve this purpose far better than an odd distribution of ⟨oi⟩. On this basis, I conclude that their purpose is to mark phonological foreignness. If I am correct, the earliest occurrences of type 4 spellings would imply at least a passive knowledge of a non-native phonology. The presence of hypercorrect forms argues that these spellings cannot be taken as evidence of active knowledge, and may indicate the subsequent use of type 4 spellings as orthographic conventions. Whichever interpretation is preferred, type 4 spellings tell us nothing about the diachronic development of Older Scots phonology in isolation. If my interpretation is correct, then at best they provide synchronic evidence for 'Anglicization' or restandardization (Agutter, forthcoming) of the phonology.

CONCLUSION

In this paper I have attempted to show how a taxonomy would be advantageous in the study of OSc orthography. I have concentrated on classifying spellings in relation to sound changes and devised a preliminary taxonomy on that basis. The proposed taxonomy could obviously be extended and modified in a number of ways e.g. to take account of stylistically motivated orthographic variation, or to cover other periods of the language. However, even as it stands, it reveals some interesting aspects of the relationship between orthography and phonology and in particular demonstrates that OSc orthography was partially but not wholly lexicalized.

This paper is clearly only a very small beginning to the very large task of classifying the orthographic forms of OSc but I hope it has served to illustrate some of the potential and some of the problems of such a taxonomy.

NOTES

1   This is a revised version of a paper given at the Languages of Scotland Conference, Aberdeen, 26–29th July, 1985.
2   Early uses are theoretically important in trying to relate an individual scribe's practice to the orthographic system as a whole. In practice, of course, because of the chance survival and loss of mediaeval texts, we can seldom, if ever, be certain whether an individual token of a spelling was an early occurrence in the system.
3   ⟨Vi, Vy⟩ cannot be used for / u: / which is represented in both southern English and in OSc by ⟨Vu, Vw⟩ — in practice by ⟨ou, ow⟩ — and additionally by ⟨Vc⟩ (⟨o v⟩) in OSc only.

SIX

Dunbar: New Light on Some Old Words

Priscilla Bawcutt

Gavin Douglas, in the preface to his translation of the *Aeneid*, paid eloquent tribute to

> Maist reuerend Virgill, of Latyn poetis prynce.

Jack Aitken might likewise be termed prince of Scottish lexicographers, and 'maister of masteris': not only of those Masters of Arts whom he taught at Edinburgh University but a host of scholars scattered all over the world. This article is written in his honour by one who has learnt much from him, although never technically his pupil; it springs from a heart-felt desire to offer him

> Lawd, honour, praysyngis, thankis infynyte.

Dunbar has received much scholarly attention in recent years, and he is repeatedly commended for his mastery of language. Yet it is remarkable how many passages in his poems are still opaque; certain words, phrases, even whole lines still resist precise explanation. In his important edition of Dunbar[1] Kinsley (1979) provides the fullest Glossary that has yet appeared; even here, however, it is striking how often a gloss is preceded by a query, or instead of a gloss there appears the phrase 'meaning and origin obscure'. (For instances, under the letter C, look at *caprowsy*, *cawandaris*, *chevalouris*, *chittirlilling*, *clucanes*, *couhirtis*, *coun3ie*, *cowffyne*, *cowhuby*, *cowkin*.) After the lapse of five centuries, the existence of such difficulties is not surprising, particularly in a poet whose vocabulary draws on the informal and colloquial registers of the language; the difficult words tend to cluster in *The Flyting* and other humorous or satirical poems. We must accept that many problems are insoluble; nonetheless it is still possible, I think, to throw fresh light on some of these obscure or misinterpreted passages. The following notes are offered primarily as an aid to understanding Dunbar, but also as a small contribution to Scottish lexicography.[2]

Dunbar's poems are chiefly preserved in sixteenth-century prints and manuscripts, the great majority of them being found in two important anthologies, the Bannatyne Manuscript (B), c.1568, and the Maitland Folio (MF), c.1570, but their modern editing and glossing derive from the eighteenth century. Many of the glosses first supplied by editors, such as Allan Ramsay and Lord Hailes, have passed unchallenged into modern editions of Dunbar. Most of these are correct, but occasionally they were the result of guesswork, and need to be eyed critically and sometimes rejected. It is here that a modern student of Dunbar can build upon the work of other scholars, and on twentieth-century progress in dictionary-making. My own study of Dunbar's language is greatly indebted not only to OED but to DOST and MED, both of which provide precious evidence for the usage of Dunbar's near contemporaries in Scotland and England. Two other dictionaries, SND and the recently published CSD, are also invaluable, since Dunbar sometimes uses words and phrases that are not otherwise recorded in Scottish literary use till several centuries later. Advances in textual criticism, in palaeography, and in the study of Scots orthography during the fifteenth and sixteenth centuries can further aid our understanding of Dunbar. In this respect it is important to re-examine an assumption that seems increasingly prevalent: that the Bannatyne Manuscript is, in general, textually superior to the Maitland Folio. Bannatyne's importance in preserving many early Scottish poems can never be over-estimated, but he has been shown to be a careless copyist of work by poets other than Dunbar.[3] Bannatyne's texts of Dunbar should not be granted an over-privileged status; where there are several witnesses for a poem, the variants should be scrutinized and their respective value assessed as carefully and impartially as possible.

> (i) Fy, tratour theif; fy, *glengoir loun* [MF: *ganʒelon*] fy, fy!
>
> Fy, feyndly front far fowlar than ane fen!
> *The Flyting of Dunbar and Kennedie* (no. 23, 83–4)

B's reading is adopted by most editors; *glengoir* (= OF *grand gorre*) is glossed by Mackenzie as 'venereal disease', and by Kinsley as 'poxed'. But why, unless the abuse is completely random, should Kennedy be called 'poxed' at this stage of *The Flyting*? In this and the preceding stanza the main theme of Dunbar's attack is treachery: 'Thow crop and rute of tratouris tressonable' (73), 'tratour theif' (83), 'Thow leis, tratour' (86). In such a context the name of *Ganʒelon* is highly appropriate, and has an opprobrious function similar to that of *Lazarus* in line 161. It was Ganelon who betrayed Roland at Roncesvalles, and thereby became for the medieval world an archetype of treachery. In *The Book of the Duchess* (1121–3) Chaucer speaks of him as 'the false Genelloun, / He that purchased the tresoun / Of Rowland and of

Olyver'; and in *The Nun's Priest's Tale* (*C.T.* VIII.3277) he couples his name with that of Sinon and Judas Iscariot. Ganelon (for which *Ganʒelon* was the usual Scots spelling) was equally notorious in Scotland. Blind Harry says 'the traytour Ganʒelon / The flour of France he put till confusion' (*Wallace*, XII, 843–4; see also VIII, 1257). Ganelon also figures as a type of guile and treachery in several poems of the late sixteenth century, published in *Satirical Poems of the Reformation* (e.g. nos. xxii, 21; xxiv, 41; xxxvi, 99). *Glengoir* is clearly a very offensive epithet, but has far less point in the context. Although DOST's first record of the word is dated 1497, the vaguely abusive uses are recorded much later — 'glengoir huir' (1547), 'grandgorie loun' (1619). It is easy to account for B's reading as a misunderstanding of *Ganʒe -lon*, particularly if in his original the last element were spelt *loun*.

It should be noted that another abusive term twice applied to Kennedy, *cuntbittin* (50, 239), is also glossed by Kinsley as 'poxed' (DOST is more tentative), but does not necessarily have this meaning. Parkinson (1983: 150, 51) has pointed out that the same or a very similar compound is recorded much earlier in the fifteenth century, in *Lyarde*, a scurrilous English poem attacking the friars: 'Salle never no counte betyne mane bycomen ther brother'. MED glosses *counte betyne* as 'impotent', and Parkinson notes that in *The Flyting* it is linked with words suggesting cowardice, or sexual failure, rather than disease: 'Cuntbittin crawdoun . . . coward of kynd'. It is usually assumed that Dunbar depicts Kennedy as suffering from syphilis, and that this rules out a date for *The Flyting* earlier than the late 1490's, when the disease is thought to have entered Scotland. But this argument is somewhat flimsy, since the two phrases under discussion constitute the most precise and definite pieces of evidence in its support.

> (ii)   Or thow durst move thy mynd malitius —
> Thow saw the saill abone my heid up draw;
> Bot Eolus full woid and Neptunus,
> Mirk and moneles, us met with wind and waw
> And mony hundreth myll hyne cowd us blaw
> By *Holland, Seland, ʒetland*, and Northway coist
> [MF: By *hiland forland getland* and norroway cost]
> In sey desert quhill we wer famist aw:
> ʒit come I hame, fals baird, to lay thy boist.
> *The Flyting of Dunbar and Kennedie* (no. 23, 89–96).

In this account of a voyage by Dunbar line 94 is particularly tantalizing, since it contains apparently specific but puzzling references to real places. The line has been discussed by several scholars, most carefully by Baxter (1952) and Kinsley. Previous discussion has focussed on B's version of the line, with little attention being paid to MF's variants; Baxter, for instance, says 'The Maitland manuscript is still less intelligible' (p. 82). Most scholars have assumed that *Holland* corresponds to modern Holland or one of the provinces of the Netherlands, and that *Northway* is Norway. There has been less agreement as to *Seland*, which is identified either with Zealand, the island on which Copenhagen stands, or Zeeland, the district around the mouth of the Scheldt; and *ȝetland*, for which either Jutland (the peninsular province of Denmark) or Götaland, the Swedish province round Göteborg, has been suggested. The most recent interpretation is contained in Kinsley's note: 'I read the stanza as an account of a rough, dark voyage from Northern Holland up the west coast of Jutland and round into the Kattegat past Zealand; and thereafter to the south of Norway on the return journey — the destination being Denmark'. This seems to imply that Dunbar made a normal trading journey through the North Sea, along the coast of Holland and Denmark; but the stanza as a whole presents rather a different picture, of mariners being blown off course into an empty sea (*sey desert*). The order in which the places are mentioned is also puzzling — why is Zealand mentioned before Jutland?

If MF's version of line 94 is examined, it is by no means unintelligible; indeed it produces excellent, if different, sense. (It should be noted that elsewhere in this stanza Kinsley has already introduced some of MF's readings: *us met* instead of B's *wes met* in line 92, and *sey desert quhill* instead of B's *desert quhair* in line 97.) In MF the line divides, metrically and logically, into two units. In the first of these, *hiland* and *forland* are not place-names but common nouns. *Hiland* is a variant of *heland*: for the same spelling, cf. 'a hiland padyeane' (MF, I, 121/109). The sense here is 'high land, promontory', as in Douglas's 'the heland Pachynnus in Scycilly' (VII. v. 12); cf. also DOST, *heland*, sense 3. *Forland* has a similar meaning, 'headland or cape': see OED, sense 1; DOST, *for(eland*, sense 2; and MED, *for(eland*. The word tends to occur in descriptions of journeys (cf. *Sir Gawain and the Green Knight*, 699), shipwrecks, or the difficulties of navigation. Douglas says

> By strange channellis, fronteris and forlandis,
> Onkouth costis and mony wilsum strandis
> Now goith our barge . . .
> (*Eneados*, III Prologue, 37–9)

The second half of the line passes from the general to the particular: Shetland and Norway. *ȝetland* and *Getland* are both recorded as early spellings for Shetland; for an excellent brief note on the divergent developments of the Norse name, *Hjaltland*, see CSD, *Zetland*. Both Shetland and Norway were long regarded, with some reason, as extremely remote. As late as 1655 the English traveller, Thomas Tucker, expressed an opinion which was probably felt even more strongly in Dunbar's time:

As for Shetland (thought to be the Ultima Thule, soe much spoken of and reputed by the ancients to bee the furthest part of the world) it lyes over against Bergen in Norway, and very difficult to get thither but in some certaine moneths of the summer.

(Brown, 1891: 175)

MF's version of line 94 tallies far better with the rest of the stanza, suggesting an involuntary northward journey along the headlands of eastern Scotland, then out into the open sea of the Atlantic. If one looks at a map of northern Europe, the expanse of empty sea around Shetland and to the west of Norway corresponds far better to Dunbar's climactic *sey desert* than does the land-locked area, studded with islands, that comprises the Kattegat.

    (iii)   Laithly and lowsy, als *lathand* [MF: *lauchtane*] as ane leik.
            The Flyting of Dunbar and Kennedie (no. 23, 102)

B's *lathand* is adopted by most editors, and glossed as 'disgusting, loathesome'; no other citation, however, appears in DOST. It seems repetitious, adding nothing to the sense of *laithly*, and grammatically is unusual (one would expect the active sense, 'loathing, feeling disgust'), although not unparalleled (see OED, *loathing*, pple. a). MF's *lauchtane* supplies a richer and far more appropriate sense. This word, which corresponds to modern Irish Gaelic *lachtna* and Sc Gaelic *lachdunn*, is recorded in Scots from the fourteenth to the sixteenth century, with such senses as 'dull, livid, discoloured' (see OED, CSD, DOST). It is applied disparagingly to the complexion in another sixteenth-century poem in the Maitland Folio (I, 206): 'My rubie cheikis . . . Ar leyn and lauchtane as the leid'. At this point in *The Flyting* Dunbar is poking fun at the appearance of 'wan-visaged' Kennedy; it is the pallid colour of leeks to which he directs our attention, as does Langland in his portrait of the sin of Envy:

        And as a leek that haddle yleye longe in the sonne,
        So loked he with lene chekes, lourynge foule.
                (Piers Plowman, B. V. 81–2)

B's *lathand* can be explained as a misreading of an original *lachtan*, with a ⟨c/t⟩ confusion, aided perhaps by the proximity of *laithly*.

    (iv)   The larbar *lukis* [MF: *linkis*] of thy lang *lene* [MF: *lenʒe*] craig
            The Flyting of Dunbar and Kennedie (no. 23, 169)

B's version of this line has been accepted by most editors, and makes adequate sense: 'the feeble appearance of your long, lean neck'. No editor considers the rival claims of MF's variants, *linkis* and *lenʒe*, yet there are strong arguments in their favour. *Linkis* makes excellent sense because of its anatomical precision: the various meanings of *link* include 'flexible part of the body, joint, vertebra'. In Middle English it was used (in the plural) to translate Latin *spondilia* (see MED, *linke* n). Although DOST does not record this specific sense, SND gives illustrations from later Scots, including this quotation from Hogg's *Brownie of Bodsbeck*: 'the links o' my neck' (SND, *link*, sense 3). By contrast, B's *lukis* is extremely vague. What is more, the repetition of the word later in the stanza — 'With hingit luik' — is weak, and lacks rhetorical force. It should also be noted that in this sense of 'appearance' the normal form in Middle Scots is the singular. The plural *lukis* most commonly means 'looks, glances', as in Dunbar's own 'Fra everylk e gois lukis demure' (no. 63, 43; cf. also no. 14, 434). DOST in its entry for the noun *luke* gives only this citation for *lukis* in the sense 'appearance'. Textually, it is easy to account for B's reading as an erroneous interpretation of three minims, *linkis* being read as *luikis*. The merits of MF's *len ʒe* are more debatable, but deserve consideration. B's *lene*, 'lean', is straightforwardly abusive. *Len ʒe* means 'fine, thin, slender', and in Scots at this time was applied both to textiles and a person's figure (OED, *lenye*; DOST, *len ʒe* and *lignie*; CSD, *leengyie*). It does not seem normally pejorative, and its use here must be sarcastic. Rhythmically, however, it seems preferable to *lene*; it is also a more specific and unusual epithet. It is arguable that the very frequency of the commonplace *lene* in the vicinity of this stanza (see lines 121, 161, 182) might have prompted B to substitute it for the more difficult *len ʒe*.

(v)   Thow pure pynhippit ugly *averill* [MF: *averhill*]
      With hurkland banis holkand throw thy hyd.
      The Flyting of Dunbar and Kennedie (no. 23, 185–6)

Averill is a puzzling form, which DOST tentatively glosses 'app. = AVER, n', and for which it provides no other citations. Editors usually gloss it as 'old horse' (Gregor in Small, 1884–93; Mackenzie, 1932) or 'cart-horse' (Kinsley). I suggest that *averill* is a ghost-word, and that we should divide it into *aver ill*. Such linking of words that today would normally be separated was a common scribal practice; it is possible also that there may have been an unconscious confusion here with the other *Averill*, i.e. the month of April (DOST, *Averill*, *Avril*). *Aver* signifies a cart-horse, and is in itself usually disparaging; but it is frequently accompanied by pejorative epithets like *farcy* or *crukit*. As an adjective, *ill* (for which DOST also records MF's spelling with initial ⟨h⟩) was applied both to animals and persons, with such senses as 'evil, inferior, of poor quality'. *Fergusson's Scottish Proverbs*, for instance, include 'An ill hound comes halting home', and 'A good cow may have an ill calf'. In line 185 *ill* is the culmination of a series of abusive epithets; its selection for rhyme position can be paralleled elsewhere in Dunbar (as in 'the malt wes ill', no. 56, 51; also no. 82, 46). Kennedy is here depicted as the poorest specimen of a horse, and the image continues into the next line, where his bones protrude not through skin but *hyd*, 'hide'.

> (vi)   Rank beggar, ostir dregar, *foule fleggar* [B: *foule fleggaris* MF: *flay fleggar*]
> in the flet
>   *The Flyting of Dunbar and Kennedie* (no. 23, 242)

This line illustrates but one of the many interpretative problems presented by the climax of Dunbar's section of *The Flyting*, with its fusillade of internal rhymes and compressed and inventive use of language. Editors have usually adopted MF's *fleggar* instead of B's *fleggaris*, and glossed as 'flatterer'; DOST has two entries, querying *flay-fleggar* but supplying *fleggar* with a definition from Jamieson: 'One who talks loosely . . . a proclaimer of falsehoods'. Yet no lexical support is provided for any of these meanings. I wish to revive Fox's (1956: 184, 5) suggestion that MF's *flay fleggar* is correct, and means 'flea-frightener'. As such it is an alliterative compound, which rhymes correctly with *ostir dregar*, 'oyster dredger', and also parallels it in word-formation. *Flay* occurs elsewhere in MF as a spelling for *fla*, 'flea' (see line 446); *fleggar*, though not otherwise recorded, is an agent-noun derived from the verb *fleg*, 'frighten, scare away'. This verb was very common in later Scots, though DOST records only late instances of its use (DOST, *fleg, fleig*, v; CSD, *fleg*[1]). Fox also quotes from EDD (*fleg*, v) 'We . . . frae our shouthers fleg the bugs'. 'Flea-frightener' may seem a bizarre compound (though not in the context of *The Flyting*), but connotes either Kennedy's extreme ugliness (cf. modern 'scarecrow') or more probably his infestation with vermin (cf. similar references in lines 102, 121, 148 and 195). *Flay fleggar* thus evokes the ignominious image of someone standing in the hall (*flet*), trying to rid himself of fleas, perhaps scratching himself to frighten them off.

> (vii)   Ane benefice quha wald gyve sic ane beste,
> Bot gif it war to gyngil *Judas bellis*;
> Tak the a fidill or a floyte, and geste —
> Undought, thou art ordanyt tu not ellis!
>   *The Flyting of Dunbar and Kennedie* (no. 23, 505–8)

In line 506 all the early witnesses (which here include a print, as well as B and MF) agree remarkably, suggesting that it posed no problems for contemporaries. Yet what is the nature of the taunt that Kennedy hurls at Dunbar? Earlier editors have offered no convincing explanation of *Judas bellis*. Gregor glosses the line as 'Unless it were to act the traitor, as Judas did who betrayed Christ', and suggests that it alludes to 'the Passion Plays'. Mackenzie provides no comment. Kinsley notes: 'for treachery. The image is perhaps that of an ass (*beste*) with bells'. *Judas* is clearly the most shameful term that could be applied to a Christian, and is used in this absolute sense a few lines later (524). it is likely that some word-play is intended in the sequence *beste . . . Jud-as*. Bannatyne includes a feeble epigram from Heywood, which hinges on the joining of 'Iude and the ase togither' (fol. 159 b). There are similar puns also in *Love's Labour's Lost*, V. ii. 623 ff. Yet such word-play does not reach the crux of the problem. DOST provides articles on both *Iudas* and *bell*, but neither includes *Judas bellis*. Yet there is at least one other Scottish occurrence of the phrase, in an inventory of church vestments, books and furnishings for the Chapel Royal, Stirling, dated 4 November, 1505:

> Item, ly Judas bellis et ly traditor pro officio
> tenebrarum in septimana dominicie passionis.

From this we learn that *Judas bellis* were real objects, used in the service of Tenebrae, on the last three days of Passion Week; *ly traditor* perhaps refers to an image of Judas, or more probably the special candle-stick, used at this time and sometimes called the *Judas*. Rogers (1882: 66 and xlix), who includes this inventory in his history of the Chapel Royal, says that he has not come across *Judas bellis* in other ecclesiastical records. But they are listed among the furnishings of various medieval English churches. According to MED (*Judas*, n, sense 3) the Accounts of St Michael's, Oxford, for 1468–9, record the payment of three pence 'pro emendacione de Judas bellys'. They are also mentioned in the records of All Saints Church, Bristol, where an inventory of 1469 includes 'Clappers all Judas bells'. According to Atchley (1904:243),

> The accounts for 1413–14 record the payment of 2d. for mending these. At Wells Cathedral Church they paid 4d. for mending the "Judas bell" in 1414–15. At St Margaret's Westminster, they paid 10d. in 1486 "for making a new clapper to Judas bell".

There is some uncertainty as to the form and material of Judas bells; most probably they were rattles or clappers made from wood, such as the object mentioned in the following entry (dated *c.* 1450): 'Ane clappir of tre for the passioun' (DOST, *clapper*). These clappers seem to have had a range of functions at different times and in different parts of Europe, but they were commonly associated with the ritual Silencing of the Bells; the ritual stipulates that church bells should remain silent from the Collect during mass on the Thursday before Good Friday to the Gloria on the following Saturday. A joyful peal of bells celebrates the Resurrection; it is to this that Dunbar seems to allude in his poem on the Resurrection (no. 4, 29):

The knell of mercy fra the hevin is soundit.

While the bells were silent the harsh sound of clappers summoned church-goers to church; in some parts of modern Germany the custom also remains of the Judas Hunt — Judas (traditonally the bell-ringer) is driven by children out of the church, to the accompaniment of rattles and clappers.[4] But for Kennedy and the compiler of the Chapel Royal inventory *Judas bellis* seem to have had a further function: they were the clappers used to make a loud and discordant noise at the most dramatic moment of Tenebrae, as the anthem *Traditor autem* was sung, the last candle was extinguished, and the church plunged in darkness.[5]

Kennedy's insult therefore has a double thrust, quite apart from the opprobrious link with Judas. Kennedy first ridicules Dunbar's pretensions to a benefice; although ordained, he is worthy not of the priesthood, but of a comparatively humble role in the church. Presumably Judas bells were rattled only by those in minor orders, children, or even by the ordinary bellman. Secondly, Kennedy mocks Dunbar's pretensions as a poet. The discordant sounds produced by Judas bells are associated with the sort of music produced by popular but low-status entertainers — 'Tak the a fidill or a floyte, and geste!' Dunbar is *ordanyt* (in a double sense of the word) to no higher office, whether in church or court.

> (viii) My mind so fer is set to flyt
> That of nocht ellis I can endyt,
> For owther man my hart *to breik*
> Or with my pen I man me wreik.
> *To the King* (no. 44, 79–82)

This poem is extant only in MF. All Dunbar's editors transcribe line 81 with a space between *to* and *breik*, treating it implicitly as an infinitival phrase, 'to break'. But this produces awkward and unusual syntax; the auxiliary verb, *man*, 'must', is regularly followed by the infinitive without *to*, as may be seen in the following line (82). *To breik* should be read as *to-breik*, 'break asunder, shatter', and is indeed so treated in the Glossary to Craigie's edition of the Maitland Folio. This verb had existed for centuries, and is found in Old English. Even Dunbar's phrasing can be paralleled in one of OED's citations from the romance *Sir Beues*: 'Me thinkyth, my herte wyll tobreke' (*tobreak*, v). This correction does not substantially alter Dunbar's sense. But it removes a slight clumsiness from his syntax, and shows him ready, in the manner of Gavin Douglas, to use what was probably a rather old-fashioned and archaic verb. The use of the intensive prefix *to*- was rapidly being discontinued in the fifteenth century, and only a few examples are found after 1500 (see OED, *to*-, prefix[2]; CSD, *to*-).

> (ix)   The tailȝeour baith with speir and scheild
>   Convoyit wes unto the feild
>   With mony lymmar loun:
>   Off *seme byttaris* and *beist knapparis*,
>   Off *stomok steillaris* and *vlayth takkaris*
>   A graceles garisoun.
>
> *Fasternis Evin in Hell* (no. 52B, 127–32, re-punctuated)

There are three witnesses for this passage. Kinsley has adopted B's version, which seems undoubtedly the best. The only significant textual disagreement is over the ending of line 131, where for B's *clayth takkaris* the Asloan MS has *cat knapparis*, and MF has *wit clipparis*. I am here concerned only with the interpretation of the italicized words in B, which Kinsley explains as follows: 'In the Tailor's entourage are subsidiary workers in his trade: seam cutters, cutters of basting-thread (used to stitch quilting loosely), those who work protective steel into horses' pectoral covers, and those who tack cloth'. This explanation is ingenious, but it is unsupported by lexicographical evidence and it does not fit the context. Dunbar's compounds are not descriptively neutral; they are abusive, as *graceles garisoun* confirms. What is more, they draw on traditional stereotypes of the tailor.

Line 131 shows the dishonest tailor in action: stealing stomachers and taking cloth. *Steillaris* is a form of *stealers*, as in 'steillaris of geis' (Roule, *Cursing*, 262). Neither OED nor the unpublished files of DOST lend any support for interpreting *steillaris* as 'workers in steel' (Kinsley, Glossary). *Stomok* can indeed refer to a horse's pectoral cover, but its most common meaning is 'stomacher, article of dress worn by both men and women, laced in front, over a jacket, gown or kirtle' (OED; DOST files). As for the sense of *clayth takkaris*, there is no dictionary evidence for the early use of the modern tailoring terms *tack, tacking, tacker*. In Dunbar's time *takkar* was a common Scots variant for *taker*, and was frequent in the pejorative sense, 'thief, plunderer' (OED, *taker*; DOST files). This loaded sense of the noun (and of the verb from which it derives) is clear in another poem of Dunbar's:

> Grit men for taking and oppressioun
> Ar sett full famous at the sessioun,
> And peur takaris ar hangit hie.
>
> (No. 80, 36–8)

In line 130 the focus is rather on the ignominious work of the tailor, who sometimes had to re-shape old and possibly dirty garments. *Seme byttaris* is literally 'biters of seams'. Tailors had to bite or press seams together with their teeth, in order to make them flat and smooth. *Beist knapparis* is the most puzzling of these compounds. The noun *knappar* seems to derive from the echoic verb *knap* (or *gnap*), which (like modern *snap* and *crack*) means 'to break, with a sharp snapping noise', and is often used of the teeth. There is no good evidence that *beist* here means 'basting-thread'. Its most likely sense is 'beast', more specifically 'small verminous creature'; although not recorded by DOST this sense was current in later Scots (see CSD, *beast*, sense 3). *Beist knapparis* would thus be an insult analogous to the better-known *prick lous*, applied earlier (line 125) to the Tailor. Line 130 mocks those whose occupation causes them to bite seams and in so doing to crack vermin between their teeth.

There is literary evidence to support this interpretation, in a poem included by Bannatyne, and attributed to William Stewart, *The Flyting Betuix the Soutar and the Tailȝour*. Here the Soutar charges the Tailor with his thefts:

> Off *stowin stommokis* baith reid and blew
> ane bagfow anis thow bur abowt
> Thay fallowit the w¹ cry and schowt
> ha hald the theif that *stall the claith*
> (fol. 140 a)

He too speaks of seam-biting:

> For lowsy *semis* that thow hes *bittin*
> Thy gwmis ar giltin . . .
> (fol. 140 a)

and calls the Tailor a *priclous* and *wirriar of lyce*. In another fragment of verse (fol. 144 b), which may belong to this flyting, there is a similar reference to the snapping sound made by the Tailor as he destroys lice.

> ȝour commone menstrallis hes no tone
> Bot Now the Day dawis, and Into Joun;
> . . . .
> Think ȝe not schame,
> To hald sic *mowaris on the moyne*
> In hurst and sclander of ȝour name?
> *To the Merchants of Edinburgh* (no. 75, 29 ff.)

In this poem (extant only in the Reidpeth MS) Dunbar here rebukes the merchants of Edinburgh for retaining incompetent minstrels with a very limited repertory. *Mowaris on the moyne* refers to the minstrels, and is clearly derisive, but its precise sense is puzzling. The moon has many possibly relevant associations, such as madness — cf. 'ilk mone owt of thy mynd' (no. 23, 53), or criminality — cf. Falstaff's 'minions of the moon' (*I Henry IV*, I.ii.26). *Mowaris* is regularly glossed by editors as 'jesters' or 'mockers'; DOST also takes it to have this sense here, and provides an excellent illustration from Douglas's *Palice of Honour* (1229–30): 'Iuuenall like ane mowar him allone/Stude scornand . . .'. On the whole phrase Kinsley provides the following note: 'those who deride, mock at, the moon. Cf. the proverbs, "to bark against the moon", "the moon does not heed the barking dog".' But this still leaves the point of the phrase mysterious. *Mowar* seems to be an agent-noun, derived from the verb *mow*, which had two closely inter-twined senses: 'mock, deride', and 'make grimaces, pull faces'. This verb and its related noun (cf. French and modern English *moue*) are recorded in late Middle English phrases which closely resemble that here used by Dunbar. MED (under *moue*, n^2) cites the following explanation: 'Vel tu facies a mowe on the mone, hoc est, tu eris suspensus per collum immediate'. In addition it also records, from *The York Plays* with reference to the crucified Christ, 'make mowes on the mone' (358/286), and 'Late hym hyng, full madly on the mone for to mowe' (361/78). It looks as if 'to mow (or make mows) on the moon' was a current slangy and cruel jest at the expense of the ugly and distorted faces of those who had been hanged and left overnight on the gallows. There is a similar reference in *The Two Noble Kinsmen* (I.i.100) to a body left not on the gallows but the battle-field: 'Showing the sun his teeth, grinning at the moon'. Even closer to Dunbar's time is the description in *Scotish Feilde* of the corpses at Flodden, who lie 'gaping against the moone'.[6] Dunbar refers in another poem (no. 34, 24) to those who 'glowir' on the gallows, and in *The Flyting* compares Kennedy's ugly face to that of a thief 'glowrand in ane tedder' (176). I suggest therefore that *mowaris on the moyne* derives from this perhaps rather vulgar phrase; it means, literally, 'those who pull ugly faces at the moon', and by implication, 'those who are destined to be hanged and make such grimaces'. The insult is prophetic in character, analogous to the later English *gallows-bird*, defined by OED as 'one who deserves to be hanged'. Comparable Scottish formations are Dunbar's *gallow breid* (no.23, 141) and *widdefow* (no.23, 101), and Henryson's *widdinek* and *crakraip* (*Fables*, 661).

This study has, I hope, lexicographical value of a general kind. But its chief purpose is to illuminate some dark passages in Dunbar. Readers of his poems sometimes have to put up with a blurred impression of what he is saying, or to guess at this sense from the context. But in his best poems Dunbar is a precise and discriminating user of words; he is rarely vague, and we should not be content with vagueness, if a more definite sense is available. Sometimes, in *The Flyting* especially, one can still retrieve only a portion of the meaning, and much remains obscure. Yet — as in a jigsaw — the correct placing of one small piece may throw light on the surrounding area and contribute to the solution of the whole puzzle. What is more, a better understanding of the words and phrases here discussed increases one's admiration of Dunbar (and Kennedy also): these passages are not only lucid but vivid, visual, and forceful pieces of writing.

NOTES

1   All Dunbar quotations are from this edition; italics are employed to identify the word or phrase under discussion.

2   For discussion of other lexical problems in Dunbar, see Bawcutt (1981, 1983).

3   See Fox (1977) and Fox and Ringler eds. (1980: xi).

4   In the mediaeval period many symbolical explanations were devised to account for the silence of the bells; see Brown (1927: lxxvi and 4). On the popular customs associated with what were sometimes termed 'the instruments of darkness', see Frazer (1930 vol. 1, Part 7: 121ff.) and Lévi-Strauss (1973: 404ff.). Van Gennep (1947, vol. III: 1209–39) records the different practices in various parts of France; many different names were given to the clappers, but there seems no French equivalent to *Judas bellis*, although anti-Jewish feeling is often evident, as in 'la crécelle de Ténèbres est nommée *jwhero*, Juif' (p. 1237).

5   I am much indebted to Dr John Durkan for discussing with me the significance of Judas bells, and for a vivid description of the service of Tenebrae.

6   The relevant portion of this poem is included in Gray (1985: 9–10).

SEVEN

DOST and Evidence for Authorship: Some Poems Connected with *Ratis Raving*

Denton Fox

In view of the occasion, it might be appropriate to make a short experiment to see if DOST can be used to throw any light on the authorship of poems. I am very far from certain that Professor Aitken will approve of this use, or misuse, of the dictionary, but at the worst this experiment may be useful as a horrid example of methods to avoid. Though some may think we have already had enough of that ever-recurring phenomenon, the scholar who finds that similar phrases occur in a number of poems, and thus goes on to prove that they are all by the same author. There is salmons in both, as Fluellen said.

The procedure is obvious enough: one finds unusual words, or words used with unusual meanings, in a poem, looks them up in DOST and contemplates the other citations. If the words or meanings are frequently cited also from another particular poem, it may be that there is some relationship between the two poems. But the dangers are also obvious enough. Some words are of little or no value as evidence. Then as now, for instance, there were presumably many words that everyone knew but seldom had occasion to use, or at least to use in writing. (An example would be *lynx*: see DOST, *linx*.) Some subjects, too, have their own special vocabularies: if there were two MSc poetic descriptions of the preparation of flax, we would doubtless find that there was a striking similarity in their vocabulary. Even apart from the certainly huge body of lost OSc literature, not all of the surviving texts have been read for DOST, though I suspect not many literary texts have been missed; excerptors for the dictionary may have missed important words (though I have not found this to be a real problem); and of course what is printed in the dictionary is only a tiny fraction of the available data — though I think that, at least in the more recent volumes, the editors would not often give, for example, only three instances of a word if they knew of a fourth (see Aitken, 1981c). Then there is the dreadful human tendency to find whatever one is looking for, whether it is, for instance, evidence to prove that a poem is by Shakespeare, or that it is not by him. This tendency is likely to take the form of a belief that bad evidence, if accumulated in sufficient quantities, will become good evidence. But a million times zero is still zero; the metaphor that frail twigs, if bound together in sufficient number, can become a strong staff does not, unfortunately, apply.[1]

If the coincidences in vocabulary between two works seem more than chance coincidences, and one posits a relationship between them, we are not much further ahead: 'relationship' is a splendidly vague word, which is doubtless the reason for its current vogue as an amatory term. The author of one work could have been influenced by, or borrowed from, the author of the other (or conceivably both authors could have borrowed from a third and no longer extant work); the coincidences might have arisen from a coincidence of dialect; just possibly, the coincidences may go back to the particular diction of a single man. There is no easy method for determining between these options, though clearly one has to start by assessing carefully all the other available internal and external evidence. But the last option does seem to me a genuine one: I assume that in a comparatively early period, when most forces for uniformity, such as compulsory courses in English, vernacular dictionaries, and copy-editors, were absent, and when few people could have the opportunity to read a great many vernacular texts, men could have had fairly diverse vocabularies and usages. This diversity may well have diminished with the spread of printing.

The texts I would like to look at are some of the poems in Part six of Cambridge University Library MS Kk. 1. 5: *Ratis Raving*, a moral poem of 1814 lines that takes the form of a father's advice to his son, and the three somewhat similar poems that immediately follow it: *The Foly of Fulys and the Thewis of Wysmen* (476 lines); *The Consail and Teiching at the Vys Man Gaif his Sone* (456 lines); and *The Thewis off Gudwomen* (316 lines). This MS is a composite one, but Part six was all written by the same scribe, perhaps *c.* 1480. All the works in Part six have been edited by Girvan (1939), in one of the best editions of the Scottish Text Society: Girvan dates *Ratis Raving* 'not later than the opening decades of the fifteenth century' (p. lxxii), and dates the other three '*c.* 1450 at the earliest' (p. lxxiv).

Some of the more interesting words are these.

DOST, *lefe*, a., sense 2, 'Pleased, willing, glad (*of* or *for* something, *to* do something); also, inclined (*to* some kind of conduct)'. DOST lists five instances, one from *Ratis R.* (I use the dictionary's short titles), one from *Thewis Wysmen*, one from *Consail Vys Man* (There is another in line 150), two from *Thewis Gud Women*, and adds the note 'Appar. only in the poems cited: cf. also *Leful*, a.². As DOST notes, however, this sense occurs in ME, where it is fairly common: MED gives about one column of examples. This sense apparently died out around 1500.

DOST, *leful(l*, a.[2], with similar meaning, has ten citations, one from *Thewis Wysmen*, four from *Consail Vys Man*, two from *Thewis Gud Women*, and three from other works. DOST adds the note, 'Appar. only Sc. verse.'

DOST, *ill*, v., 'to speak ill of', 'to harm'. The only examples under this entry are from *Ratis R.* (in an unusual intransitive sense, 'to do harm'), *Thewis Wysmen*, and *Consail Vys Man*. But from the entry for *illing* and from 'Additions and Corrections' one can garner four more examples of the verb or verbal noun, two of them from the Records of the Burgh of Prestwick (1528). The verb has some slight currency in English, especially in Northern dialects. See MED, *illen* (example only from Rolle); OED, *ill*, v.; EDD, *ill*, 12, but is not recorded in SND.

youthage, n., 'period of youth'. DOST has not, of course, published this entry, but Professor Aitken kindly gave me access to the relevant slips. I have not found it in other dictionaries. The slips contain eight examples, one from *Thewis Gud Women*, one from *Consail Vys Man*, two other fifteenth century ones, and four sixteenth century ones. This is not very strong evidence for anything, but the two other fifteenth century instances, which I will return to below, are interesting.

the law and profesy. This phase appears in *Ratis R.* 1439, and, with some variations, in *Thewis Wysmen* 2 (*in prophesy and in lawis*) *Thewis Gud Women* 310 (*profecy & lawis*). As Girvan suggests, this is presumably a version of *lex et prophetae* (Matt. vii. 12, etc.), used in the New Testament as a compendious term for the books of the Old Testament (see OED, *prophet*, 3): in the passage in *Ratis R.* the poet is following Matt. xxii. 37–40, where the phrase occurs. This phrase (whether with *prophesy* or with *prophets*) is not commented upon in DOST (see however *law*, n.[1], 7b), though the instance from *Ratis R.* is given under *prophecy*, n.; I may be too sanguine in thinking that it would have been commented upon if it had occurred frequently. But the translation of *prophetae* as *prophecy* is striking: it seems unlikely that the reoccurrence of the phrase is a chance coincidence.

Other examples could be given, but anyone interested can, with Girvan's excellent glossary and DOST, explore for himself *ladry* and *chastiment* (though I have tried to avoid words in the A-G range, since the citations in the first two volumes of the dictionary are much sparser). There are of course some words in the S-Z range, for which DOST is not yet available, that look as if they might be relevant, but one cannot really argue on the basis of OED entries, since their citations of early Scots are too sparse.

If enough evidence has now been amassed to suggest that there may be some relationship between these four works, we are left with the question of what kind of relationship. As far as the three poems that follow *Ratis Raving* in the manuscript are concerned, there is, I think, no real problem, since there is some other evidence, of three sorts, to indicate that they are all by the same hand: (1) There are no significant disparities in the rhymes and the language of these poems, and they are likely to be of about the same date (See Girvan's Introduction, especially pp. lxxii–lxxiv); (2) Each of these poems contains lines that are very similar to lines in one of the other poems;[2] (3) The final 22 lines of *Thewis Gud Women*, the last of these three poems in the manuscript, form a sort of epilogue to all three. The author refers perfectly clearly to *Thewis Wysmen* ('. . . how ȝe suld knaw men that are wys, / and als ful men') and more obliquely to *Consail Vys Man* 'sindry documentis, / To scharp ȝong men in thar ententis').[3]

So it seems fairly safe to assume that these three poems are by the same author; indeed, some may think that I have only added superfluous and uncertain proof to an assumption that was already safe. But the situation is more interesting with *Ratis Raving*. I am not inclined to question Girvan's work or his cautious conclusion that *Ratis Raving* is considerably earlier than the other poems. The most striking evidence is that the author of *Ratis Raving*, like Barbour, but unlike later poets, including the author of our three poems, does not rhyme words such as *dey*, *de*, 'die', with words in pure *é*, such as *tre*.[4] While it is true that the quantity of evidence for this distinction in *Ratis Raving* is not large, all of Girvan's other evidence goes to support an early date.

However, the evidence from vocabulary connecting *Ratis Raving* to the other three poems seems, if not quite as strong as the evidence connecting the three poems to each other, fairly strong, so we are left with a puzzle. The puzzle is made worse by contemplating the work that immediately precedes *Ratis Raving* in the part six of the manuscript, *Dicta Salomonis*, a prose paraphrase of Ecclesiastes. There are few interesting coincidences of vocabulary between it and the three shorter poems: (1) The word *youthage*, discussed above, also occurs here twice (lines 158, 493); (2) The only instances of *glaikitnes*, 'foolish behaviour', in DOST are from *Thewis Wysmen* and this tract (though the word has some limited use in nineteenth and twentieth century Scots and Northern English: see SND, *glaikit*, and OED, *glaikitness*); (3) The use of *mak of* (someone), 'to esteem or value highly', is recorded in DOST with four instances, one from *Consail Vys Man*, one from this tract and two from the late sixteenth century: the idiom was not uncommon in Scots from that time on (DOST, *mak*, v.[1], 15b; see SND, *mak*, 1 (8)).

This is not, perhaps, evidence that one would care to hang a dog on. But Girvan (p. xxxii) has noticed two very interesting passages in the tract. When the author came to Eccl. vi. 7, 'All the labour of man is for his mouth: but his soul shall not be filled',[5] he paraphrased it as 'Item he sais that al the vismanis wyt is in his mouth, and thinkis that he has neuir yneuch of It' (lines 293–5).[6] This somewhat opaque sentiment is repeated and clarified in *Thewis Wysmen* 84, 87–88: 'The mouth schawis wysdome of the vys [Prov. xv. 7] . . . The wysman venis he wantis ay wyt / Suppos he have Ineuch of It'. Again, when the writer was paraphrasing Eccl. vii. 22, 'But do not apply thy heart to all words that are spoken: lest perhaps thou hear thy servant reviling thee', he changes this to, 'a man sulde . . . trow nocht al vpone thar seruandis that men will say, for percas It may be for Inwy of thaim' (lines 359–63). This is the other side of the advice given in *Consail Vys Man* 389–92, following Prov. xxx. 10, 'Accuse not a servant to his master, lest he curse thee, and thou fall':

> Ill neuir na seruand to thar lord;
> he sal the neuir luf the bettir ford,
> Fore he wyll traist it is leisinge
> For enwy, hattrent ore flechinge.

Various explanations are possible. Girvan cautiously remarks that these similarities 'may suggest that the poems are later than, and that they borrowed from, the prose, but the evidence falls a long way short of demonstration.' (He has some linguistic evidence to indicate that the prose work may be earlier than the three poems.) This is possible but seems unlikely: in both examples the verse is closer to the Bible, and it would be a clever man who could untangle the prose of the first example. I would cautiously suggest that the similarities suggest a single author. One might guess that when the paraphraser came to Eccl. vi. 7, with its not very lucid beginning, *Omnis labor hominis in ore ejus*, he mistranslated it to approximate Prov. xx. 7, 'The lips of the wise shall disperse knowledge', a proverb naturally close to the heart of any professional giver of wise advice, and then attached to it another statement that was presumably coupled with it in his mind, to the effect that a wise man thinks he lacks wit. When he came to Eccl. vii. 22, he was perhaps baffled by the last phrase (if your servant is reviling you, don't you want to know about it?), and so turned to another verse he knew well that also has the words *servus* and *maledico*, and then added the bit about envy because that was attached to it in his mind. (Envy is not a very likely motive, in fact: why should a master think your accusation of his servant was made out of envy, unless you were a servant yourself and wanted his place?) In the poem, the cues are different, but the same mental associations are made. The details of this hypothesis are of course very speculative, and it is perhaps impertinent to think that one can follow the mental processes of a nameless poet five hundred years ago. But the parallels are real enough, and some such hypothesis seems to me the best way of accounting for them.

In any case, we are still left with our puzzle, now made slightly worse: we have *Ratis Raving*, related in some way to the three other poems, which in turn may be by the author of the *Dicta Salomonis*; at the very least two of these three poems are apparently related to the *Dicta*. Various solutions can be found, but they are mostly repugnant to common sense. Do we suppose a very long-lived poet, who changed his dialect and his rhyming patterns as he aged? Or a nest (perhaps a dynasty) of advice-giving poets, all living in the same place and having the same vocabulary, and all assiduously perusing each other's works? Some light on this puzzle may possibly be cast by part of the epilogue to the three poems mentioned above, the final 22 lines of *Thewis Gud Women*. The poet speaks of 'sindry documentis'

> of wysmen, that befor has ben
> and mekil honor knawin & sen,
> quhilk thai drew out throw thare gret wyt,
> And eftir maid seir bukis of It,
> Quhilk thai drew out of bukis old
> quhar It lay as in myne the gold.
> quhat thank serf I þocht it gud bee,
> Sen gudnes cummys nocht of me
> Bot of thir worthi mennis sawis . . .

These lines are not as lucid as they might be, but the author seems to be speaking of previous writers that he has followed who made their books out of both 'gret wyt' and 'bukis old'. We are now all trained to discount 'modesty' prologues and epilogues, but some indication that these lines are to be taken seriously is given by the speaker's following request, that his readers and hearers 'pray for hyme that maid the buk, / And fore al cristyne man and me', which seems a clear enough statement that he does not think of himself as the man 'that maid the buk'. There is a somewhat similar epilogue to *Ratis Raving* that I would like to think was written by the same man: there is no proof of this, but the style, sentiments, and lengths of the two epilogues are much the same, and both begin with 'Now'. The writer of this epilogue is plainly not the author of *Ratis Raving*: he criticizes the title (as he well might), and prays for both the man 'That trawall tuk of this treting' and for himself, 'the vrytar'.

The texts of poems such as these are notoriously unstable: people seem to have regarded them, fairly enough, as miscellaneous collections of good advice rather than poetic masterpieces, and writers seem to have felt completely free to make additions, deletions, and changes as they saw fit.

Mustanoja's edition gives plenty of evidence for the textual instability of English poems of parental advice. A Scots example is the other text of *Thewis Gud Women*, in St. John's College, Cambridge, MS G. 23 (a manuscript of Barbour's *Bruce*). Although the manuscript is also fairly early (1487), its version of *Thewis Gud Women* is very different from the one in Kk. 1. 5. While the two versions differ in length by only 10 lines, each contains about 70 lines not represented in the other, and in addition there are a large number of lines which correspond only roughly to their counterparts in the other manuscript (the rhyme-words tend to be the most stable elements).[7]

A similar situation exists with some of the verse prophecies that are extant in Scots versions (three of them are in part four of Kk. 1. 5). The composite nature of some of these prophecies has long been recognized, and indeed is obvious: for instance, one part of a prophecy may be in alliterative verse, another part in non-alliterative rhyming verse, and still another part in something that seems to be a distant ancestor of *vers libre*. The poems we have been dealing with are not so obviously composite, but there is some interesting evidence in *Thewis Gud Women*. Part of this poem is cast in the form of general statements, some of them addressed to men ('men suld considyr / That womenis honore is tendyr & Slyddir', 7–8), but parts of it use the imperative ('Fle fra defamyt cumpany', 117), which would be more natural in a poem cast in the form of a mother's advice to her daughter, and on occasion the second person singular pronoun is used, which could only be appropriate to a poem of this type. It seems very likely that this confusion results from a poem of the parental advice type having been partially turned into a poem of general advice, or, perhaps less probably, vice versa.[8]

The hypothesis that *Ratis Raving* and the three shorter poems are not, as we now have them, works that were composed by single authors, but the results of the revisions, additions, and deletions made by various hands, has at least the merit of fitting all the evidence. There is considerable evidence to show that the three shorter poems all show the touch of the same man — it would be safer to call him a redactor than an author. The resemblances between these poems and *Ratis Raving* may have been introduced by him, or by an earlier redactor, or may have arisen because passages were borrowed from works by the same author. The curious resemblances between the prose *Dicta Salomonis* and two of the short poems may indicate that a redactor of the poems wrote the prose piece, or may simply indicate that all these works were revised or rewritten by the same man.

This hypothesis may also cast some light on the puzzle connected with the first word in the title *Ratis Raving*, which presumably means 'Rate's Raving'. (The second word is also a puzzle, though perhaps a long poem of good advice might attract a derisory nickname; Trautmann's suggestion to connect it with a reflex of ON *raða*, 'advise' (ME *rede*) is tempting but difficult.) The puzzle arises because of MS Ashmole 61 (Bodleian 6922*), a manuscript dated probably c. 1500. Eighteen items, about half the number of English items in this manuscript, carry the colophon 'quod Rate': these items are various, and include three romances, but also include versions of 'How the Wise Man Taught his Son' and 'How the Good Wife Taught her Daughter'. J T T Brown's suggestion that the poems in his manuscript ascribed to Rate and *Ratis Raving* should all be connected with a David Rate who was King James I's confessor is impossible on chronological grounds alone and was rightly dismissed as an absurdity long ago (see Girvan, 1939: xxxiii–xxxiv, xxxviii). The current theory is that the colophons in the Ashmole manuscript indicate only that the scribe was named Rate, and that this Rate has no connection with the Rate of *Ratis Raving*. But there are two difficulties in this theory. The first is that the colophon 'quod X' is used, either always or almost always, to indicate that the scribe thought X to be the author of the piece.[9] The second is that Rate is a very uncommon name, and it is preposterous, when it is almost the only name attached to early poems of advice, to suppose that two Rates are involved. Is it not simpler to suppose that there was a poet named Rate, real or legendary, whose name became attached to various poems? He would presumably have been a northern poet, though perhaps on the English side of the border. The Ashmole manuscript is from the northern or northeast Midlands, though Bliss (1966: xxv) remarks that some rhymes 'suggest that it was copied from a very northerly or Scottish exemplar'. Girvan, who suggests that *Ratis Raving* 'is a rehandling of an earlier work', gives some reasons for thinking that this earlier work was not written by a Scot (p. xxii). And a Northern English pedigree is congruent with some of the unusual elements of *Ratis Raving*'s vocabulary (see the discussion of *lefe* and *ill* above), though this is not strong evidence. It seems to me very possible that 'Rate' wrote poems of advice, including an ancestor of *Ratis Raving*, and perhaps also some of the poems attributed to him in the Ashmole manuscript, but it is also possible that his connection with these works is as tenuous as the connection between the historical Solomon and his *Dicta*, or between King Alfred and his Proverbs: I argue only that there was thought to be a connection.

The question raised at the beginning of this paper, whether DOST can be used to throw any light on the authorship of poems, must, I think, be answered with a wary and guarded affirmative: the dictionary throws light readily enough, and often suggestive and enticing light, but the light may be only the *ignis fatuus* that leads men into bogs. Very seldom can a dictionary alone be used to make a convincing case for authorship. In a case where there is other internal and external evidence, as with the five works treated here, DOST can assist in forming an hypothesis that is, I hope, digestible. Without such evidence, we are left all too often with a suspicion that two works must be connected, a suspicion that may well be correct but, since it cannot be proven, is not of much use.[10]

NOTES

1   The mathematical metaphor is Ephim G. Fogel's; the other is Arthur Sherbo's: see Erdman and Fogel (1966: 96–7, 10–11); my reference to Fluellen is also borrowed from Fogel. A quantity of bad evidence, to quote Fogel again, provides not 'a tidy, tight little bundle of twigs, but a random array of dead leaves, withered stalks, and bits of bark.'

2   Some convenient examples are given in *The Good Wife Taught her Daughter* . . . (Mustanoja ed., 1948: 137–88); further examples are in Girvan's notes. Mustanoja considers that the poems were 'probably written by the same person' (p. 155).

3   It is sometimes said (e.g. by Mustanoja, 1984: 136) that this epilogue refers also to *Ratis Raving*, but I can see no evidence for this.

4   The first is Vowel 11, the second Vowel 2 in Aitken's (1977a) system.

5   Biblical passages and references are to the Vulgate (Douay version), which, in the Wisdom books, is sometimes, as here, at some distance from the King James and later versions.

6   Conceivably he was influenced by an explanation in the *Glossa Ordinaria: hoc est quod laborando didicit homo id est, rationis in ore habet, quia alios docet*. (I quote from a a Venetian edition of 1603; the version in the *Patrologiae Latinae* (vol. 133, 1122), while superior, is less close.)

7   The versions are edited on facing pages by both Girvan and Mustanoja; the later also gives a table of correspondences (p. 153).

8   Mustanoja, who comments on this confusion, explains it by saying that 'the poem was imitated from some parental instruction', and suggests that it was imitated from *Consail Vys Man* (p. 137). But this does not seem a plausible explanation.

That the change was probably from a poem of parental advice to a poem of general advice is suggested by the tendency, in both MSS, to avoid the second person singular pronoun, sometimes with awkward results. The St. John's MS, for instance, has the sensible lines, 'But leif set nocht þi hert to luff, / for eftir followis gret repruff. / leiff þi awn will and tak consale / Or it sall turn þe to tynsale' (211–14). Kk. 1. 5. destroys most of the sense by substituting, for the three second person pronouns, *hir*, *thare*, and *thaim*. Conversely, Kk. 1. 5. has the line 'In thrift stryf ay with thi nychtboure' (81; *stryf* is of course imperative); the St. John's MS turns this into nonsense by substituting *hir* for *thi*.

9   Girvan (1939: xxxiv) gives the Naples MS of *Libeaus Desconus* as an instance of this formula being used to indicate the scribe, but this example will not hold. See Rickert (1940: 377–8).

10   An example relevant to these five works is provided by two poems, 'Man of maist fragilite', Bannatyne MS, f. 69b–70a, and 'Be nocht lefull to lie', Maxwell MS, Edinburgh University Library MS La. III. 467 (1584–1607), f. 6b. They are both clumsy or corrupt poems of moral advice, in eight-line stanzas, *aaabaaab*; the *a*-lines have three or four stresses and the *b*-lines two or three stresses. (The six stanzas in the Bannatyne MS keep the same rhymes throughout; the two stanzas in the Maxwell MS do not.) The two poems look as

if they must be related, but the only line they have in common is 'Be not lefull to lie' (line 22 of the Bannatyne MS poem; the incipit of the other). These are two of the three other instances of the word *leful(l*, discussed above. It might be added that in five of the seven cases of this word in the three poems connected with *Ratis Raving* it occurs in the phrase 'Be nocht lefull to', or 'Be nocht lefull . . . to' (cf. also'leif to lee', *Consail Vys Man* 150). One is probably right in suspecting that there is something more than chance coincidence here, but to speculate further is to enter the bog.

EIGHT

The Middle English and Scots equivalents of 'hence', 'thence' and 'whence': some word-geographical facts, principles and problems

Angus McIntosh

In a paper in a volume honouring a distinguished historical lexicographer, I may be forgiven for offering a few preliminary remarks which attempt to 'place' the study of the regional distribution of words that are part of the vocabulary of mediaeval English and Scots within the broader framework of what the makers of historical dictionaries aim to encompass.

We may look upon lexical variation as manifesting itself along two main axes, one of which has to do with the passage of time and the other with position in geographical space; consideration of both these 'planes' is or should be part of the business of historical lexicography. But the frequent and highly respectable association of the adjective 'historical' with the noun 'lexicography' and, conversely, the rarity of the phrase 'geographical lexicography' has not been without attitudinal and procedural consequences: the result has tended to be that problems of change in vocabulary through time have received far more systematic and voluminous treatment than those of diversification over space.

In what follows, though I shall be primarily concerned with variation over space, I shall try to show how inextricably interwoven are the two kinds of phenomenon. And since any kind of treatment of such matters demands a realistic assessment of the nature of the material available for investigation, I shall put forward and illustrate two or three principles which I believe should govern the approach to, and the handling of, word-distribution studies bearing on that large and chronologically and geographically diverse body of mediaeval English that is still accessible to us. I propose to do this by way of a necessarily brief look at a very small and fairly readily delimitable set of words and some consideration of the wide range of problems with which even so small a set confronts us.

Some years ago I mentioned in a brief note (McIntosh 1978b: 141) the existence in different parts of the Middle English area of two sets of equivalents for the modern English adverbs 'hence', 'thence', and 'whence'. The first set consists of a trio of words which descended from Old English; the various manifestations of these I shall label *henne(s)*, *thenne(s)* and *whenne(s)*. The second trio consists of their Scandinavian etymological equivalents, which I shall refer to as *hethen*, *thethen* and *whethen* though of course these also occur in a wide variety of spellings. Since all three members of each set (and compounds of these) would appear to behave quite similarly, distributionally speaking, in mediaeval times, I shall normally use the term *hethen*-type' to designate all three Scandinavian items and compounds thereof, and '*henne*-type' all three native items and their compounds.[1]

It is well-known that Middle English words of Scandinavian origin had greatly differing areas of 'domain' and widely varying subsequent histories. The important pioneer work of Alarik Rynell (1948) on such matters has never been followed up with the thoroughness and energy which it should have inspired[2] and the rivalry of our three pairs of words was not among the 101 items he considered. In respect of breadth of domain, our three borrowed words occupy a sort of middle position between those which seem never to have been at all widely current and others which, far from being narrowly restricted, gradually spread widely beyond any of the areas of Scandinavian settlement, sometimes from quite early in the Middle English period.

In mediaeval times the *hethen*-type was current in Scotland, the north of England, the north Midlands and the northern half of East Anglia — to describe the situation only very roughly for the moment. The *henne*-type would seem to have been the one in normal use almost everywhere south of these areas. One or two apparent violations of this broad dichotomy will be considered in due course but given this rather neat pattern of distribution, it is evident that the geographical domains indicated by the respective places of occurrence of each of the two types promise to be of considerable interest from a word-geographical standpoint. Even at the present stage of our knowledge of these areal configurations, which is far less detailed than need be if we consider the amount of as yet quite unused material readily available for their study, it is also clear that the results of a scrutiny of them may be expected to be of far more than merely linguistic interest.

I now come to the principles that I believe should underpin any study of this kind and to some of the complexities in which we can scarcely avoid being embroiled when engaged therein. We must begin by asking: how can one most efficiently and accurately establish the domain of a particular form or of a certain sub-set of variants of that form? Part of the answer is simply this: that we are seldom entirely without prior clues or hints about the probable area of origin of the material in which our form is attested. For there will almost always be other, to some degree similar, material available, the origin of which *is* known and whose characteristics will enable us to suggest, though necessarily with widely varying degrees of precision and certitude, the place or district or region where what we are now considering originated. To exonerate this procedure from over-hasty accusations of circularity it should be observed at this point that any such hypotheses about place of origin would have been made at a time when as yet we had no information about the domain of the form in question, since this will only now for the first time be coming under scrutiny. From the point of vantage attained by having these hypotheses we shall thereafter be in a better position to associate, however tentatively, instances of our word with particular areas or perhaps even places.

We may also note as a sort of reverse procedure that a hypothesis on any other than the above grounds about the total probable extent of the domain of a particular form, as distinct from the place of origin of any particular attestation thereof, may properly — with the exercise of due caution — provide a reasonable basis for placing more precisely than would otherwise have been possible some newly encountered text or texts in which that form crops up. This manner of advancing may be regarded as being complementary to the previous one.

If one encountered no additional factors which complicated the exploitation of these two lines of attack, one could expect, simply by proceeding on both fronts in an interactive step-by-step way, gradually to reduce the number and the dimensions of our uncertainties, both about the domain of a given form and about the place of origin of some Middle English text or other which contained it. This gradual progress towards greater precision in these two directions is in general only possible if one promotes a continual interplay between the two facets of what, in a wider perspective, should be regarded as just one larger single entity. This entity lurks immoveably behind the two parts of the question which necessarily dominates the *modus operandi* of any mediaevalist involved in word-geographical problems: where does each of my source-texts stem from and just what variant or variants does each manifest for every lexical item included in my enquiry?

In these circumstances, a doctrinaire horror of circularity may merely be inhibiting even where no circularity exists; the way forward is to devise and execute the appropriate heuristic strategy for ordering as satisfactorily as possible each of two distinct but related sets of phenomena, making the fullest use of all the available information bearing on each of them. It would not be difficult to show that some such strategy (though the word perhaps too strongly suggests carefully formulated rules for proceeding) underlies almost all kinds of progress in the frequently slow and long-drawn-out cultivation and development of numerous fields of knowledge.

So much for the principles. If I now add a brief word here about what I have described as additional complicating factors (and I shall consider some of these in due course) it is because I detect a marked reluctance among many of my colleagues to discuss such matters openly and rationally. Yet these things manifest themselves continually in nearly all realms of scholarly and scientific enquiry; they well illustrate what I learnt a long time ago from Michael Frayn to call the sheer *knobbliness* of things.[3] Besides, scholarship would be vastly the poorer without them because what may seem to bedevil or obfuscate one line of enquiry will usually serve to illuminate, or at least call attention to, interesting new problems perhaps quite unsuspected hitherto. But they deprive the present paper of any semblance of neatness or well-roundedness; it will pose as many questions, overt and implicit, as it attempts to answer; *seðe bet cunne, gecyðe his mare*.

Now for some facts and problems relating to my main subject. I have already indicated the approximate territorial domains in Middle English times of each of the two trios of words, the *hethen*-type and the *henne*-type. The two must of course have overlapped to some extent, but the domains seem nevertheless to have been remarkably distinct; it is extremely rare for examples of the Scandinavian type to crop up in manuscripts known to have been written in the *henne*-type area and it is unusual for the native forms to intrude in the north and north midlands.[4]

I shall, however, consider here a clear example of the *hethen*-type being attested (several times) in an anthology of verse almost certainly produced in the London area and therefore well to the south of the *hethen* domain. This is the Auchinleck Manuscript[5], which is generally believed to have been compiled in London around 1330. At least two of its six scribes use the Scandinavian form, those numbered 1 and 5 by A J Bliss, and M L Samuels places the scribal origin of 1 in East Middlesex and of 2 in S W Essex. The instances known to me are in *Reinbrun*, *The Harrowing of Hell* and *The Four Foes of Mankind*. It is beyond doubt that the latter has a northern textual background; the antecedents of the other two poems require close investigation but clearly lie considerably further north than the Auchinleck versions themselves. The use of the *hethen*-type in this manuscript is no more proof of its being current in London in the fourteenth century than is its use by Chaucer, on the lips of John, the northern clerk, in the *Reeve's Tale*.[6] In Auchinleck, as with comparable phenomena in Harley 2253 in another area, its appearance indicates a readiness, perhaps less common a century later,[7] to accept alien forms for reasons other than mere technical obligations or pressures to preserve rhymes, rhythms or alliteration.[8]

It may now be appropriate to cite two examples of the contrary procedure, whereby scribes *altered* the original forms of our words in the process of transcribing texts written in the dialect of one area into that of another area.

The first has to do with the equivalents of 'hence' in the surviving texts of the *Proverbs of Alfred* (there is nothing, in any of the versions, answering to 'thence' or 'whence').[9] The instances are:

line	J	T	C	M
166	heonne	henne	—	henne
168	heonne	he*nn*e	—	heþen
486	—	henne	henn(e)	heþen

Everything we know about the poem points to its being of southern origin but the surviving texts are all midland. Both T and J are western; T was probably the work of a scribe from somewhere west of Worcester and J that of someone from only slightly further south in east Herefordshire; both fall just a little south of the southern limit of the *hethen* type on the west Midlands.[10] M and C are Midland re-workings from much further east; there is evidence associating M with Northampton at a very early date and various linguistic forms in C point to its being the work of a scribe from somewhere a bit to the south of M.

These suggested placings are not based in any way on hints provided by the forms evinced in the texts themselves of the words for 'hence'. However to assign M to Northampton or thereabouts is to put it sufficiently far north for it to fall within that part of the east central Midlands — as roughly established recently from a considerable body of information — where *hethen* was current. Since M itself was not a source of that information it is pleasing to find that it uses the *hethen*-type twice where three other manuscripts attest the native form and that it retains *henne* only once. As for C, its solitary instance of *henn(e)* (and none of the other form) is too flimsy a piece of evidence to adduce as proof of a rather more southernly origin for that text than for M. But it is entirely consonant with other bits of evidence which suggest the very same thing. Typologically, therefore, C would seem — from a linguistic viewpoint — to stand to M in the same sort of geographical relationship as that of J to T. We may perhaps, therefore, tentatively assign it to the south Bedfordshire or Hertfordshire area.[11]

My second example of a text which deviates from the other (and 'better') versions in the forms of the words it uses answering to the modern English 'hence' trio is that of the *Ancrene Wisse* in British Library manuscript Cotton Titus D XVIII. From the dialectal point of view this may be described as a considerably modified version — perhaps through an intermediate stage or even several — of the original Herefordshire text and with characteristics suggesting for Titus itself a west Midland origin somewhere in the region of south Cheshire.[12] It would appear that this is the only text of *Ancrene Wisse* in which the *hethen*-type is found. Since (as I have noted) there is good evidence for the occurrence of this type as far south in the West Midlands as the northern half of Worcestershire, its absence in the other *Ancrene Wisse* texts suggests that we should be reluctant to locate any of these as far north as that. Conversely, however, we should perhaps, on the same grounds, hesitate to place Lambeth 487 any further south than north Worcestershire.[13] It is evident, however, that much more work is necessary if these and similar matters are to be clarified; again here I should emphasize how ill-explored so far much of the relevant (and readily available) source material is.

The final matter I wish to touch on involves a complication that I have hitherto avoided. Up to now I have spoken as if the *hethen* and the *henne* types were always unambiguously distinguishable. However, Middle English also attests, though probably not till the fourteenth century,[14] for each of our trio of word forms such as *hine, hein, hyne, heyn* (which I shall label 'hine' forms); the source of these has been sufficiently in doubt for them to have received differing etymological treatments in the dictionaries and elsewhere. So we must ask: do they — since they must almost certainly descend from one or the other — derive from the native or from the Scandinavian forms? The question is important, apart from other reasons, because if we cannot answer it, then our information about the respective distributions of our two sets of forms must necessarily remain imperfect. But how to approach this problem?

There is no space for detailed discussion of this matter but it must be noted that the word-geographical facts are of critical importance. And taking these into account one may say with some confidence that 'hine' forms are derivatives of *hethen* and not of *henne*. From a phonological point of view they are, I suppose, somewhat odd anyhow. But apart from a small cluster of exceptions to which I shall return they occur only in the domain of the *hethen* type and only in parts of that domain. As I have noted, they probably did not develop anywhere until the fourteenth century. Their subsequent formal history is closely similar to that of the adverb *syne* 'afterwards' and this not only by way of positive resemblances but also because *syne*, like the 'hine' forms (and indeed like the *hethen*-type as a whole) seems never to acquire the -*s* suffix that produces *since, hence, thence* and *whence*.

The 'hine' forms share with *syne* and its variants several characteristics. Not only do both types first appear rather late in the Middle English period but both are extremely rare except in the north and far north midlands of England and in Scotland. Furthermore both display the same tendency to manifest *ei, ey, ie, ye* variants beside the *i/y* forms and to occur in rhyme with both *ei/ey and with ī/ȳ* words, but never with *ai/ay* words. It is therefore probable that OED s.v. *syne* adv. is correct (*pace* DOST s.v. *hyn(e)* adv.) in deriving *syne* from *sethen*, in exactly the same way as the 'hine' forms from *hethen* etc., rather than from *sithen*.

If so, however, these explorations will have the discomforting (but I hope

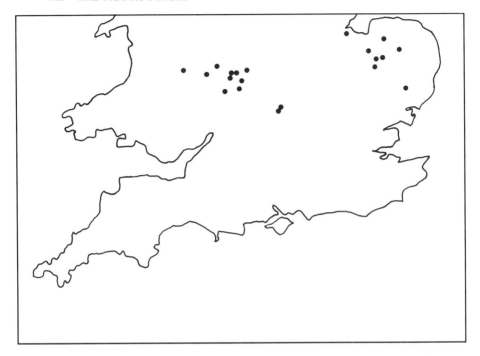

MAP showing the southern limit of occurrence in later Middle English of 'hethen' type forms of the items 'hence', 'thence' and 'whence'; cases of the 'hine' sub-type are not included. 'Non-indigenous' examples of the 'hethen' type attested in *Sir Ferumbras* (Devon), the Auchinleck MS 'hand E' (SW Essex) and Chaucer's *Reeve's Tale* have been omitted. The map is based on material presented in *LALME*: vol. iv, items 148, 234, 250; vol. i, dot maps 1024, 1076, 1101.

ultimately meritorious) result of opening up several new problems. Some of these I shall, by way of conclusion, merely list. Do the *heythen*-type forms cited in note 6 represent an intermediate stage between *hethen* and *hein*? If so, what is the explanation of this sequence and are there any parallels to it outside the group of words under discussion? And if there are, is the regular use in Fairfax of *siþen* (and not *seiþen* or *seyþen*) a further indication that all monosyllabic forms of this adverb are likely to derive not from *siþen* but from *seþen*? And if they do, can *seþen* be shown to preponderate over *siþen* at the appropriate date in the areas where the monosyllabic forms appear or must we merely assume that it did? And how early did the disyllabic forms disappear in Scots and why earlier there than in English? And are there no indications in verse, e.g. in Barbour's *Bruce*, of disyllabic forms being required by the metre even if not preserved as such in the extant texts? It would appear that the main result of an effort to throw a little new light on one knobbly problem has been to reveal how many others there are which call for fuller exploration.

NOTES

1 I shall not discuss here the earlier history of the two trios and their ultimate formal identity. Nor would it be relevant to consider variations in stressed vowel within the Scandinavian trio because these seem not to be replicated in their Middle English or Scots descendants. I shall also say nothing about the development in the thirteenth century of the type 'hennes' with the adverbial genitive -(e)s suffix. It is of some interest however that this suffix is attached only very rarely if at all, then or later, to any *hethen*-type form.

2 For some references to further work see Hudson (1983), especially footnotes 1 and 2.

3 See *Observer Weekend Review*, 1 December 1962, and *Review of English Literature* VI, 1965: 17–18.

4 The occasional and rather late appearance of *hens* (but not, it seems, *henne*) in Scottish texts raises other questions relating to intrusions of English elements into the literary vocabulary of Scots. For instances of *hens* see DOST *hens* adv. and *hensfurth(e)* adv. On the general problem, see McIntosh (1979b) esp. 12–16. I take this opportunity of correcting a statement in that paper (page 15) to the effect that the short forms *thine* and *thyne* are attested only in Scots; for northern Middle English examples see OED *thyne* adv.

5 National Library of Scotland, Advocates' MS 19.2.1. For full details see Pearsall and Cunningham (1977) vii–xxiv. For the scribes who contributed to the manuscript see Bliss (1951). For the northern origin of *The Four Foes of Mankind* and related matters see McIntosh (1978b).

6 Tolkien (1934) examines seven 'good' texts containing passages spoken by the two northern clerks. Of these, five have the Scandinavian form (correcting P's erroneous *hepen* — an example which authenticates an underlying *heþen*). Three of the five (E, H and O) have the unusual variants *heythen* or *heithen*. Tolkien, commenting on these (p. 21), suggests possible influence from *ei/ai* forms of the word for 'heathen'; these would have to derive from Scandinavian *heiðinn* and not from the OE word (cf. Bjorkman 1900–2:45). However this may be, recorded instances of *ei/ey* forms in the *whethen* trio are extremely rare except in the Fairfax MS of *Cursor Mundi*, which originated in or near Lancaster. A search for further such examples in the north might throw some light on the source or sources of Chaucer's entire inventory of northern forms; scores of northern manuscripts survive which have never been examined even cursorily for such a purpose.

7 However, the late fourteenth century Vernon Manuscript (Bodleian Engl. poet. a. 1) and its companion volume BL 22283 still display an evident readiness to copy poems which must have been composed some distance away (in these cases mostly somewhat further north in the West Midlands) without obliterating by

any means all linguistic traces of their origin in the process. Cf. McIntosh (1978b: 138 and footnote 8).

8   Another manuscript which is commonly believed to be in a language characteristic of the London area is Trinity College Cambridge B. 14. 52. But it has — at least in certain parts — forms which suggest an origin fairly far north in the East Anglian area, e.g. *cnolles* 111, *skilede* 119, *fundi* 119, *buertut* 123. It also has (cf. McIntosh 1978b: 141) at least eleven examples of the *hethen*-type words. Of those I have noted all but one occur in passages written by scribe II, for whom see Ker (1931). The underlying problems call for detailed investigation. There are possible parallels between the nature of the East Anglian ingredient in the homiles in the Trinity manuscript and that of the Suffolk forms which Samuels and Smith (1981) have shown to be one basic component of the English of John Gower.

9   For the material here cited and the abbreviations, see Arngart (1942: 7–8, 65 and 1955:185). For notes on the dialect of the manuscripts, see especially Arngart (1942: 125–136).

10   In the preparation of the *Linguistic Atlas of Late Mediaeval English* (LALME) the ME equivalents of 'hence', 'thence' and 'whence' were only collected for the southern half of the country. The material, for which see the Map on p. 113, suffices to indicate that the domain of the *hethen*-type reached (in the west) no further south than the northern half of Worcestershire where, however, it is very well attested in later Middle English texts; this makes it somewhat surprising that the type is not found in even the A-text of Laȝamon's *Brut*. The Scandinavian forms would seem to be common a good deal further south in the Worcestershire area and in East Anglia than anywhere in between.

11   It cannot well be assigned a position any further east than Hertfordshire because this would put it in East Anglia, an area where in the thirteenth century the dialect forms and the orthographic conventions would be recognizably different.

12   Much later in the Midddle English period there is a parallel further east to this 'northover' conversion process in the 'U' revision of the *South English Legendary* in the Lincolnshire area; for this see Görlach (1976) and cf. Hudson (1983: footnote 9). Another is provided by a manuscript containing Wycliffite material written by two scribes in which the language of both is of N. Nottinghamshire (Leicester CRO, Leicester Town Hall MS 3). The vast majority of such 'translated' texts, being unprinted, remain an untapped resource for lexicographical and word-geographical studies.

13   The form þeðð*an* occurs in Morris (1867: 93). I owe this and much other information to the kindness of Professor R E Lewis, editor-in-chief of MED, University of Michigan, who very kindly put at my disposal unpublished material in the archives of the Dictionary. The textual history of Lambeth 487 is, of course, complicated, cf. Sisam (1951).

14   MED s.v. *henne* adv. 1(a) cites the word *hine* (rh. *erðe-dine*) *Genesis and Exodus* 1107 as the first example. But this is far earlier than any other case and Morris is probably right to take it as being the accusative 3 person sg. pron. masc. word for 'him'. The same form in clearly that sense, is found rhyming with the same word *dine* at line 3467. The form *heyn* (validated by rhyming with *certein*)

is found, very puzzlingly, at a much later date in Lovelich's *Holy Grail* 21.304, a text with strong south Essex characteristics. This should perhaps be compared with the rare forms *þeyn* and *wheynnes* which occur, exceptionally, in two other texts from the south east, LALME nos. 6200 (Essex) and 6530 (east Hertfordshire). A derivation of these from the Scandinavian rather than from the native words should not be assumed, any more than for similar forms found occasionally elsewhere in the south, e.g. *theyn*, LALME no. 5040 (Devon).

NINE

Past presences of Older Scots abroad[1]

Hans H Meier

The following notes are offered to the most learned recipient of the present collection in the hope that, since he cannot be further instructed in anything to do with the language of his ancestors, he will at least be entertained, while for other readers both purposes advocated by ancient rhetoric may be served. Starting from casual remarks about OSc, in contrast to MLG, having had no geographical radiation to speak of (Meier, 1977:202; Görlach, 1985:21 n. 4), the question arose whether it had thus no existence outside Scotland at all during the period of its greatest vigour. Of course, on closer view, it did have *some* presences, some of which, however, will not be eligible for exemplary treatment.

Whenever Lowlanders went abroad their speech would go with them, but where written records of it are lacking a historic language is philologically unattainable. The most successful export of this kind was the plantation of Ulster, from 1606. This was the only thing James VI ever did exclusively for his Scottish subjects. But are there any of their writings extant? Not until 1642 was the first presbytery established there, in Carrickfergus. Were its records anglicized? We know that until 1707 Ulster was simply looked upon as an extension of Scotland, after which date the mother country lost interest, though folk went on calling themselves, 'people of the Scottish nation in Ulster', repudiating the label 'Scotch-Irish' by which they became generally known (Heslinga, 1979: 152–66). And there were Scots in England, France, the Netherlands, and the Baltic, all no doubt retaining their native tongue for a considerable time. Then there were indeed Scots writings and prints from beyond the kingdom. Of these, however, two categories cannot claim to be testimonies from outside. The first are private documents penned by Scotsmen abroad for their own use, such as the ledger of Andrew Halyburton, 'Conservator of the Privileges of the Scotch Nation in the Netherlands' (1493–1502). The second category are books printed and published abroad but chiefly for home consumption, for which reason they cannot be viewed as independent presences, though the number of Scottish works printed (often first printed) in England, France, the Low Countries, Denmark, and Sweden is rather impressive.[2]

116

What concerns us here as being the nearest thing to geographical radiation, i.e. the spread of the language itself, are cases of Scots being offered by foreigners for foreigners, from clearly non-Scottish motives. And these cases again, must be distinguished from those of literary borrowings from Scots which, among Anglo-Scottish relations, 'are so interesting because they are so rare' (Kratzmann, 1980: 228). Since Kratzmann has diligently scraped together the rare instances of such transfer — though omitting Harrison's Englishing (1587) of Bellenden's Boece (1531) — they will not be reconsidered. Only Surrey, exploiting Books II and IV of the *Eneados* for his *Certain Bokes of Virgiles Aenaeis* (1557), might deserve special mention because Douglas, as is now hardly remembered, came to be a notable factor to seventeenth century scholars. But translations do indeed count, and we shall see the Dutchman Jacobus Koelman coping successfully with no small quantity of Scotticisms. It can hardly be doubted that, from the later Middle Ages, Englishmen were acquainted with Scottish speech, and sometimes baffled by it, but we shall now proceed to a survey of eligible written witnesses through four centuries.

(i) The talk of the two 'northern clerks' Aleyn and John in Chaucer's *The Reeve's Tale* (*c*. 1386) has been associated with Scots: Angus McIntosh points to the most characteristic Scots features as against Southern English and remarks that 'Chaucer was aware of all these phenomena in the English of his time' (1978a: 39). Now in spite of some misgivings I suggest that we call it Scots as much as Northern English, since the two are not generally considered as distinct at this period, and we could do worse than return to the 'Northumbrian' view of Skeat (1912: 25–35) and Murray (1873), who maintained that up to 1400 the Border was no language bar between Northumbria to the north and Northumbria to the south of it. The more typically northern forms in some manuscripts (such as ⟨qu⟩ for ⟨wh⟩, *boes* for *behoves*, *howgates* for *how*, *gar vs haue* for *get vs som*), played down by Blake (1981: 28–33), may well show the scribes' interpretation to have been in the right direction. Taking seriously Chaucer's own localization of the students' birthplace as Strother, there is a specific reason for considering their speech to be 'Scots'. According to Manly, Castle Strother lay ten miles west of Wooler, near Kirknewton, and this is a subregion that embraces part of South East Scotland and the non-Scandinavianized north of Northumberland, which to this day the best judge of that dialect sees as a 'spreadover to both sides of the political border' (Mather, 1980: 40). And there is good evidence that the adjoining East Roxburgh and Berwickshire were formerly identical with Northumbrian speech.[3] I would even submit that the spellings *geen* 'gone' and *neen* 'none' are brilliantly phonetic, demonstrating the stage / ɛ: /in the development of Northern ME / a: / to modern / ɪə / in this very region (cf. Zai, 1942: 58 n.9).

Only two further observations: First, since 'at no point during the period [i.e. to the end of the Middle Ages] was there a standard variety of English accepted as such wherever the language was spoken' (Leith, 1983: 7), it is slightly incongruous for Blake to cite the students' speech as non-standard language. Indeed, he is hard put to make out a case for some kind of social satire. The fact is that even in the absence of any country-wide spoken standard any unexpected use of a very divergent, but of course intelligible, dialect is itself comical, and it is this that makes the two students' idiom here so jolly and liberating. Second, Chaucer's rendition is not only the first but is an all-round imitation of regional speech, i.e. of phonological, morphological, grammatical and lexical features, such as was not again to be achieved in comic representations of Scots abroad.

(ii) As the old Selden colophon to *The Kingis Quair* (1437), claiming that it was 'maid quhen his Maiestie was in England', has been discredited and Craigie's view that its language is basically the English of Chaucer contaminated by Scottish scribal interference is widely accepted (Kratzmann, 1980: 35–36 n.4), this work now appears as an early, surely the earliest, literary entry of Southern English into the northern Kingdom — and this is exactly the opposite of what I was looking for. So it must here be left out of account. And even if a suspicion lingers that its Scottish features might after all be due to an authorial substratum rather than a scribal superstratum, and that James I might at least have begun it before his release, we should still only have a Scotsman's unpublished manuscript once existing in England, which would hardly amount to a witness in the sense intended. Still, it is a pity one cannot plead otherwise for James, since the length and the nature of the *Quair* would have predestined it to have originated in captivity like the English courtly songs of his fellow royal, Charles d'Orléans. Because at times, prison, like the plague, has proved a powerful promoter of poetry.

(iii) Though coming two centuries later, the short speechs of Captain Jamy in Shakespeare's *Henry V* (iii.2) (c. 1599) are comparable to those of Chaucer's clerks. Like the story of a Scotsman ordering a 'bare heade', i.e. a boar's head for an inn sign, in the *Hundred Merry Tales* (1540), they show that Scots must have been familiar to Londoners, for dialect that has to be explained falls flat. By now indeed London English was *the* standard, so that the English of the Welsh, the Irish, and the Scots would strike a humorous note. Yet, as with Aleyn and John, without satire, indeed with some pride in the English forces in France comprising a diversity of nations. In contrast to Chaucer's northern speech, however, Jamy's Scots is stereotyped, with a restriction to a few shibboleth-like tokens piled up: *gud*, with its funny vowel, occurs six times, *sall* four times, *aile* 'I'll' three times, with a sprinkling of *de* 'do', *vary* 'very', *bath* 'both', *lig* 'lie', *grund* 'ground' and *wad* 'would'. Thus we have a kind of stage Scotch where mere 'accent' has replaced the full body of regional speech in Chaucer, which included strange meanings like *hope* 'expect', *wight* 'swift', *kepe* 'catch', strange words like *lathe* 'barn', *fonne* 'fool', *capul* 'horse', *ilhail* 'misfortune', and racy idioms like *step on thy feet*; *com of, man*; *I sal been hald a daf*; *swa have I seel*.

In Shakespeare too we have the fatal restriction of what is now considered dialect to low characters. Any more serious northern figure, say in *Macbeth*, or Archibald Douglas in *1 Henry IV* (v.2), speaking Scots is unthinkable. All the characters found by Blake to speak some kind of Scots in plays of this period are either low or satirical. He discusses Caconas in Nathanial Woodes, *The Conflict of Conscience* (1581), Bohan in *The Scottish History of James VI* by Anthony Munday and others (*a*. 1592), *The Northern Lass* (1632) by Richard Brome, and the anonymous *Late Lancashire Witches* (1634) (1981: 74–77). Unnoticed by Blake, we may note Ben Jonson's fragment *The Sad Shepherd, or A Tale of Robin Hood* (*c*. 1636). About this, Henry Bradley, calling it 'the first extensive attempt in dramatic writing to represent any midland or northern variety of provincial English', observes that 'the shepherds of Sherwood Forest speak a jargon which, so far as it is anything at all, is Scotch' (1916: 571). This was perhaps not very wide of the mark, since even James Murray's educated Scottish audience found a reading from Richard Rolle to be 'Old Scotch', whereas Rolle 'wrote in the extreme south of Yorkshire, within a few miles of a locality so thoroughly English as Sherwood forest, with its memories of Robin Hood' (1873: 41, quoted in Skeat, 1912: 35 n.6).

(iv) Less popular but more significant philologically than the occasional stage Scotch in England is the appearance of the vocabulary of Gavin Douglas in learned circles there. More than a century after Surrey's plagiarism, Franciscus Junius (1591–1678), famous Oxford scholar of Dutch descent had compiled a glossary to the *Eneados*, entitled *Index Alphabeticus Verborum Obsoletorum quae occurrunt in versione Virgilii Aeneadum per Gawenum Douglas*, which, though unprinted to this day, was known and used by English scholars of Saxonist interest centred at Oxford. It was extensively used in the Third Appendix of Stephen Skinner's *Etymologicon Linguae Anglicanae* (1671) (Kerling 1979: 26 and 141),[4] in Edmund Gibson's notes to his edition of *Polemo-Middinia* (1691), and in George Hickes's *Linguarum Veterum Septentrionalium Thesaurus* (1703–1705) (Duncan, 1965: 51). This English interest in Douglas led Thomas Ruddiman to edit the *Eneados* and append a glossary that was the first 'dictionary to the old Scottish language' (1710). It was part of a movement in quest of the ancestry of English, and its proponents and lexicographical heirs constantly named Douglas together with Chaucer, Gower, Lydgate and Langland as a prime source for old words. However, it is only fair to recall that a century before this 'Douglas boom' in England Peter Levins discriminated 200 words, either Northern or Sots, in his *Manipulus Vocabulorum* (1570) to discourage their use — as the later lexicographers were to do. In the preface he singles out *kirke*, *myrke*, and *ken* as warning examples so that 'the rude may reforme their tong', which apparently did not prevent Spenser from lifting a dozen of them straight from Levins for display in his *Shepheards Calender* (1579) (Kerling, 1979: 48, 49 n. 16).

(v) From the late sixteenth until well into the eighteenth century, the proportion of Scots among Anglophone residents in the United Provinces of the Netherlands was always high. They had their own Scottish churches and ministers at Amsterdam, Dordrecht, The Hague, Leiden, Veere, and Rotterdam, the last having the largest Scottish trade and by 1700 up to a thousand Scots residents.[5] That their preachers, mainly banished Covenanters and dissenters, all acquired Dutch is less surprising than that some Dutch theologians in sympathy with their cause translated Scottish works and so had to struggle with some Scots. Thus one Jacobus Borstius lost no time in translating James Stirling's *Naphtali, or the Wrestlings of the Church of Scotland* (1667) (Scherpbier, 1933: 82) under the title *Historie der kerken van Schotland tot het jaar 1667* (Rotterdam, 1668),[6] as well as sermons by Samuel Rutherfurd, *Vijftien predicatiën* (Utrecht, 1696) (Sprunger, 1982: 435 n. 19). The most productive translator was the notorious dissenter Jacobus Koelman (1632–1695), banished from his Zeeland parish of Sluis in 1672, who provided Dutch versions of work by Hew Binning, John Brown, David Dickson, James Durham, William Guthrie, Robert McWard, and Samuel Rutherfurd (Krull, 1901: 352–57).

To propagate the fame of the last-named, whom in admiration of his style he re-christened Rhetorfort, he tackled the formidable and famous *Letters* that Robert McWard had published at Rotterdam in 1664, bringing them out in Dutch 1674–1687.[7] Apart from showing a masterly understanding of English, we find him producing excellent renderings of Scots words and expressions: *zijn klein troetelkind* 'his little dawted Davie', *een arm bankroetier* 'a poor dyvour', *als je Christus dagh gestelt hebt* 'when ye have a set tryst with Christ', *de vier kwartieren* 'the four airts', *zuur zien* 'gloom', *kleeft aan* 'hing on', *valt Hem moeyelijck* 'fash Him', *een ydel dingh* 'a blaflume', *te staan kijken* 'to tarrow', *uitgelezen spijs* 'waled meat', *geschud* 'brangled', *schuw zijn* 'scaur', *blinde koopmanschap* 'a blind block'. In some cases, Dutch had a cognate equivalent that English would lack: *vreemd / fremed, lid / lith* 'members', *(bij) (uit) roep (verkopen) / rouping (and selling), gespalkt / (have broken legs) spelked, (wettige) borgen / (law)-burrows.* In *noch bod noch huur* for 'neither bud nor hire', Koelman with *bod* 'offer' for *bud* 'bribe' instinctively hit upon the true etymology and derivation from Dutch of this curious Scots word. He can even be used to correct Bonar's editions, where we read of the believer 'that is infested in heaven', which doesn't make sense (1891: 489). Here Koelman has *die den Hemel in verbandt heeft* 'who holds heaven as a legal bond', proving that his original had *infefted* 'enfeoffed'.[8]

(vi) The London publication in 1692 of the anonymous *Scotch Presbyterian Eloquence Display'd*, which continues to attract attention (cf. Carnie, 1976; Aitken, 1979: 94; Meier, 1985: 80 n. 23), is in itself, with its many satirical illustrations from sermons, a notable example of pre-Revolution Scots appearing abroad. It is also a further proof of parallelism in the life-story of Scots and Low German in that the same age in both regions saw popular sermons in the folk-speech beginning to be noticed as odd, with specimens being collected and printed, to be read for amusement by the next age.[9] But what *Scotch Presbyterian Eloquence* affords us in our context is evidence that not only at home but also in Holland the Kirk maintained some Scots in her oratory. For in the 1789 edition there is a letter to the publisher telling about 'the famous Mr. Hogg' (i.e. John Hogg, minister at Rotterdam 1662–1689), a fierce anti-Episcopalian, one day exclaiming: 'O Lord, thy kirk was once a bony, braw, well-fac'd kirk, but now 't is as bare as the birk at Yool-even, we've done our part in telling thee of it, if thou wilt not do thine, to thyself be it'.[10] Yet in spite of such surviving humorous gems, popular preaching was no doubt the last literary genre in which Scots was used for serious prose.

(vii) Finally, the most pregnant if somewhat precarious portion of OSc is to be found in Thomas Percy's *Reliques of Ancient English Poetry* published in 1765. Though England was now no longer abroad and Scottish could be subsumed under English, the *Reliques* both in their record and their 'Glossary of the Obsolete and Scottish Words in this Work' contained a genuine reflex of the language, since the ballads date back to its period of prosperity.[11] Their immense influence on Scott, and on German Romanticism, with two editions in Frankfurt by the turn of the century, may in part be due to their not being published in Scotland. My only point here is, however, that even if 'Percy did not know Scots', the *Reliques* first made the world of letters conscious of what Henderson called 'the non-vulgarised Scots of the seventeenth and later centuries' (1912: 25). For although only 20 of 180 pieces (11 per cent) are Scottish, about 470 of 1977 entries in the glossary (24 per cent) are so marked, and dozens more should have been.[12] One may deplore Percy's editorial shortcomings but, as with Burns and the Brothers Grimm, tampering with folk-texts turned out to be a recipe for literary success.

Thanks to Percy, the rudiments of the language could at that time be learnt abroad. Titles themselves would greet readers with the required stamp: 'The *Gaberlunzie* Man', 'The *Bonny* Earl of Murray', 'The *Braes* of Yarrow', 'The Ew-*Bughts*', 'Marion', 'The *Auld Goodman*'. Some forms might strike them as mere spelling variants: ⟨quh⟩ for ⟨wh⟩, ⟨z⟩ for ⟨y⟩, *sweit* for *sweet*, *thrie* for *three*, and even *gude, guid* for *good*. In others they could note systematic vowel correspondences: *sair / sore, kame, kem / comb, blaw / blow, drap / drop, dule / dole, rin / run, lee / lie*. Or consonantal changes: *brig / bridge, kauk / chalk, faucht / fought, brocht / brought*. Or morphemic differences: *-is / -e)s, -it / -ed, dois / does, filland / filling*. In greater need of interpretation, in 1765, would be strange lexical items such as were to become familiar to educated English speakers, some being signalled as Scottish in the glossary, e.g. *bairn, dicht, eldritch, gar, glen, gowan, graith, haggis, hooly, ilk, ingle, loon, mavis, mense, mirk, pauky, pibroch, sark, sonsie,* *tryst, whang.* Others were included without being so marked, e.g. *buskit, byre, canty, ettle, ferly, flyte, lither, mickle, speir, stour,* and *tine.* If to us the set looks quite modern, the *Reliques* no less significantly do fall between the old makars, who were yet to be discovered, and the revivers of Lallans who, except for Allan Ramsay, were still to come.

It will be clear that no such lexical finds as enrich the peerless DOST are to be unearthed from these stray foreign deposits of OSc. But for all their fragmentary nature, they may still be found either symptomatic or consequential for the outside reception of Scots at given points of time. Motivation for broaching Scots may be seen to vary with each draught: With Chaucer's northern clerks, it is simply good nature and good humour, though their love of proverbs and of legal arguments might well suit them as Scotsmen. In James I, if indeed he composed in English captivity, we should have a residue of native idiom reasserting itself in the midst of Chaucerian imitation. Shakespeare, like Chaucer, makes use of Scots with inoffensive humour, possibly setting off the laconic Scot against the loquacious Irishman and Welshman. The philological discovery of Douglas in England was occasioned by learned, antiquarian, Saxonist interest — an early demonstration that one way to Scots, and to lexicography, is through a search for Anglo-Saxon roots.[13] In Koelman it was serious admiration for Scottish divines that entailed the skilful unknitting of much Scottish texture. Only in *Scotch Presbyterian Eloquence* is the aim unmistakably satirical, though the sting is stylistic rather than sociolinguistic.

With Percy, finally, the inclusion of Scottish texts is ultimately the result of a universal sympathy with folk literature. With Percy begins the influx of hallmark Scottish words into General English, whereas those due to pre-Percy borrowing, such as *narrate, outcome, shortcoming, uptake,* and *vote* do not show any sign of their origin. Before Percy, as we have seen, Scots had presented more than one image of itself to the world, but never that of the poetical and the romantic which it has since preeminently borne.

NOTES

1   Research for this paper was carried out as part of the Free University (Amsterdam) VF-programme 1985 VUA LETT 3 84/14.
2   See Geddie (1912).
3   For relict vowel stages, see Zai, 1942: §136; Wettstein, 1942: §88. For 'Scottish' isoglosses taking in parts of Northumberland in the East Marches, see Glauser (1974); Speitel (1978).
4   Kerling was preparing an edition of Junius's MS Douglas glossary.
5   For a general account of the Anglo-Scottish presence in Holland, see the excellent first two chapters of Osselton (1973); for an extensive study, Sprunger (1982).

6   See Scherpbier (1933, Appendix: 207–220) for an annotated list of translations from English and Scottish theological work.

7   On Rutherfurd's *Letters* and their background, see Meier (1985).

8   For the Dutch version, *De brieven van Mr. Samuel Rhetorfort*, the first edition at Vlissingen (1674) and the Leiden reprint (1886–1887) were compared.

9   Compare James Row's *Pockmanty Preaching* (1638) and the specimens in *Scotch Presbyterian Eloquence* with the *Plattdütsche Predigten* by Jobst Sackmann, pastor at Limmer near Hanover 1680–1712, which were collected in the eighteenth century (ed. by Insel Verlag, Leipzig, n.d.).

10   On John Hoog (surname dutchified from Hogg?), see Sprunger (1982). The quotation is from *Scotch Presbyterian Eloquence* (1789: 129).

11   Murison (1978) mentions 1550–1650 as the most productive period but considers some Scottish ballads to hark back to the fifteenth century or earlier.

12   The Everyman's Library reprint (n.d.), which combines into one the separate glossaries to the three volumes of the first edition proved sufficient for my purpose on comparison with Schröer (1893).

13   Such was Murray's way: cf. K. Murray (1977: 45–59).

TEN

Teaching Middle Scots by Computer

Arne Zettersten

Ever since the microcomputer revolution started in the latter half of the 1970s, the interest in using personal computers for language learning has increased slowly but steadily (see Zettersten, 1985). However, most linguists working with CALL (computer-assisted language learning) have concentrated on writing software for the teaching of modern languages, primarily English, French, German, and Spanish. There are occasional programs dealing with Latin but very few on, for example, ME or MSc. The purpose of this paper is to indicate one way of teaching MSc by microcomputer.

My intention is to describe some experiments in using the authoring system *BrainLearn* (1986) to produce exercises in MSc carried out in the English Department, University of Copenhagen. Besides showing some types of exercises dealing with MSc, I shall explain how teachers can use an authoring system for creating such exercises without any knowledge of programming.

The MSc texts on which the exercises are built are inserted in the computer (an IBM PC or an IBM-compatible one) just as in ordinary word-processing or typewriting. These texts or sentences are used for text manipulation, cloze exercises, grammar exercises, etc. These types of exercises are pre-programmed in the system, and the teacher (author) just follows the instructions on the screen or uses a manual.

An authoring system is usually menu-driven (see fig. I), i.e. the teacher (author) moves around in the system by selecting from a series of choices on the screen in the form of a menu. The following types of exercises are used in the system:

1. Text reconstruction
2. Cloze exercises
3. Grammar, translation
4. Stylistic exercises, dialect
5. Vocabulary acquisition
6. Spelling

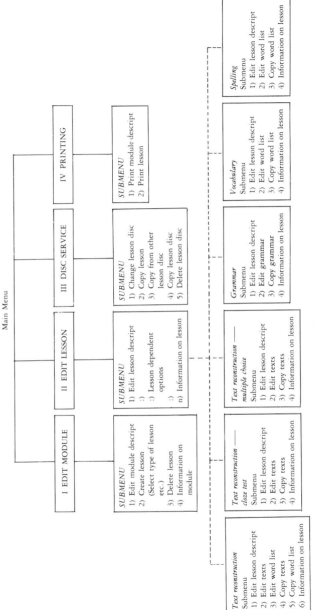

Figure I

These six basic types can be combined in different ways and also changed to suit different purposes in language learning. It is the author's own imagination that sets the limits for the capability of the learning system.

An authoring system like BrainLearn can be used in many different ways. Of the six types of exercises mentioned above, Spelling is the only one restricted to language applications. All other exercises and especially combinations of exercises can be used in subjects where the aim is to learn new facts and to reinforce knowledge.

I should like to emphasize these different ways of using the above-mentioned types of exercises:

1. A series of exercises within fairly large and well-defined subject areas can be made, such as business administration, computer science or business English. A business company can use the authoring system for inserting its own texts or terminology lists and for preparing specialized language exercises.

2. It is also possible to base a lesson diskette on a specific textbook like William Dunbar's *Poems*, edited by Kinsley (1979) (see figs. VII and VIII). All types of exercises and combinations of exercises may be used as applications of what has been learnt by reading the textbook. Introductory material or final tests may be inserted on a diskette and saved for future purposes.

3. Computer-based exercises may also be concentrated on specific linguistic areas like grammar, stylistics, textual knowledge, vocabulary, morphology, spelling, etc. Again, it is important to emphasize that several basic types of exercises can be combined. In learning words and phrases, it is important to practise vocabulary in context and to avoid learning words in isolation.

In order to show how the system runs, a few figures will be given in order to show how the selection of choices is made. The system starts from the Main menu (fig. II). If a student wants to take a lesson, he or she selects '5' and reaches the Lesson menu (fig. III), from which he can select the type of exercise he wants to practise. He is now in 'student mode'. If the user is a teacher and wants to produce lessons, he or she presses Edit module and gets into 'authoring mode'. Starting from this menu (fig. IV), the author first 'creates' the lesson, i.e. reserves a place for it on the diskette and then proceeds to write a description for the module he is working on, inserting the text needed to describe the aim of this set of exercises. After that the teacher turns to the menu called Edit lesson (fig. V), and inserts the texts he wants the exercises to be based on. If he has chosen to produce multiple-choice exercises, the form for inserting comments turns up for each word that should be practised. See figure VI.

Examples of exercises dealing with verbal forms are shown in fig. VII and linking words (prepositions, conjunctions, and adverbs) in fig. VIII.

```
┌─────────────────────────────┐
│          Main menu          │
│  1. Edit module             │
│  2. Edit lesson             │
│  3. Diskette service        │
│  4. Print                   │
│  5. Take a lesson           │
└─────────────────────────────┘
```

Figure II

```
┌─────────────────────────────┐
│          Lesson Menu        │
│  1. Text construction       │
│  2. Cloze exercise          │
│  3. Multiple choice         │
│  4. Grammar                 │
│  5. Vocabulary              │
│  6. Spelling                │
└─────────────────────────────┘
```

Figure III

```
┌─────────────────────────────┐
│          Edit module        │
│  1. Edit module description │
│  2. Create lesson           │
│  3. Delete lesson           │
│  4. Information on module    │
└─────────────────────────────┘
```

Figure IV

```
┌─────────────────────────────┐
│          Edit lesson        │
│  1. Edit lesson description │
│  2. Edit text               │
│  3. Copy text               │
│  4. Information about lesson │
└─────────────────────────────┘
```

Figure V

```
┌─────────────────────────────────────────────┐
│  Ryght as the stern of day begouth to schyne, │
│  Quhen gone to bed war Vesper and Lucyne,     │
│  I raise, and by a rosere did me rest:        │
│  Up sprang the goldyn candill matutyne,       │
│  With clere depurit bemes cristallyne         │
│  Glading the mery foulis in thair nest;       │
└─────────────────────────────────────────────┘
```

```
┌──────Correct choice:────────── Comments:──────┐
│                          ─                     │
│  Wrong choice:                  Comments:      │
│  1.                                            │
│  2.                                            │
│  3.                                            │
│  4.                                            │
└────────────────────────────────────────────────┘
```

Figure VI

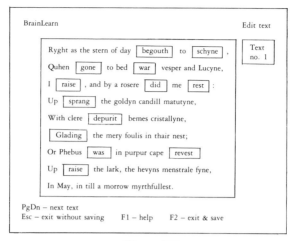

Figure VII

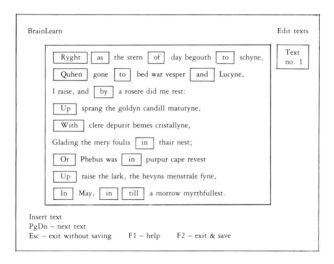

Figure VIII

Tools similar to this authoring system are likely to change attitudes to microcomputer software. By using pre-programmed software all language teachers will have a better chance to produce their own software and to tailor their exercises to the needs of their students.

MODERN SCOTS

ELEVEN

Teaching in the Vernacular: Scotland, Schools, and Linguistic Diversity

Richard W Bailey

In the Bullock Report of 1974, the issue of linguistic diversity in England received some attention. For one of its recommendations, the Committee of Inquiry extracted these words from the lengthy text of its Report:

> No child should be expected to cast off the language and culture of the home as he [sic] crosses the school threshold, nor to live and act as though school and home represent two totally separate and different cultures which have to be kept firmly apart. The curriculum should reflect many elements of that part of his life which a child lives outside of school. (*A Language for Life*, p. 286).

Though these words occur in a chapter devoted to 'children from families of overseas origin', they apply equally to autochthonous multicultural classrooms throughout the English-speaking world. And 'multicultural' needs to be construed to take account of diversity of all sorts, especially in democratically organized school systems like those found in Scotland and the United States (among many other places) where most children are enrolled on the basis of their home communities rather than on the ability of parents to pay school fees to ensure that their youngsters are grouped with others of like social class.

As in so many other matters, the London government in the Bullock Report gave relatively little attention to Scotland. (Members of the Bullock Committee visited schools and Colleges of Education in more than fifty communities in England and at half a dozen locations in the United States. No visits were made to Scottish schools or teacher training centres.) This omission was especially unfortunate because Scottish educators have long attempted to cope with a sociolinguistically complex culture. Scottish schools and their linguistic environment thus merit much greater attention than they have usually received abroad.

SCHOOLS AND THE SCOTS VERNACULAR

When education in the vernacular began to supplement and later supplant the study of Latin, the declared purpose of schooling was to provide instruction in the Scots language. In 1559, the court authorized a monopoly for William Nudrye to issue textbooks, two of which were titled *Ane Schort Introduction*: *Elementary Digestit into Sevin Breve Tables for the Commodius Expeditioun of Thame That are Desirous to Read and Write the Scottis Toung* and *Ane Instructioun for Bairnis to be Learnit in Scottis and Latin*.[1] Early in the seventeenth century, Heriot's Hospital employed a master to 'teach the Scholeris to read and wreat Scottis', and later schools in other places followed the example of the capital: Peebles (1655), Glasgow (1663), Dumfries (1663), Leith (1681), and Stranraer (1686) (Law, 1965: 222).

Written conventions gradually changed to follow the English norms of London publishers which in turn became models for Scottish printers, most particularly through the Geneva and Authorized Versions of the Bible (1561 and 1611) (see Devitt, 1982). But written conventions had only the most gradual influence on the spoken language, and not until the elocution movement in the second half of the eighteenth century did lingusitic practices in schools enthusiastically reject Scots norms in favour of spoken English shaped by fashions of the south.[2]

These developments influenced schools programs and the models of spoken English deemed appropriate for the pupils. By 1761, Arthur Masson, a popular Edinburgh schoolmaster, had employed an English assistant whom he declared to be 'of excellent pronunciation', and Masson himself made an extended visit to London to seek 'improvement in the English language, which above all others ought to be the study of every Briton' (Law, 1965: 151). The mid-eighteenth century was the point at which earlier tendencies in popular attitudes toward the vernacular coalesced, though not with immediate success, to oust Scots from the classroom. (At the same time, there arose a remarkably persistent nostalgia about the Scots that was presumed to be vanishing or at least retreating into the wynds and braes. See Aitken 1981b.) The language chosen for emulation by parents seeking education for their children came more and more to be that associated with the prestige dialect of London. The focus of educational attention, however, was not the English language that children were urged to revere but the one that their schools attempted to eradicate — the Scots vernacular. Pedagogy was directed toward cleansing and purifying Scots by expunging its distinctive features; the result of this educational laundry was supposed to be standard English (though the term *Standard English* apparently did not arise until 1836).

DISENCUMBERING THE SCOTS FROM THEIR LANGUAGE

Thanks to the remarkable trove of personal journals and papers discovered in this century at Fettercairn and Malahide Castles, we have in the Boswell papers a source of insight into the daily life of Scotland at the height of the Scottish Enlightenment (see Pottle, 1982). James Boswell (1742–1795) represents ambitious Scots professionals whose later influence (in the nineteenth century) helped to suppress or romanticize things Scottish and to foster the ideals of polite behaviour contrived by upper-class London society.

Alexander Boswell (1707–1782), James's father, was a distinguished member of the Court of Session (with judicial title Lord Auchinleck) and a substantial landowner in Ayrshire. Alexander Boswell represents Scottish respectability, and he viewed with emotions ranging from indifference to scorn his son's enthusiasm for the intellectual and political life of the southern capital. James Boswell's twentieth-century biographer, drawing on the assumptions of the son, provides this rather patronizing characterization of the father: 'He scorned modern literature, spoke broad Scots from the bench, and even in writing took no pains to avoid the Scotticisms which most of his colleagues were coming to regard as vulgar' (Pottle, 1966: 11). Contrary to this judgement, I see in Alexander Boswell, through his linguistic practices, the beliefs of a political leader whose ideology was then in decline but who remains a possible model for Scottish patriotism; his son displays the emerging perspective of a modern 'North Briton', and his beliefs, though underlying much modern educational and political practice, have created for many of his present-day descendents a disabling schizoglossia.

In the selection from his journal that follows, James Boswell presents testimony from the trial of John Reid in 1774 before the Court of Session and implicitly suggests something about the sociolinguistic setting for Scots and English at that time. Reid, who had formerly been in difficulties that put him in a bad state of 'habit and repute', was tried, convicted, and executed for the theft of nineteen sheep, but not without a vigorous defense mounted by Boswell, who though fully occupied with the task of representing his client, kept a minute daily record of his efforts. Here, Boswell has disputed the prosecutor's attempt to introduce a thirteen-year-old youth as a witness. Citing a legal authority, Boswell says that evidence should not be received from a child but fails to convince his father (whose words begin this extract):

AUCHINLECK. I remember in the first trial I was on, which was for a murder, a little girl swore to having seen the panel [i.e., the accused] mix a powder, which clenched the evidence of poison.
COALSTON. There is a great difference between civil and criminal questions. In the first, people have the choice of their witnesses. In the other, they have not. *He was called.*

JUSTICE-CLERK. Boy, do you go to the Church? — to the Kirk?
BOY. No. I gang to the meeting house.
AUCHINLECK. You know that God made you?
BOY. (Stupid).
AUCHINLECK. Wha made you?
BOY. (with shrill voice). God!
AUCHINLECK. You ken it's a sin to lie?
BOY. Ay.
PITFOUR. You know you are always in the presence of God, and that an over-ruling Providence superintends us all, and that you will be severely punished both in this world and the next if you say what is not true? (Wimsatt and Pottle, 1960: 254–55)

Boswell here abandons his literal representation of the testimony, though it is surely reasonable to assume that the boy was unresponsive to the questions raised about Reid's conduct if they were presented to him in the latinate and anglicized style of Lord Pitfour's concluding question. Unsurprisingly, the judges failed to learn anything beyond 'trifles' from the boy.

As this example illustrates, Alexander Boswell uses 'Scots from the bench' to excellent effect, though the words just quoted are hardly 'broad'.[3] His command of the vernacular has just that flexibility and range one would expect from a figure in authority charged with carrying out public business in a multicultural community.

James Boswell represents the generation that was abandoning Scots in writing and on occasions of serious speaking. Elsewhere in his journals, he reported a discussion with Edmund Burke on the question of accent and dialect:

> I maintained a strange proposition to Burke: that it was better for a Scotsman and an Irishman to preserve so much of their native accent and not to be quite perfect in English, because it was unnatural. . . . I said it was unnatural to hear a Scotsman speaking perfect English. He appeared a machine. (Ryskamp and Pottle, 1963: 124–25).

That this view seemed to Boswell 'a strange proposition' is sufficient evidence that he regarded it as a minority opinion amid the prevailing enthusiasm for English styles of speaking.

Boswell and Burke shared some slight distance from the prestige dialect of London in that the former was a Scot and the latter Irish. Both agreed that public figures from those portions of the United Kingdom other than England should not strive to be 'quite perfect in English'.[4] Years before, when Boswell made his first extended visit to London, he expressed these linguistic preferences by joining with two other Scots to condemn the first performance of a play written by one of their compatriots, David Mallet. Mallet (c. 1705–1765) had aroused the well-deserved hostility of the London literary establishment, but among his faults in Boswell's view was his having changed his name from the manifestly Scots name *Malloch* on the grounds that 'there is not one Englishman that can pronounce Malloch'.[5] Mallet's perfection in acquiring the accent of Anglo-English was, from Boswell's viewpoint, carrying the extinction of Scotland too far. As he later counselled in the *Life of Johnson*:

> . . . let me give my countrymen of North-Britain an advice not to aim at absolute perfection in this respect; not to speak *High English*, as we are apt to call what is far removed from the *Scotch*. . . . a small intermixture of provincial peculiarities may, perhaps, have an agreeable effect, as the notes of different birds concur in the harmony of the grove, and please more than if they were all exactly alike. (Boswell, 1934: vol 2, 159–60).

Alexander Boswell differed from his son on the question of linguistic diversity, his view apparently founded on the aptness of language for its purp se rather than a single idea of correctness to which all would be obliged to adapt. In June 1761, Thomas Sheridan had appeared in Edinburgh to offer lectures on the English language that he had already presented in London, Oxford, and Cambridge: 'These lectures, with considerable enlargements, concerning those points with regard to which Scotsmen are most ignorant, and the dialect of this country most imperfect, he delivered in St. Paul's chapel, Edinburgh' (*The Scots Magazine* 23 (July 1761): 389). In the 'nrhusiasm for anglicization that followed, some of the principal intellectual leaders of the city formed a body they called 'The Society for Promoting the Reading and Speaking of the English Language in Scotland', and among the directors of the Society was Alexander Boswell (*The Scots Magazine* 23 (August 1761): 440–41).

However distinguished its membership, the Society did not immediately prevail in influencing attitudes toward English, though James Boswell submitted himself enthusiastically to Sheridan's tutelage.[6] Most prominent Scots, Alexander Boswell among them, were not very assiduous disciples, however. In the 1780s, the sons of gentry attending the justly famed Edinburgh High School had no great regard for Anglo-English speaking. According to Henry Cockburn, a pupil in those days, 'among the boys, coarseness of language and manners was the only fashion. An English boy was so rare, that his accent was openly laughed at' (Cockburn, 1856: 10–11). In 1813, the situation had not much changed, and George Borrow recalled his own days at the High School in similar terms:

> I certainly acquired here a considerable insight in the Latin tongue; and, to the scandal of my father and horror of my mother, a thorough proficiency in the Scotch, which, in less than two months, usurped the place of the English, and so obstinately maintained its ground, that I still can occasionally detect its lingering remains. (Borrow, 1931: 47).

PUBLIC OCCASIONS AND DOMESTIC USES

As the century wore on, schools more and more stressed the 'improvement' of spoken English (which meant the eradication of Scots). By 1852, one writer in the *Scottish Education and Literary Journal* found it 'highly creditable to Scottish teachers [that] there are two accents in Scotland, two styles of speech — one which is set apart for public occasions and one for domestic uses' (Williamson, 1982: 73). Were this evaluation accurate, one would surmise that the balance of public and domestic styles found in Alexander Boswell had become generalized to other social classes. Teachers, lawyers, and clergymen, this author opined, commanded the two styles to good effect: one for reading and public discourse, the other for conversation and the ordinary business of life. Balance was not regarded as the ideal, however. When school inspection was inaugurated in 1845, the official visitors grew increasingly critical of *any* use of Scots in the classroom. After 1872, with the requirement of universal primary education throughout Britain, anglicizing of all forms of English became the goal for all schools. In language precisely contrary to that of the Bullock Report, the inspectorate in 1898 praised the disjunction between public and domestic varieties: 'This seems to show that the average child carefully divests itself of its school language as it leaves the school door; and all the more credit is thus due to the teacher who is able to maintain so correct a standard of reading and conversation within the school'.[7]

Until quite recently, Scottish schools have continued to discourage vernacular varieties and to promote anglicized forms without much discrimination among lingusitic levels or functional settings for varied stylistic performance. Some attempts have been made, of course, to include the national literature in the curriculum, but even these initiatives are sometimes viewed by teachers as disturbing to the larger national interests of Britain.[8] Tolerance for linguistic diversity is even more threatening to the ordained view of one monolithic and standard variety of English.

The present-day situation shows glimmerings of change. Aitken's essay of 1976, 'The Scots Language and the Teacher of English in Scotland', apparently stimulated discussion among teachers, though the educational officer who edited the collection in which it appeared felt obliged to insert a prefatory disclaimer describing it as a 'personal statement' and not necessarily reflective of 'the views of the S[cottish] C[entral] C[ommittee on] E[nglish]' (p. 47). A further pamphlet prepared for pre- and in-service teachers was likewise described as not an 'official policy' but was even richer in raising questions about linguistic variety. Among many other interesting statements are two that call into question much of Scotland's historic educational language policy:

What is being argued is that a concentration on superficial aspects of language like accent or 'correctness' may not develop the ability to use language for a variety of purposes.

Can Scottish teachers not accept that diversity in language may be a source of strength and not of weakness? (*Scottish English: The Language Children Bring to School*, pp. 5, 15).

Progressive teachers and the educational authorities in Scotland have thus reached a position where the long and unsuccessful struggle against the vernacular must now be considered anew. A J Aitken, Lorna S Borrowman, the late John T Low and J Derrick McClure (among others) have provided these educators with the insights of contemporary sociolinguistics and accounts of the history of English in Scotland. Through workshops and their writing, they have described varying models for schooling and the language of children and thus have offered a range of options and priorities. Public opinion is only now beginning to shift toward the view that the door of the schoolroom is an entrance rather than a barrier. And it is up to teachers to decide how to teach the children now in school.

PLANS AND DREAMS

More than two centuries of lively discussion about the state of the language in Scotland have not yet led to consensus, but there are well-articulated positions that have consequences for schools.

One view of the contemporary linguistic scene is suffused with historical nostalgia. From this perspective, what Aitken has called 'Ideal Scots' was the national language at some earlier time (typically seen as the great literary culture of the Makars) and persisted until disrupting influences diminished its value as a lingusitic system and brought it into disrepute among Scottish people. David Murison is among the most learned to present this view, and his conclusion is gloomy indeed: 'the stark fact remains that the Scots language is in a bad state of decay and will assuredly pass into such a vestigial condition as to be virtually dead' (1971: 179). Elsewhere he declares that this form of Scots is so rapidly vanishing that 'by the end of this century very little indeed will be left' (1977: 57). If this estimate is correct, educational planners need hardly trouble themselves with Scots since the children now entering school will be leaving it just at the time this Ideal Scots has vanished from the linguistic scence. While this view is distinctly idealistic about language history, it is also — obviously — profoundly pessimistic. Still, since Scots has been regarded as at the point of death for two hundred years, we may assume that the catastrophe Murison foresees may not come quite so soon as he predicts.[9] For educational planners, however, a language on the brink of extinction hardly merits their attention.

A second view draws its inspiration from the linguistic revival movements of the past century, with the exemplary figures of Ivor Aasen (1813–1896)[10] and Eliezer Ben Yehuda (1858–1923) (see Black, 1985: 13, 14) who 'revived' and modernized Nynorsk and Hebrew, respectively, and showed them to be fit for contemporary use. Other parellels, almost exclusively drawn to the minority languages and dialects of Europe, are occasionally presented in the search for support for revivalist efforts to plan a distinctive language for Scotland (see Görlach 1985). What makes these comparisons unpersuasive for Scottish educational policy is that the social conditions that favoured the development of Nynorsk and modern Hebrew are lacking in Scotland. Public enthusiasm verging on linguistic zealotry is essential for the success of such linguistic reforms, and the Scottish public is ambivalent about its national language. Even the effort toward devolution of governmental powers from London to Scotland in 1979 did not reveal the nationalist movement as making language an important part of its platform (Macafee, 1981: 32). Without a foundation of strong public support, it is unreasonable to expect that any artificially codified variety of Scots can have a significant role in schooling.[11] While synthetic varieties like Lallans may continue to excite some literary efforts, even the magnificent translation of the New Testament by W L Lorimer is unlikely to kindle the sort of linguistic restoration desired by the language planners. As Karl Inge Sandred concludes: 'the revival of Scotticisms which are going out of use . . . is a middle-class phenomenon which seems so far to be of small practical consequence, even if it is supported by the press' (1983: 118).

A third view seeks to identify cultural traitors and foreign agents who are responsible for the decline of the Scottish vernacular. Popular objects for these attacks include the sixteenth-century Scottish printers who imitated London English rather than the Scottish written tradition, King James VI and the subsequent Stuart monarchs who first removed the court to London and then succumbed to anglicizing its language, the proponents of the Act of Union of 1707 who shifted parliamentary authority to the south and completed the linguistic anglicization of Scottish politicians at the national level, Robert Burns whose Scots poetry attached itself to English literary fashion rather than extending native lines of development, Walter Scott who anglicized the language of narration and thus made Scots dialogue into a mere colloquial and rustic form of English, and the Kailyard novelists whose evocation of rural folklife relegated Scots to a kind of quaint rusticity unconnected with contemporary reality. But the most popular villains in the panoply of those who are 'responsible' for the present state of the language are teachers and educational policy-makers.

Attacks on Scottish educators (especially school inspectors) are so common among those who decry the loss of Scots in the public life of the nation that it would be tedious to chronicle them. McClure's assertion can represent this view sufficiently: 'the entrenched hostility to and contempt for Scots which the Scottish educational system has instilled into all of us is now very deep-rooted' (McClure, 1980: 36). Needless to say, it is difficult to persuade people to one's cause who are obliged, during their wished-for conversion, to accept the blame for the plight of Scots and the erosion of a full range of styles in the vernacular. Those teachers who merit the approbation of the Scots-language establishment find themselves obliged to interpret unpopular viewpoints to a public of parents and pupils who have little sympathy for efforts to make what they see as a despised dialect into a vehicle for educated discourse. As David Black asserts in describing the evolution of anglicized norms, 'the Scots, very largely, have done it to themselves' (Black 1985: 12); the schools, in short, have given the middle-class public what it has wanted, a device to control the entry of the urban poor into its ranks. Schools are profoundly conservative institutions, and Scottish schools for the past century have transmitted the linguistic values of the middle-class to their children and, with rather less success, attempted to convey these values to the children of the classes below them. Whether such linguistic change can be imposed by the schools is seldom questioned; whether these efforts ought to be a primary purpose of schooling is even less often considered. Yet these issues must now be examined for reasons increasingly clear; as the Professor of Education at Glasgow has recently written: 'there are so many groups in our society denied access to the full range of opportunities that something has to be done not only in the name of common justice, but in order to avoid social distintegration' (Grant 1982: 42).

SCOTLAND AND THE WORLD OUTSIDE

A recent study of attitudes in Edinburgh toward various covert and overt Scotticisms confirmed that schools provide an important source of (mostly prescriptive) information about the vernacular. Even when they acknowledge words and structures to be 'good Scots', teachers feel obliged to admonish the pupils who use them on the ground that a fluent command of colloquial styles may be an obstacle to employment (though their rationale is usually stated in terms of individual features that will allegedly lead to instant rejection in the interview or hiring hall). As one teacher said, 'I correct the kids to prepare them for the world outside' (quoted by Sandred, 1983: 76). Teachers apparently feel that they must decry and correct forms that they believe to be stigmatized without actually investigating the opinions of employment interviewers. One observer believes that those teachers who are themselves comparatively 'broad' in their own speech are the most severe with their students.[12] Their prophecies may become self-fulfilling, of course, and subsequently legitimize hiring practices that deny opportunities to vernacular speakers (see Macaulay, 1974, 1977). Yet 'the world outside' may not have the same view of Scots that the educational community imagines. Within Scotland, employers need not (and certainly do not) consistently deny themselves the services of talented people by limiting themselves only to those who have rid their language of shibboleths. Abroad, Scots has a certain cachet — in Canada and New Zealand, for instance — and it is probably true that 'a Scots accent in England, other things being at all equal, carries a suggestion of competence and of a purposeful career sense that cannot fail to be an advantage to the speaker' (Phillipps, 1980: 79).

The 'world outside' no longer offers the same opportunities that made emigration an attractive alternative in the past. Scots who now depart for other nations are not the landless (like those who went abroad as a consequence of the Highland clearances) nor the mechanically minded who made Scottish engineering and maritime technology so namely around the world. The emigrants from Scotland today are fewer in number and better educated than those who left the country in the past. Many who remain in Scotland face the tragic future of continued structural unemployment, but, paradoxically, by having fewer choices they may have more options. They can, if they choose, please themselves with the kind of language that is best for their children and scorn the repeated claim, never fulfilled, that employment near at home awaits all those who perfect their English in school. With this shabby promise now obviously discredited, their schools can prepare today's children in a way that will contribute to the economic and cultural future of the nation. Liberated from foreign prejudice, imagined or real, Scotland is free to select from a greater range of possibilities than ever before. In short, the curriculum can reflect many elements of that part of life which a child lives outside school. Schools will necessarily take account of increasing linguistic diversity — more languages are now spoken in central Scotland than at any previous time (see McClure, ed. 1983b). The challenge of dealing with the riches of multilingualism — South Asian languages, Cantonese, West African languages, and the English-based varieties of the Caribbean — may help provide a richer context for understanding the divisiveness that has animated disputes about English over the past two centuries and more.

In a forum held at St. Andrews in 1978 to consider issues of nationhood, Angus McIntosh raised an issue of central importance for education in Scotland:

> . . . if you feel you need to foster a local tongue you should regard it as no betrayal of that need to foster along with it something of broader currency. If you want a form of language which accords with your ethnic or cultural instincts as a man [sic] of Buchan, it should somehow be tied up with your wider instincts as a man who will root for Glasgow Rangers against Tottenham Hotspur at any time. And if you thus enlarge your horizon to be a man of

Scotland as well as a man of Buchan you should also try further to enlarge it so as to feel your language and your culture to be part of that of Britain as a whole and to have at your disposition along with whatever else you may command one form of English which can function in any part of the world where English is spoken. (McIntosh, 1979a: 146–47).

And from this point, he goes on to suggest, those who command a local language within English should also command 'a language which lies beyond English altogether'.

These concentric circles of linguistic competence that McIntosh foresees open in an ever widening circumference of knowledge and opportunity. The centre lies in one's linguistic home. The boundaries between accent and dialect are not so different from those between dialect and yet another language, and Scottish educators are poised to encourage the enlarging of their pupils's ability across all these boundaries. In this respect, the youth of Scotland find a kinship with other young people in communities abroad.

Scotland's diverse linguistic community allows schools to recognize and reward children who have linguistic breadth, an educational approach clearly more promising than the long-failed attempts to eradicate one or another of a child's linguistic domains of competence. Upper-class deprivation means that some of the families who command hereditary wealth and power are unable to communicate effectively with their fellow Scots; many of them, or their children, will wish to repair their linguistic deficiency (see McCrum *et al.*, 1986: 144). Working-class deprivation means exactly the same and has exactly the same consequences for the generations that follow. The young who display stylistic virtuosity across social, regional, and register boundaries — and Scotland seems to have an abundance of such youth (see Reid, 1978) — provide role models for successful educational programs.

The kind of 'perfect, high English' that James Boswell found distasteful in his countryfolk is no longer in fashion. Even the elegancies of the Morningside/Kelvinside accent are falling into disrepute (see Johnston, 1985). The notion of 'the harmony of the grove' made melodious by the differing varieties of world English is now emerging as the ideal polyphony of our language, not the monotone of some sterile, standard English. But perhaps the ideal will have been reached when all Scots are able to command, with the same natural facility displayed by Alexander Boswell, the full range of styles and languages that are required by our multilingual world.

NOTES

1   To a great extent, when a contrast was made between *Scottis* and *Inglis*, the distinction reflected ideological rather than purely linguistic sentiments (as for instance in the debate between Ninian Winȝet and John Knox). See McClure (1981).

2   This period was marked by widespread acceptance of ideas that arose earlier. Keith Williamson describes the setting in these words: 'certainly, among the gentry and educated people unease with Scots forms of speech — which was to become something of a neurosis by the mid-eighteenth century — was apparent at the end of the seventeenth century. Nevertheless, a fairly full Scots must have remained the everyday spoken tongue for most people in Lowland Scotland, even allowing for the availability of more English options compared with two or three generations before' (Williamson 1982: 61). The following report suggests that Charles I (1600–1649) retained at least a Scots flavor in his English: 'I haue heard that an Englishman Scottizing once to our King, was roundly reproued for it, blessed be his Maiesty that so hateth flattery' (L'Isle 1639: C-3).

3   These usages are 'thin' Scots in McClure's terminology (1979: 30).

4   This view is certainly the dominant one today among speakers of various regional varieties of English around the world. Consider the following observation by T T B Koh, Singapore's Representative to the United Nations: '. . . when one is abroad, in a bus or train or aeroplane and when one overhears someone speaking, one can immediately say this is someone from Malaysia or Singapore. And I should hope that when I am speaking abroad my countrymen will have no problem recognising that I am a Singaporean' (Tongue 1974: iv).

5   *Dictionary of National Biography*, s.v. Mallet. See Pottle (1950: 152–55). In his essay on Mallet in the *Lives of the English Poets*, Johnson wrote: 'Having cleared his tongue from his native pronunciation so as to be no longer distinguished as a Scot, he seemed inclined to disencumber himself from all adherences of his original, and took upon him to change his name from Scotch *Malloch* to English *Mallet*, without any imaginable reason of preference which the eye or ear can discover. What other proofs he gave of disrespect to his native country, I know not; but it was remarked of him, that he was the only Scot whom Scotchmen did not commend' (Johnson 1905: vol. 3, 402–03).

6   See Boswell (1934: vol. 2, 159). Alexander Boswell subscribed for two copies of Sheridan's *Course of Lectures on Elocution*; see p. B-2.

7   Quoted from the *Annual General Report of HM Chief Inspectors* for 1898 (Williamson 1983: 59). Another dubious evidence of progress is the shift in pronoun for a school child from *it* in this Report to *he* in Bullock.

8   See the responses to a questionnaire circulated in 1985 to teachers in the Grampion Region quoted by McClure (1985: 7).

9   Aitken regards the immanent death of Scots as a 'myth' (1982: 30–31).

10 Aitken (1980: 48), however, is not persuaded that Riksmål and Nynorsk offer a suitable model for the diglossic situation in Scotland.

11 Spelling reforms that extend the principles of the *Scots Style Sheet* (1947) are unlikely to have much influence on the mass media, and the '*Sunday Post* Scots' of popular culture does not enjoy the support of those most active in the Scots linguistic establishment. See Macafee (1981: 36–37).

12 Joy Hendry, personal communication, August 1986.

TWELVE

Languages of Childhood

David Daiches

When, some time in the early 1930s, I first read T S Eliot's poem *The Waste Land*, three lines in section III ('The Fire Sermon') struck a strange note of half recognition. They were

> O the moon shone bright on Mrs Porter
> And on her daughter
> They wash their feet in soda water.

It is a reminiscence of a song brought to Britain by Australian troops in the First World War, and the original went something like this:

> O the moon shines bright on Mrs Porter
> And on the daughter
> Of Mrs Porter.
> They wash their feet in soda-water,
> And so they oughter,
> To keep them clean.

(I doubt if the original parts were as respectable as 'feet'.)

In 1915, during the disastrous Dardanelles campaign, there emerged another version. Charlie Chaplin was then beginning his career as a popular comic screen actor, and the coincidence of the Dardanelles campaign and the beginning of Chaplin's popularity produced the following, which I heard sung by small boys in Edinburgh in the spring of 1919, and I listened with fascination:

> O the moon shines bright on Charlie Chaplin,
> His boots are cracking
> For want of blacking,
> And his little baggy trousers will need mending
> Before they send him
> To the Dardanelles.

I heard this version again a few years ago sung in the play *O What a Lovely War*, and my recollection was confirmed.

The First World War echoed for several years in children's songs and rhymes. Another chant associated with children in the Meadows of Edinburgh in 1919 was:

> When I was young I used to be
> The bonniest lad that you could see.
> The Prince of Wales he wanted me
> To go and join the army.

A ruder one was:

> Kaiser Bill went up the hill
> To play a game of cricket.
> The ball went up his trouser leg
> And hit his middle wicket.

The war eventually faded away as a subject for children's rhymes and a variety of mindless chants succeeded. I remember

> I spent all my money
> On an old tin cuddy
> And the old tin cuddy wouldn't go.
> I hit it on the belly
> With a piece of sugarellie,
> But the old tin cuddy wouldn't go.

Sugarellie (or *sugarally*) was liquorice, and a *cuddy*, to Edinburgh schoolboys of the early 1920s, was not a donkey but a horse. It was a cuddy that pulled the coal-cart and the cart loaded with Leitch's mineral water, and it was cuddies that drank in the horse's drinking-trough at the foot of Marchmont Road. Jamieson glosses the word as 'ass' and Warrack (1911) as 'donkey', but CSD (following SND) after giving the primary meaning as 'donkey', gives 'horse' as a local meaning in the twentieth century.

Some years ago I heard two American linguists arguing about the *greasy-greazy* line, that is, the geographical east-west line that divides those Americans who pronounce the word *greasy* with / z / and those who pronounce it with an unvoiced / s /. When they asked me which way I pronounced the word, I could not be absolutely sure: I thought perhaps that if something was terribly greasy I would call it greasy with / z /, but in less drastic situations I would say the word with an / s /. Then I remembered my early childhood rhyme:

> Salvation Army free from sin
> Went to Heaven in a corned-beef tin.

> The tin was greasy,
> They slipped out easy.

There 'greasy' rhymed with 'easy', with / z / in both words. (This rhyme bothered me even as a small boy, because I had already a precocious sense of the difference between an adjective and an adverb and thought that there must be something wrong with the last line).

There were counting-out rhymes, with a different person being pointed to in each word. The most vigorous of these was:

> My mother and your mother were hanging out the clothes.
> My mother gave your mother a punch on the nose.
> Was it sore? Yes or no?

You then spelled out the answer. If, for example, the answer was 'yes', you continued:

> Y – E – S spells 'yes'
> And out of this game you must go.

The person landed with the word 'go' was 'out'.

For some reason potatoes figured in one counting-out chant. Every one clenched his or her two fists and held them out while the counter-out went round with his or her clenched fist bopping each of the held out fists in turn while chanting:

> One potato, two potato, three potato, four,
> Five potato, six potato, seven potato, more.

The plural form 'potatoes' was never used.

There were rhymes that must have been rooted in social history, such as this about the sausage vendor:

> Hi the wee polony man,
> Ho the wee polony man,
> Put a penny in the can
> For the wee polony man.

Polony was originally Bologna sausage, which the Americans call 'baloney'.

There was also the mysterious 'merry-ma-tanzie' which figured at the end of dancing and circling rhymes ('here we go round . . .') in the line 'Around the merry-ma-tanzie'. Chambers, in his *Popular Rhymes of Scotland*, says that 'this apparently meaningless term is probably a corruption of Merry-May-dance, having been perhaps a sport practised in the festivities of the 1st of May in former times' (1826: 268). CSD (following SND) describes it simply as 'corrupted phrase found in the refrain of a children's ring game etc.' Warrack calls it 'an expression in the girls' singing game of "jingo-ring"; a children's singing game'. Jamieson says the same, more elaborately, also specifying it as a girls' game 'in Tweeddale, Fife, Edinburgh, and other parts of Scotland': he spells it *merry-metanzie* and gives examples of the rhymes with the refrain ending in this word. I suppose it was a girls' game in my childhood: I learned the rhyme including it from my sister and don't now recall any game involving the word that I played myself.

Chambers' *Popular Rhymes*, I might mention incidentally, contains a richly documented and fascinating account of children's rhymes in Scotland in the first half of the nineteenth century, and it is interesting to compare them with those one recollects from one's own childhood. There was a schoolmaster at Watson's in the 1920s (and earlier), nicknamed 'Dub-Dub' (he was W W Anderson) who introduced us to Latin at the tender age of eleven and used to tell us of a country boy who on arriving home at the farm after his first term at the grammar school was asked by his father whether he could now speak in Latin. When the boy rashly said 'yes', his father asked him to ask for his breakfast in Latin, at which the boy recited: 'Porridgebus, porridgebus, come to silver spoonibus' (a *silver* spoon in a farmhouse!). For some reason Dub-Dub thought this extremely funny, and used to chuckle every time he told the story, which was often. Now there is a version of this in Chambers:

> A whimsical summons to breakfast, said to have been made by a female servant at a school, in consequence of hearing Latin words amongst the scholars —
>
>> Laddibus and lassibus
>> Come in to your parritchibus,
>> With milkibus and butteribus,
>> And ram's horn spoonibus!

A horn spoon seems more plausible in this context than a silver one.

There were ice-cream men, but no polony men, in Edinburgh in the 1920s, one with a barrow in Archibald Place, beside the old Watson's, waiting for the boys to come out in the lunch interval. They were all Italians, and some of the well-known Italian caterers in the city today started with ice-cream barrows or small ice-cream shops. The boys used to chant

> Ikey keema, pulla bella,
> On a warma day.

That is the sort of thing a small boy would chant on a summer evening while scooting down the streets in his *bogey* or *guider*. This was a home-made vehicle consisting of a wooden box on wheels with a movable front axle steered with string. A second boy would start it off with a push before jumping on to squeeze in behind. 'Can I hae a hurl on your bogey?' Some envied older boys had bicycles, and if you were very lucky you could get a back-step on a bike, perched precariously behind the cyclist.

One shared bogeys and bikes — and even sweeties. 'Gie's a sook,' a child would cry, hoping that another child would remove a *strippit ba* (striped mint humbug) from his mouth and give him a brief suck before receiving it back. You could ask for a sook (really a lick) of someone else's ice-cream cornet (always cornets, never cones, in those days). An ice-cream slider lent itself less readily to sharing. It was towards the end of the next decade, in the summer of 1939 to be precise, that I heard the term *ice-cream slider* used figuratively in a way new to me. It was in the bar of the Grandtully Arms, in the village of Grandtully on the River Tay, and two farmers were talking over their beer. 'She wasna muckle tae look at,' said one, 'but between the sheets she was like an ice-cream slider.'

Besides the ordinary sliders there were *Black Men*, known in some parts of Fife (and according to the SND Supplement also in Angus) as *Lochees*, where the wafers containing the ice-cream were thickly coated in plain chocolate. These were very expensive, and I don't remember ever being in a position to buy one.

If one wanted to proclaim a truce while playing a game, one would *cry a barley*, at the same time holding up one's thumbs and licking them alternatively. *Barley*, which is suggestive of *parley*, seemed much more expressive than the Latin *pax* of English schoolboys, which I read about in school stories. Expressiveness was all. *Umberella* was much more expressive than *umbrella*, especially in such a description as

> Skinnymalinky long-legs
> Wi umberella feet.

The message boy from Cameron the grocer round the corner used to tease us small boys with threats about the coming of the Gaggies Man. I pictured him as a horrible giant. Years later I heard the expression *Big Aggie's Man* and realised that *the Gaggie's man* was a corruption of a very different kind of name. I can get no help in this matter from any Scots dictionary.

In 1923 and 1924 my family spent summers in Port Seton and I used to listen fascinated to the chanting tones of the fishwives as they auctioned off on the harbour side the fish their husbands' boats had brought in. Each fishwife would stand over her share of fish, neatly laid out in rows on the ground, and, raising and lowering her arm with extended hand and pointed forefinger, would chant the price, moving up as the bids from the attending fishmongers came in. Often they would start with 'ae shillin, ae shillin, ae shillin' (the finger moving up and down, pointing at the fish and then rising), then go on to 'thirteen, thirteen, thirteen' (i.e., thirteen pence, never one-and-a-penny), 'fowerteen' (never one-and-tuppence, but at least once I heard 'yin an'twa') and so on to 'auchteen, auchteen, auchteen'. At two shillings they gave up counting in pence and the price became 'twa shilling, twa shilling, twa shillin'. I don't remember any price higher than that.

Most of our summer holidays, however, we spent in Fife. It was in the village of Kilrenny in 1920 that I learned that to Fife boys apples were *aipples* and was reproved by my parents for adopting this pronunciation from the locals. Fife was glorious for its seaside entertainers, popularly called *pierrots*. The men wore navy blazers with brass buttons, white trousers and nautical caps, and the ladies wore white dresses. It was at Leven in 1922 that I first heard Bob Merry give his much loved rendition of 'That's how you do it' and 'The red-blue sea'. These songs were not in Scots, but in a kind of music-hall English.

> While strolling one day to a music-hall I went,
> I put my hand in my pocket and I hadn't got a cent.
> I just turned my trousers round about:
> Instead of going in they thought that I was going out.
> So that's how you do it.
> That's how it's done,
> That's how you diddle-iddle-iddle-iddle-um.
>
> An old friend of man, Brown he was called,
> Was very very sad because his head was bald.
> He went to an artist, and, so he declares,
> He painted rabbits on his head;
> He thought that they were hares.
> So that's how you do it, etc.

And so it went on and on.

There seems to have been a fascination with problems of baldness, for Ian Maclean, another of the troupe, who sang Scots songs of a sub-Harry-Lauder variety, discussed the same topic in one of *his* songs:

> I'm a man o learnin
> As you can plainly see,
> Arithmetics and politics as easy as can be,
> Theology, zoology, literature and law,
> I hae them at my finger-tips,
> In fact I ken them a.
>> Zinty tiny haligolum,
>> Mebbe you think I'm just in fun,
>> If you don't believe me
>> Come up and feel ma pooches.
>> Kneel doon, kiss the groon
>> An kiss the bonnie wee lassie.

Old Mr Macintosh
He cam tae me indeed
To see what was the best thing
For a baldy heid.
Says I, 'Mr Macintosh, to you I do declare
The best thing for a baldy heid, my man, is hair.'
    Zinty tinty haligolum etc.

A herring man frae Paisley
Cam aw the way tae me
To see if I could keep his fush
Frae smellin, don't you see.
Says I, 'My man, I'll tell to you
Wi'oot the slightest chaff,
The way tae keep your fish frae smellin's
Cut their noses aff.'
    Zinty tinty haligolum etc.

I was puzzled by 'Come up and feel ma pooches', but eventually I decided that it meant that a learned man was traditionally poor and if you felt his pockets you would find that they were empty and that was proof that he was indeed a 'man o learnin'. I thought there was something wrong with this reasoning, although at the age of nine I had not the training in logic to realise that 'all x are y' does not necessarily mean that 'all y are x'.

Another of Ian Maclean's songs was a curiously debased version of a common Scottish folk theme:

Wull ye gae lassie gang
And walk we me ma honey?
Ah'm no Carnegie but
Ah've got a lot o money.
Ah've got the brass, my lass,
And it I mean tae scatter.
It's in the Bank o Scotland near the Banks o Allan Watter.
Wull ye gae lassie gang?

There were several stanzas in this vein, with the penultimate line always sung very fast. I could never figure out the grammatical sense in which the verb *gang* was used at the end of the phrase.

The songs of the Fife pierrots of the 1920s were primitive even by the standards of later Scottish seaside entertainers such as Harry Gordon, who packed them in at the Pavilion at Aberdeen in the years just before the war. I heard him in the mid-1930s, when I was a research student looking some things up at King's College Library (it was an excuse to visit my fiancée who was then working there), and I remember comparing a Harry Gordon song such as 'I am the keeper of the lighthouse' with Bob Merry's 'Right in the

middle of the red-blue sea (Nobody there by myself and me)' and realising
the greater sophistication of such lines as

> . . . Me and the sea and the seagulls,
> And the foghorn with its warning.
> But I'm a richt
> When the lichthoose licht
> Shines bricht through the nicht
> Till the morning.

This is to move away from the seaside entertainer to the 'Scotch Comic',
though the line between the two is sometimes hard to draw. The comic I
admired most when I was a teenager was Dave Willis, who had a real Scots
wit:

> Wi ma Indian feathers
> Listen tae me talkin Indian blethers.
> Wi ma squaw an ma wee papoose
> Ma wigwam's better than a cooncil hoose . . .

And the famous opening:

> Ye'll hae heard o Hiawatha.
> If ye havena, dinna bother.

Dave Willis was master of a particular kind of Scottish deadpan. Acting
the part of a pirate tried and condemned to death, he is asked if he has any
last words and replies: 'Aye. Ah feel rotten aboot the whole thing.' This
somehow reminds me of the Aberdeen minister who referred to Bethlehem as
on the Stonehaven side of Jerusalem.

To go from school rhymes, chants in the Meadows, Fife pierrot songs and
Edinburgh street speech ('Keelie language' the genteel called it) to the
domestic scene was to enter a rather different language world. My father, a
polyglot rabbi and Hebrew scholar who regularly received visitors from all
over Europe and talked with them in their own language, took it for granted
that educated people read the Greek and Latin classics in the original and of
course had picked up modern languages simply as part of growing up. I
myself could read Hebrew before I could read English, with the result that
when I went to school I wrote English either left to right or right to left
(mirror-wise), believing that one had the option to do it either way until I
was disillusioned in Class B of Watson's by an astonished teacher. I was
aware from early childhood that the world was full of different languages,
and occasionally failed to distinguish between them, using the odd Hebrew
or Yiddish word that was common in our family discourse in a quite different
context, with disturbing results. I have written elsewhere (1957) about the

Scots-Yiddish that older immigrant members of my father's congregation spoke. The amalgam is not as odd as it may seem. The two languages have much in common, Yiddish being essentially an early form of Low German (with a small admixture of Hebrew) containing many Germanic words akin to or even identical with the Scots equivalents. Douglas Young once pointed out that Goethe's alleged last words, 'Mehr Licht', would have been the same in Scots as in German, only spelt differently 'mair licht'), and they would be the same in Yiddish. A retired Fife station master wrote me many years ago saying that he used to have mutually intelligible conversations with Jewish *trebblers* (travellers, who went round the Fife coast towns selling haberdashery to housewives), he speaking in Scots and they in Yiddish.

There were words found in Scots Yiddish, and I believe in the Yiddish spoken by Jews in the north of England, which were quite mysterious in their origin. One was *bleggage*, a term of abuse for an ill-mannered boy. (My father once hazarded the guess that it was a confused mingling of *blackguard* and *baggage*.) The other, also a term of abuse for an ill-mannered keelie, was *baitzemah*. The origin of this word is totally mysterious, though a Liverpool correspondent once suggested to me that the word, as he knew it used among Liverpool Jews, may have originally referred to young Irish egg-sellers who came over from Ireland and went round Liverpool houses with baskets of eggs peddling their wares. The Hebrew word for egg is *baitzah*, so *baitzemah* might originally have meant 'egg boy'; if so, the suffix remains morphologically odd.

I remember Motty Rifkind, a shambling, grizzled man, the elder of two extremely pious brothers. He sat next to me once in *shul* one Passover morning, and was indignant with some young men, infrequent visitors to the synagogue, who were chattering loudly throughout the *chazan's* repetition of the *Amidah* (an important prayer, with 'eighteen benedictions', which the congregation recite first, standing, and then the *chazan* repeats). As old Motty himself used the synagogue as if it were his club, sleeping, snoring, talking, arguing, or praying as the spirit moved him, I was a little surprised at his stern view of the talkers, and indicated as much. In reply he told me a story. 'Two men', he said, 'vent into a poob and ordered a glass beer. Dey hadna been in dat poob more dan vonce or tvice before. Vell, day sip deir beer un' dey sit talking un' *shmoosing* (chatting). Dey sit un' talk un' talk. At lest de barman leans over de counter und he says to dem: "Drink op yer beer. Get oot frae here. Ye coom into ma poob vonce a year un' ye tink ye can sit here un' *shmoos* for hours as do' ye owned de place. Ma regular customers can sit un' talk over deir beer as long as dey like. But no' you. Oot!" *Nu*, dat's hoo it is mit a *shul*, I come here every veek und *Hakodosh boruch hu* ("the Holy One, blessed be He", that is God) kens me vell, un' he don't mind if I take it easy. But dese bleggages, dat come vonce or twice a year — no! Dey *daven* (pray) or dey shot op.'

There is nobody left who speaks Scots-Yiddish now; the language flourished, I suppose, from just before the First World War until about 1935. That was before the days of tape recorders, so there is no record of that richly expressive tongue. My own memory of it has grown dim with the years, and soon there will be nobody with even that degree of recollection.

THIRTEEN

A Northeast Farmer's Working Vocabulary

Alexander Fenton

In 1932, the late Eugen Dieth published *A Grammar of The Buchan Dialect*, building on the earlier work of H Mutschmann in 1909, in order to provide 'a full and accurate record of the living speech of a small but, on the whole, uniform area'. Dieth found that his students (when he was at Aberdeen University) could for the most part speak 'braid Scots', but few could pass as reliable dialect speakers. He therefore sought out, as his best authority, 'the intelligent but not over-educated man in the country'. He recorded his material on the farm of Yonderton, three miles north of the town of Turriff, much of it being supplied by Alexander Henry, the farm bailie (in charge of the cattle) and his wife (Dieth, 1932; Mutschmann, 1909).

Since the accidence and phonology of the dialect is available in print, though sadly Dieth's second volume on syntax never appeared, it is not the intention of this paper to repeat what is readily available elsewhere. It concentrates instead on outlining parts of a working vocabulary from one source, James Hunter, farmer at Brownhill, Pitglassie, Auchterless, gathered by the present writer during 20 years of talking and working with him in the fields and about the houses, and entered into notebooks during the late 1950s and 1960s. What is given here is a sample. On occasion the words of the speaker are reproduced as they were given. The aim is to place this vocabulary within its work environment. It does not look for phonological differences between the speaker's language and that of Mr and Mrs Henry of Yonderton, though these do exist: as Eugen Dieth told the present writer in a letter dated 30 January 1955, 'remember Turra isna Auchterless in every detail'. Nor does it try to give an analysis of equipment used, beyond what is necessary to contextualize the vocabulary, since such information can be found elsewhere (Fenton, 1976). It does, however, try to reproduce with as much accuracy as possible, within specific contexts, the working vocabulary of an individual who spent much of his life in the Howe of Pitglassie, Auchterless, and his earlier life a few miles away at Tollo Croft, where he was born in 1887, and at the farm of Carlincraig, just over the border into Banffshire. He entered the farm of Brownhill in 1922 with his father.

The bulk of the information relates to the days of horse draught, for Mr Hunter was a great horseman. Although a David Brown tractor came to the farm in the late 1940s, horses were not immediately dispensed with, and a black mare, Jip, was kept as an old-age pensioner for light jobs like *shimmin* 'horse-hoeing drills' and *shaavin neeps* 'sowing turnips' until she died in 1964. In the following notes, two main areas of activity, the major preoccupations of all farmers, are touched on, cultivation and cropping. Mr Hunter's own diaries and those of his father are used to give a framework over the farming year, and his own words, as recorded in my notebooks, provide a flavour of his attitude to the jobs and show his keen ability to characterize, and to see what is droll.

CULTIVATION

Ploughing with horses took up much more of the year than after the tractor came. In 1937, it absorbed 57 days or parts of days, not always in good conditions. The Diary entry for 26 March is 'plowin in bad order', and work went on also on 25 December, 'a green Christmas'. It took a good deal of skill to be a good ploughman, and some planning and preparation was needed before entry to a field with a plough. The first step was to take a spade and set up a line of sods, *props*, along the line of the old *midses*, where two *rigs* 'ridges' had come together. The *mids* marked the line of the dividing furrow or rather pair of furrows, one turned to the right and one to the left, so that a hollow remained in the field. Later working of the ground chamfered the sides and partly filled the mids in, so that it appeared as a shallow depression only, and not as a positive ditch. The row of props was a guide to the ploughman, the number of lines of props depending on the state of unevenness or otherwise of the ground, to let him see where he was going and divide the field tidily into the right number of rigs.

For those who pined for greater precision, *feerin-poles* about three or four feet high were sometimes stuck in the ground, but though Mr Hunter spoke of them, he had never seen them used. In the special case of ploughing matches, actual lines were laid along the ground to avoid as far as possible all risk of 'gaan aff 'e stracht'.

When the props had been set up, the first stage in ploughing began. This was *tae caa tae the props*, when a shallow *scrat* 'scratch' was made and not a *fur* 'furrow' of full depth. The first pair of scrats, one up and one down, was at a depth of about one and a half inches or a little more, leaving 'just a little rimmie turned ower'. The two slices turned by making these scrats came against each other in a shallow inverted V-shape. The next two furs were then ploughed up and down, the point of entry being about six inches away from the scrats, but still not all at the full ploughing depth, which was reached only after four or five furrows had been ploughed. In technical terms, this procedure meant that at the middle of each ridge, underneath the ploughsoil and not visible on the surface, there was a slightly raised area. Any field consisting of two or more ridges, therefore, had a slow-moving wave rhythm of 'positive' ridge-centres and 'negative' midses at the ridge junctions. In effect, this was a flattened-out version of the older, narrower and much more exaggerated ridges and furrows that belong to the days before the systematic underground drainage that began in the 1840s. The whole operation of reaching the proper ploughing depth was what was called *feerin*, a term which has more of a connotation than simply the cutting of the first furrow in a field (CSD). Real art was shown in keeping the *feerin* level with the rest of the ploughing. It is to be seen, therefore, as the set of six, eight or ten furrows at the centre of a rig, and practically speaking, this core is the real, even though invisible, representative in present-day fields of the high-backed *burrel rigs* of earlier days.

When *feered*, the ploughman continued to plough his rig, up one side, down the other. At ploughing matches, a quarter of an acre was reckoned as a rig for competition purposes. At each end he turned his plough and team on the *eynrig* 'end ridge', also called the *heidrig* 'head ridge' or *fleed*. *Fleed*, a word of obscure origin, can be traced back to 1808 in Aberdeenshire (SND). To the published references can be added a note for 20 January 1868 in a MS diary of G Gall relating to Atherb, near New Deer: 'the lea being all done except the fleeds in the Wright Park', which shows that the end ridges were ploughed up at the end of operations in the field.

Amongst special cultivation techniques mentioned by Mr Hunter was *brak-furrin*. For this, 'ye *ebb-plooed* [shallow-ploughed] aa 'e time, just deep eneuch tae turn a bittie ower, in 'e aatumn, an left it tae lie aa winter that wye, syne a gweed teer up in 'e spring wi a harra or spring-tine, syne a gweed deep fur. Aa deen awa wi lang syne. It gied a fine tilth for neeps.' It was also done in weedy ground to help to kill the weeds. There was also *cross-plooin*, not much practised, but on some lands there was a regulation that if a tenant was going out, he had to cross-plough land already ploughed, and the incoming tenant had to put it into turnips. 'It wisna a gweed job cross-plooin, the yird widna come aff o 'e cleathin [mould-board]'.

Since the nature of the ground could vary, the ploughman had to be able to make rapid adjustments as he went along, or else had to adjust the lie of the *sock* 'share' or coulter, or the place of linkage at the bridle. *Tae gie 'e ploo mair yird* 'earth' is to give the point of the plough a steeper pitch, so that it ploughed a little more deeply. The command to do this — if an experienced hand was watching a tyro — was *'Haad 'er up ahin!'* 'hold her up behind'. *Tae gie 'e sock yird* is to bend down the tip of the sock, an operation which had to be done in the smiddy, to make it dig in more. For lateral adjustment, the plough could be given *mair lan'*, so that it cut a wider furrow slice.

The ploughman stood between the *stilts* of the plough, and was sometimes jocularly referred to as the *docknail*, the indispensable nail at, so to speak, the plough's posterior. Linking the stilts were *steys* 'struts, stays'. The mould-board which turned the furrow slice to the right was the *cleathin*. The flat side of the plough-body that moved next the unploughed land, in line with the vertical coulter, was the *lan' side*. Overlapping the sole that ran on the ground, and the front of the *breist o the ploo* was the *sock*, which penetrated the soil horizontally and was so shaped that the furrow slice began its flow up and along it to the mould-board.

The sock consisted of three elements: the *pint* 'point, the *fedder* 'feather' and the *barrel*. The feather was the flange that undercut the grassy roots as it passed through the soil. If new iron was added in the smiddy to the edge of a worn feather, or to a worn point this was known as *layin 'e sock*. There was a *feather lay*, and a *pint lay*. The coulter could also be laid in this way.

The method of fastening the coulter to the beam had a part to play in plough adjustment also. Older coulters had flat shanks and passed through an opening, or *box*, in the beam. They were held in place by four wedges, two wide ones at the sides, and two narrow ones at the ends. By tightening or slackening one or more of these, the lie of the coulter could be slightly altered as required, or the tip could be raised and lowered. More recent coulters had round shanks and were fixed to the side of the beam by means of an iron *buckle* that straddled it. It was possible to turn such a coulter slightly to the left for the plough to be *gien mair lan'*, if necessary, or back, for less.

For the type with wedges, a *ploo-haimmer* was a necessity. 'Ye set 'e coulter first, syne tappit 'e wedges in. I've seen fyles 'e coulter fine set an ye'd come yark against a steen — knockit 'e wedges aa oot.' The coulter was set so that the point should be about three finger breadths above the tip of the sock, or more in stony ground. It should be set very slightly into the land, which helped it to turn down the grass that was to be ploughed under.

The ploo-haimmer hung in an iron loop inside the body of the plough. One at Brownhill was specified as having been the hammer of the second plough at the farm of Carlincraig in the time of Mr Hunter's father. Though its main purpose was to adjust the coulter, it was also sometimes used to hammer down the point of the sock, cold, when it was 'scarce o yird', though this was not a good thing to do since it was liable to break off the point altogether. As an aside it was mentioned that this example had been used latterly for hammering *sharps* into horseshoes in frosty weather. *Sharps*, also called *pikes* or *cogs*, were fixed into *cog-holes* on the shoes. If cog-holes had to be made in new shoes, the process was called *frostin 'e sheen*, so a cog-hole might also be called a *frost-hole*. *Frostin* was done at the approach of winter.

For ploughing *ley* 'grass', a *cuttin wheel* was buckled on to the forepart of the beam. According to Mr Hunter, 'some fowk used wheels steady, bit fin I startit first we wisna alloo't tae use a wheel for stibble or clean lan'.' He started ploughing at *Cyarlins* 'Carlincraig', but 'didna get muckle learnin — pitt'n awa wi a pair o horse an a ploo an mak 'e best o't.' The cuttin wheel, which cut the firm turf in front of the coulter with its sharp disc-shaped blade, was regularly used in ploughing matches, however.

Another attachment was the *skreefer*, which replaced the coulter, in appearance like a mini-mould-board. The name derives from *scruif*, 'the layer of vegetation on the surface of the ground' (CSD). It turned the grass and muck well into the bottom of the furrow, and in fact, many modern tractor ploughs only use a skreefer, and no coulter.

As an extra refinement at ploughing matches, 'files they vrocht [worked] a cheyn wi a ball on 'e eyn',' which helped to flatten out unevenness.

The front or muzzle of the plough-beam contained a number of openings set above each other. By fixing the pin of the *bridle* lower or higher, the plough could be adjusted for depth. The bridle itself was notched, and by fixing the *yoke* more to the right or more to the left, adjustment for land could be given.

The substantial five foot long wooden yoke held the pair of three foot *swingletrees* by means of an iron hook and *hesp* at each end. From the ends of the swingletrees, the *theets* 'trace-chains' ran forward, being supported by hooks on the *backbin* 'back band' and continuing to the hooks in the *haims* that hugged the collar of each horse. The backbin was a broad, leather strap over the horse's back, having no particular function other than to keep the theets from falling among the horses' feet, and to support the reins.

As a point of sophistication, a very short swingletree, only one and a half foot long, was put on when the last furrow was being ploughed close to a fence, since one of normal length would have caught on the *palin posts*.

The horses that drew the plough often had their special positions, and were named accordingly. The one that was used to walking on the land-side or near-side was the *lanner*; the offside horse was the *furrer* or *fur-beast*. A fur-beast that tramped in the fur was no use at a ploughing match. Expressions used of horses with particular attributes were: *A gran' lanner! a gran' furrer! a gran' aff-sider! tidy in 'e fur!*

Plough harness was simple, consisting of the collar and haims, the backbin that supported the theets, and the *rynes* 'reins' which were attached to the rings of the bit and brought back through the metal loops of the haims and the leather loops of the backbin. The bridle on the horse's head consisted of the *broobin* 'brow band', and two *lipstraps* which were fixed to the bit.

HARVESTING

Reaping with a *hyeuk* 'sickle' was long over by Mr Hunter's time, but the scythe remained in active use. This was the type with a Y-shaped *sned* 'shaft' with two handgrips, and a blade fixed to the end of the shaft by means of an iron ferrule and wedge, and a single metal strut, the *grass-hyeuk* or *girse-hyeuk*. In latter days the blade was sharpened with a long carborundum *scythe-steen*, round in section, but earlier on with a bat-shaped, wooden *scythe-brod* 'board' or *straik*, with an emery mixture attached to each side. The scythes were supplied by the local blacksmith at Pitglassie.

Mr Hunter related that during scything, 'fin corn wis stannin gey stracht up, it wis like tae faa i the bout [line of scything] an mak a lot o rakins, especially gin 'ere wis nae win'. A loon [boy] wis got tae walk alangside 'e scythesman wi a gad wand — a rodden [rowan] stick or a bittie o saach [willow] wid be fine — an held it awa fae 'e blade so 'at 'e corn wid faa richt'. He had heard of this, but had not seen it done. By the time he left school binders had come in and the scything of entire crops was finished, though it continued for *reddin roads* around fields to give entry to the binder without destroying any crop. 'Cuttin roads' is mentioned in his 1937 diary on 31 August and 1 September. This was an average to good year, but not so 1938, when stormy weather *laid* much of the crop. Then the scything of roads and flattened patches went on, alongside cutting with the binder. The entry for 22 August is 'start hairst, corn flat'. Scything is mentioned on 24 to 31 August inclusive (31 Aug.: 'scythin roads on clean land'), and on 1, 2 and 8 September, i.e. 11 days in all, and the ley was actually cut with the mower in this year, on 6, 10, 12, 14 and 15 September, before they 'Took Clyack' (end of cutting) on 19 September.

In the days before the binder, three or four scythes would normally work together on a three-pair *toon* 'farm-town'. The horsemen handled them. If three scythes were in use, there would be three women gathering. They gathered, made the band, and laid the sheaf on it, but did not tie the band. This was the job for the two men who 'bun' an stookit', serving the three bouts. Each man, therefore, served a bout and a half. They took the centre bout sheaf about, 'ilky secont shafe i the middle bout', and called that a 'scythe an a half'. The women were *lifters* or *gaitherers*, and the men were *bansters*.

In the days of the scythe, if the corn was badly laid and twisted, it was not possible for the scythers to work neatly one behind the other. 'They vrocht rig an rig — they hid gey nerra rigs at 'at time. There wis files a gey hash tae see fa'd gotten throwe 'eir rig first.'

After the horse-drawn reaper came into use, lifters and bansters worked behind it also, but 'it wis a gey hing-in ahin a reaper'. Binders came in after the reaper, self-knotting so that the need to tie bands virtually

1 *Ruck-foons* of Peterhead granite, at Brownhill. Photograph AF 1950s.

2 James Hunter tidying *corn rucks* with a rake at Brownhill. Photograph AF 1960s.

3   James Hunter with a completed *edderin* for roping thatch on stacks. Photograph
AF 1960.

disappeared. With the binder, five bouts was the common thing for
stooking.

The topic led to a reminiscence about Francis Finnie, grieve and manager
at the farm of Tollo. He was a character, who wore moleskin breeks that were
always 'as fite's a doo [dove] on Monday mornin'. When they first got a
binder he said, 'I dinna ken foo we'll get on this hairst, we've got een o yon
binner things.' In the words of my informant,

> he wis a queer kinna lad, files it [the crop] widna been in verra great order, he
> wid a been leadin [carting home the crop], idder days fin ither fowk wis leadin,
> he widna been leadin. He niver wore a flannen just a cotton sark. He wore a
> shaftit [sleeved] weskit [also called the *shafter*]. He niver hid bit ae pair o
> mittens an 'e sellt them at a profit, ye'd see 'im on 'e caalest day teerin up at 'e
> neeps wi 'is bare hans. If 'e wis wirkin doon on 'e laich [low] grun near a burn
> on a warm simmer day an' 'e wis thirsty, he widna teen a drink. 'Oh', he says, 'I
> micht be awa up on 'e hill 'e neist day far I couldna get a drink.' Files if ye met
> in wi 'im he'd a newsed, neist time he'd niver a spoken. Great big, strong chiel.
> I div a kinno jist min' on 'im, he'd a been in ma father's time.

Whether cut with scythe or binder, the crop of oats was set up into *stooks*.
Each stook consisted of five pairs of sheaves, though sometimes on the *clean*

lan only four pairs were set up, because of the grassy sole. It was easier to shift eight sheaves to a new stance, two men taking four sheaves apiece, so that the grass should not be spoiled by having stooks staying too long in one place. In this area the injunction was 'stook aye tae Bennachie', because stooks aligned with that hill lay north and south for maximum exposure, and would *win* 'dry' better.

There was a story about Willie Tocher o Yokieshill. '[He] couldna see Bennachie, sae he just stookit tae Mormon Hill. The fairmer, he gee'd roon. "Aye, Tocher", he says, "that's nae 'e wye tae stook". "Weel, I couldna see Bennachie, sae I just stookit tae Mormon." '

The tail of the sheaf was the *butt*. The word *gavel* was also known, but only through its currency in the song, 'Johnny Sangster'. The proper way to stook the sheaves was to set them with the knot of the band to the inside, so that the shear of the butt lay to the outside and the smallest possible area sat on the ground. With a straw band, it was the corn ends that were *knottit*, and the corny knots were set in to prevent them from growing 'in a weety time'. With binder sheaves, Mr Hunter normally stooked with the knot out. As he said, they sat better like this, but all the same there was a better run on the sheaf with the knot in and this was probably the best way to do it. About three weeks was the average time for drying in the stook.

One of the least pleasant jobs during harvest was *stook parade*, when stooks demolished by storm and wind had to be set up again. The stookers inevitably got a thorough soaking. Mr Hunter noted such occasions in his Diary. The stooks were levelled on 13 September 1937, for example, and had to be set up again on the two days after. On 19 September, he noted, 'Stockie [sic] Sunday in New Deer district'. The discomfort of the job is clear.

In pre-tractor days, leading with horse and cart took a considerable time. The farm had three horse and two carts then. Two horse and two carts required four folk to work to them: 'a forker on 'e lan', a bigger [builder] on ilky cairt, an een biggin 'e rucks'. The Brownhill practice was for Mr Hunter to do the skilled job of building the stacks, the *fee't* 'hired' man took one cart, one *quarterer* (a tramp given quarters in the barn or byre) took the other cart, and another did the forking. The quarterers turned up regularly for seasonal work for many years.

Mr Hunter's grandfather used to 'fee hairsters aboot Cornhill at a kinno a market for 'e hairsters, 'e Berry Market o Cornhill. Fin 'e cam hame, 'is wife said till 'im, "Hae ye gotten onybody?" "Aye", he says, " 'e Lang Laddie an 'e Blue Flee". "Oh", she says, " 'at wis aafa names". "Oh", he says, "ye canna get gentlemen tae work yer work". Anither time 'e fee't an umman hairster an fin she cam hame she hid on skiry [gaudy] kinno claes. 'Ey were badderin 'er about 'er claes, an she said, "I'm nae prood, I'm tasty an airy." '

The 1937 Diary shows that in that year, harvesting with the binder started on 27 August, roads having been *redd* with the scythe around the fields, the *yavel* 'second year oats on the same ground' being cut first and then the *clean lan* (after a root crop). As it happened, no *ley* 'grass land' had been *crappit* 'put in crop' in that year. Cutting finished on 7 August, and leading followed with its usual urgency. All was in by 22 September.

When forking onto the cart, a skilful forker could help the *bigger* by turning the sheaves with his fork so that they not only lay to hand, but also in the right position for being built into *gyangs* 'rows' above the frame of the cart, or for *hertin*, i.e. filling in the heart. In the field the two-pronged fork was full-sized, of the type used for either straw or hay, but for forking at the ruck, where the correct positioning of sheaves was more critical, and only one at a time was forked, a *shafe-fork* was often used. Its prongs were around two and a half inches apart and just under five inches long. The small size let the sheaf slip off easily. It was also more useful than the standard forks for shoving in the tails of sheaves when tidying a ruck that was being built.

When all the corn had been led and the fields were left with clean *stibble* 'stubble', a neighbour might say, 'Ay, ye've gotten winter'. Similarly, for the end of cutting, the phrase was 'ye've gotten clyack', but Mr Hunter had experienced no special ceremonies with regard to the *clyack shafe* 'last sheaf'.

In the *cornyard*, the *rucks* were built on *foons*, 'foundations' usually consisting of a circle of stones covered with branches of broom, or simply a layer of branches arranged in a circle. More rarely there were foundations made of a circle of stone uprights of Peterhead granite, and one in the centre, each with a granite cap so that they looked like stone mushrooms. Spars of wood were laid across. On these, stacks could be built completely clear of the ground. A single fencing post was hammered into the centre of the *foon* with the *mell* 'heavy-headed hammer'.

When building began sheaves were stooked against this post, if there was one (it was not needed for a good, dry crop), so that the *hert* could be kept well up. Sheaves were added all round, at a continually lessening angle, until the outer ring was reached. This made the first *gyang*. The basic principle to be observed as the ruck grew was always to keep the heart up so that water would always run off along the lie of the stalks. In Angus and South East Scotland, there were much bigger stacks with wide bodies that rose for some distance before the head began to be formed, but in the Northeast generally, the inwards curve began more or less at shoulder level. At this point, the builder started *draain in*, making the gyangs a little smaller in circumference each time he went round, until at least there was room for only the *heedin shafe* 'heading-sheaf'. This was often stood on its head, and the tail curled down over the band.

The point at which draain in began was the *easins* 'eaves'. Some specialists who took pride in their work sometimes built the *easin gyang* farther out than the others, so that it slightly overhung the gyangs below it. In this case it was known as the *turned gyang*, with the shear of the sheaf underneath. A main practical reason was that it helped with *thackin* 'thatching'. The *thack* was carried down to this point and slightly beyond, so that it threw water well clear.

In a busy cornyard a man was given the job of keeping an eye on the shape of the stacks, pulling out a sheaf here, pushing in another there with a fork, and making sure that all was on the plumb. If, in spite of all, the stack tilted a little to one side, one or more *ruck-posts* had to be leaned against it as supports. 'That ruck wid need an oxter-stav [crutch]' was a jocular reference to a leaning stack, implying derision of its builder.

The thatch was of *sprots* or *rashes* 'rushes' and reedy plants, cut in the bog alongside the burn below the farm just before they were required. They were laid green. *Strae* 'straw' from the year before might also be used. It was laid in place from a *ruck-ledder* 'stack-ladder', and the next and final stage was to *raip* 'rope' it down well against the winter storms.

At one time, a double-thick raip, the *bag-raip*, was fixed around the stack at, or just below, the *easin*. Another name for this was the *eave raip*. The raips on the *heed o' 'e ruck* were taken once round the bag-raip before being tied into the side of the stack. Latterly bag-raips were not used and the ends of the raips were simply tied in, the end of the raip and a tuft of straw from the tail of a stacked sheaf being twisted together till the raip was tight, and the end tucked in behind it.

Raipin 'e thack was a sophisticated exercise. First of all, the raips were twisted in the barn during wet days, of straw or latterly of binder-twine, by means of a metal hook shaped like a car starting handle, with two wooden handgrips within which the body rotated. This was the *thraa-hyeuk, thraa-crook*, or *twiner*. An older form of twister was a rod with a walking-stick shaped head that acted as a hook, and at the other end a swivel that provided a hand hold. It was generally called a *tweezler* or *tweezlick*, and was made of 'hard wun sach [willow]'. A piece of *tow* 'twine' across the head served as a stay to hold the curve firm so that the straw did not slip off, and also to keep the raip from slipping into the middle of the hook. Use of the tweezlick required a good deal of motion with the hand that held it well along its two foot length. If used to it, a good job could be done, and as Mr Hunter said with reference to the smoother-turning new type, 'some fowk took ill wi this thraa-crooks fin they cam in first'.

The job of twisting required least skill. The operator simply moved backwards slowly, twisting as he went. On the straw before him sat the *latter-oot*, the man who fed the straw in an even stream through the space between the thumb and forefinger of one hand, meanwhile using the other fingers to tuck in loose ends and smooth rough patches. It was possible to twist a short rope, a *thoom raip* of hay or straw, for some temporary job, without using an instrument, but using the hands only. The thumb served as the hook. Hence the saying, 'makin a thoom raip wi yer first finger', to indicate an impossibility.

The completed ropes were coiled into round balls called *cloos*, up to the size of a football, or bigger, or else they were twisted with considerable ingenuity into a smaller shuttle-shaped form, about a foot long and containing twelve to fifteen foot of rope, called an *edderin*. Cloos and edderins reflected two forms of thatching, the first called *swappin* and the second *edderin*. In swappin, raips were laid alternatively across the shoulders of the stack, using the cloos, so that the end result gave a diamond-shaped appearance. In edderin, however, ropes were first put on vertically, often three in number to give six uprights, from one side over the top and down to the other, and fixed firmly. Then the specially-shaped edderin was used to thread another rope round each of these verticals, from top to bottom, so that the final appearance was one of a set of squares. Edderin made a tighter job than swappin, but more work was involved and in latter days it became less common.

In applying the raips, one man worked off a ladder at the top of the stack and another stood on the ground, ready to catch the cloo as it was moved from one side of the stack to the other. Mr Hunter's habit, as he threw the cloo down on the opposite side from which it was first thrown up, was to shout 'Look up!'. If you did you got it in the face.

A hairst-supper was often held when "e biggin o 'e rucks' was finished, before the extra hands had left. It consisted of a meal, something to drink, and maybe some dancing afterwards.

In latter days stacks were not built with the same care and pride, partly because hands were becoming more expensive, and therefore fewer. As *strae-raips* were replaced by twisted binder-twine, then by coir-yarn, and finally by nets, the older skills faded, and even stacks are scarsely part of the farming scene any more.

As the year wore on, and the cattle began to be kept again in the byre overnight, the need for straw as food and bedding meant that the summer's respite from threshing was over. In 1937, there was a threshing with the barn mill, driven by an Allan Oil Engine, on 29 September. On 20 October a stack was taken into the barn, and thereafter the driving in of stacks, and their threshing, occupied ten of the November and December days. Earlier in the same year, between 7 January and 12 August, at least 26 days were taken up with these activities. Even though the taking in of a ruck and a threshing occupied only up to half a day in each case, the input of labour was still considerable.

In addition to this regular bread-and-butter (for the cattle) type of work, there was an occasional visit from the travelling threshing mill, when the last of the stacks in the cornyard could be threshed, and neighbours joined in turn at each other's farms to help. The travelling mill started to come round in Mr Hunter's father's time, in the third quarter of the nineteenth century. As he put it:

At 'e start o 'e traivellin mull, they hid tae haal them wi 'e horse [plural]. They didna ken much foo tae dee wi 'em an they'd gotten an Englishman tae gie them a han'. At ae place 'e got milk-broth an 'e says, 'We got milk-broth tae wir denner bit I just gave them a milk-broth thresh.' He wis aafa ill aboot whisky, if ye'd jist noticet 'im wi a suppie whisky at 'e time, ye'd a gotten a gran' thrash. They were aakwird kinna things tae work wi the horse.

This paper is concerned with a working vocabulary, in the most literal sense of work. Two subject areas have been touched on, but much of the yearly cycle of activity remains: the driving out of dung, potatoes, neeps and hay, cattle, harrowing, rolling, grubbing and weeding, sowing, fencing, fairs and markets, the men on the farm. A round the year picture could and should be constructed, so that the full pattern of words and expressions of an individual farmer could be put on record. The present extract gives a sample of the working vocabulary within two of the major activities only, but nevertheless demonstrates how much remains to be gleaned.

FOURTEEN

The Heteronomy of Scots with Standard English

John M Kirk

Like so many studies of Scots, this paper (as well as the larger study on which it is based) is motivated by the work and the personal example of the man, lexicographer and mentor to whom this volume is so happily dedicated.

The application of the concept of 'heteronomy' to Scots appears in A J Aitken's seminal paper on the identity of Scots:

> As a spoken language it lacks 'standardisation'; it is *heteronomous* with — bound up in a sociolinguistic continuum with and constantly being influenced by Standard English, and therefore conspicuously lacking in the . . . attribute of 'autonomy' (Aitken, 1981b: 72).

According to the *Longman Dictionary of the English Language* (1984), *heteronomy* is the 'subjection to the law or determination of another, especially a lack of moral freedom or self-determination' and may be compared with *autonomy*.

The heteronomy of Scots with StE has recently been examined in an investigation of primary and modal auxiliary verbs (Kirk, 1986). In this study, the syntax and semantics of Scots is shown to be inextricably bound up with the syntax of StE at every level, included a common core of syntactic systems and structures. Such a common core, according to Quirk *et al.*, *A Comprehensive Grammar of the English Language* (1985) (CGEL) 'is present in all . . . the varieties [of English] so that, however esoteric a variety may be, it has running through it a set of grammatical and other characteristics that are present in all the others. It is this fact that justifies the application of the name *English* to all the varieties' (CGEL: §1.19). The idea of a common core also forms an indispensable part of the model of Scottish speech behaviour put forward by Aitken himself (1979: 86).

The empirical evidence in this study comes from a corpus of dramatic texts, representing two different styles of Scots available to the present-day writer, and this paper continues their detailed comparison, in a tradition of recent stylistic criticism which begins with McClure (1974) and includes Macafee (1982) and Morgan (1983).

The texts in question are Robert McLellan's *Jamie the Saxt* (Campbell and Jack eds., 1970) (JS), Billy Connolly's *An Me Wi Ma Bad Leg Tae* [1976] (LE), Bill Bryden's *Benny Lynch* (1975) (BL), and John Byrne's trilogy, *Paisley Patterns* (PP) comprising *The Slab Boys* (1981) (SB), *Threads* (1980) (TH) and *Still Life* (1982c) (SL).[1] *Jamie the Saxt* is considered to represent 'Traditional Scots' (TrSc) and is contrasted with the 'Glasgow Scots' (GSc) represented by the rest, and it is as exponents of these two literary dialects that the language of these six plays is treated.

As a variety, TrSc is ahistorical, being contemporary neither with the events of the play nor with the author's own day; it follows a technique much deployed in Scottish literature and exploited, for instance, by Walter Scott (in *The Abbott* or *The Monastery*). In regional terms TrSc is delocalized. It happens that McLellan came from, and spent his life within, the West Central Scots dialect area, but his literary dialect is essentially metropolitan Scots, by intention representative of the entire Lowland Scots-speaking area. For his purposes, McLellan believed that it was sufficiently localized as Scots (i.e. not StE) and the question of greater local realism was irrelevant insofar as his intentions were not documentary or realistic but purely literary. In social terms, *Jamie the Saxt* distinguishes the dialect of the Scots-speaking characters from that of the StE-speaking characters Sir Robert Bowes and the Stranger, and the Pidgin-Scots of the Danish-born Queen. But no further distinction is made in the Scots to reflect social differences between characters (between, for instance, the King and Mistress Edward, wife of Bailie Nicholl Edward, an Edinburgh cloth merchant, with whom the King lodges). In this respect, TrSc may be said to be '*a*social'.

Literary though TrSc is, it has some basis in actual speech. The basis usually cited is the rural Scots typified by Buchan, the Black Isle and parts of the Borders. There is thus a link between conservative, rural, largely working-class and uneducated Scots speech and conservative, metropolitan, delocalized literary Scots (perhaps most comprehensively set out by Murison, 1977, and confirmed in general by Aitken, 1981b). The appeal of *Jamie the Saxt*, as vivid in performance in 1937 as it still is in the 1980's, is thus attributable to McLellan's ability to suggest that rural Scots speech could have been spoken throughout the whole of Scottish society, including the Monarch himself; and at the same time to suggest, conversely, that even the King himself can be imaginatively shown to have the qualities of mind and character usually associated with rural conservative speech or its ordinary speakers ('the countrified, blunt-spoken quality, of the earth earthy, traditionally associated with Scots speech', as Buthlay writes of Hugh MacDiarmid, 1982: 29). McLellan's achievement was the generic extension of TrSc from its use in poetry and prose fiction to its use in drama.

Here is a brief extract from a discussion in the King's private chambers between the King himself, who happens to be trouser-less, and some of his noble lords:

> BOTHWELL: Gin ye dinnae gie in I'll cairry ye ower to the winnock juist as ye are!
> THE KING: (Almost in tears) Aa richt. I'll gie in the nou. But by God wait!
> BOTHWELL: (To Atholl) Whaur are his breeks?
> THE KING: They're in the closet.
> BOTHWELL: Fetch his breeks, Lennox.
> LENNOX: (indignantly) My Lord ye forget yersell.
> OCHILTREE: I'll fetch them . . . (coming in from the closet) This is the only pair I can fin.
> BOTHWELL: They'll dae. Help him into them.
>
> (from McLellan, 1970: 55)

Since the early 1970's, however, a new literary dialect has emerged, based on Glasgow speech. In historical terms, Glasgow Scots is contemporary with the events of the five plays and nearly contemporary with the date of writing and first performance. All the variables point to a fairly homogeneous historical dialect of the mid-twentieth century. It is the intention of the dramatist (as interviews with Bryden (e.g. Bold, 1974) and Byrne (e.g. McMillan, 1982) indicate) to represent the actual speech that such characters might have spoken in real life. In regional terms GSc is localized to the West Central Scots which centres on Glasgow. The representation of local speech is also part of what these plays are about, for their intention is to extend the range of the dialect, from its purely vernacular use, to its use as a literary (and specifically dramatic) vehicle. In social terms, GSc also differentiates between those characters who are presented as though they were speaking in the vernacular and conforming wholly (or predominantly) to its norms, and those, usually middle-class, characters who are presented as assimilating to a greater or lesser extent to the norms of StE (such as the Doctor in *Benny Lynch* or Miss Walkinshaw in *Paisley Patterns*).

Here is an extract from Connolly's play *An Me Wi Ma Bad Leg Tae* in which, after a year in the army, Peter arrives home to his parents Bob and Jean and his brother John:

> BOB: Och it's yersel', nice tae have ye hame again son, come away in. Here, gi'es that case, ye must be sick lookin' at it.
> PETER: God aye, yer no' kiddin' there faither, ma back's near broke.
> JOHN: Whit have ye got that's so heavy in there Peter? Yer wages is it?
> PETER: Aye, that'll be right.
> JOHN: How's it goin'?
> PETER: No' bad.
> JEAN: Aw, ma wee son, wid ye look at ye. Tae think o' ma wee boy.

JOHN: Aw, come on, gi'es a wee look at 'im.
JEAN: A think ye've lost a bit o' weight son, whit are they dae'in tae ye?
JOHN: Have they cut ye doon tae six plates o' mince a day Peter, eh?
PETER: Och, it's the exercise Maw, ah'm as fit as a fiddle. A've only lost yon kite A hid wi' the beer, an' A wis glad tae see the back o' it A might add. Hey, . . . (he winks at John) . . . Y're lookin no bad yersel' auld yin.
JEAN: Away an' gi'e yersel' peace you. Aye, an' less o' this auld yin stuff by the way.

(from Connolly MS, pp. 3–4)

The descriptive categories of dialectology are more readily valid for GSc. In these terms, TrSc is not realistic — it might rather be called 'bourgeois' and 'gentrified', even 'anachronistic'. By contrast, as a literary dialect, GSc represents nothing short of a shift of medium, creating on the basis of speech a written form or overall register which previously did not exist. It lacks the simplified formality of the written language and bears many of the characteristics of 'informality' associated with conversational speech. This is shown in the behaviour of auxiliary verbs, to which attention is now turned.[2]

HAVE got

Especially in British English, it is claimed (CGEL: §3.34) that the HAVE *got* construction expressing Health, Possession and Relation (which although perfective in form is nonperfective in meaning) is 'informal' and is preferred in speech as an alternative to the use of stative lexical HAVE. In these senses, there are 119 occurrences of HAVE compared with 148 of HAVE *got* in the GSc subcorpus. In TrSc, by comparison, there are no occurrences of the HAVE *got* construction. These figures are presented in Table 1.

Table 1
GSc — HAVE and HAVE *got* forms — Occurrences
and Percentages (from Kirk, 1986: Table 2.59)

	N	%
Stative HAVE	119	44.6
HAVE *got*	148	55.4
Totals	267	100.00

Table 1 shows that the speech preference in favour of HAVE *got* froms is 55.4 per cent. GSc examples of the HAVE *got* construction include:

LE JE 520 As for you, you're only jealous because he's *got* a better view o' Ben Lomond than you.
TH SA 6374 See that bugger I'*ve got?*
SL SP 8405 You want to see this joint . . . even the close'*s got* flock wallpaper.

The copiousness of the tokens arises from the fact that all characters use the HAVE *got* construction, including the middle-class characters, as in:

SB AL 345 I'*ve got* a young brother who's earning that and he's only sixteen.
SB CU 5901 And for your information Jimmy Robertson'*s got* hammer toes.
TH MW 8018 'If you're thinking of marrying that, Elsie, you'*ve got* another think coming.'

CGEL's claim that the HAVE *got* construction is particularly common in negative and interrogative clauses is also confirmed by the GSc subcorpus, as Table 2 shows:

Table 2
GSc — Lexical HAVE and HAVE *got* — Occurrences (from Kirk, 1986: Table 2.60)

	Negatived Declaratives N	Interrogatives N	Negatived Interrogatives N	Totals N
HAVE *got*	13	14	0	27
Lexical HAVE	6	4	0	10
Totals	19	18	0	37

In these two constructions, HAVE *got* is half as frequent again as the HAVE construction. Examples of negative declaratives include:

BL ST 1363 Annie an him — they *havenae got* a chance.
BL PU 2968 I *havenae got* a torch.
SB HE 5745 Ah'll be gaun wi' Wullie . . . he *husnae got* a ticket.

Examples of interrogatives include:

SB SA 3889 Noo, *hus* yese au *goat* yur tickets fur the Staff Dance the night?
TH PH 7823 What'*ve* you *got* on your hair, Jim?
TH CU 7968 Sacred heaven! *Has* he *got* a tourniquet on his arm?

There are only five examples in the GSc subcorpus of the more 'formal' HAVE construction (as an operator without DO-support), including:

SB SP 3694 *Hud* yese much bother last night?
TH LU 5977 *Have* you such a thing as a comb with soft teeth you could lend us?

Miller and Brown's corpus of Edinburgh speech, elicited from schoolchildren in both the state and private sectors, [3] the HAVE *got* construction is between two-and-a-half and three times as frequent as stative HAVE (Miller, 1982b). The distribution of these HAVE constructions thus matches up to the formality represented in each subcorpus.

MUST

A second example concerns the distribution of senses expressed by the modal verb MUST. Table 3 compares TrSc, GSc and StE. The latter is represented by the London-Lund corpus (Lund) which comprises informal conversations in spoken StE (cf. Svartvik and Quirk, 1980), and the Lancaster-Oslo/Bergen Corpus (LOB), which comprises written texts in British StE, representing four principal registers: journalese, nonfictional prose, learned and scientific prose, and fiction (cf. Johansson *et al.*, 1978).

Table 3

MUST Meanings — Percentages — Inter-corpus comparisons (from Kirk, 1986: Table 5.13) [4]

	Lund %	GSc %	TrSc %	LOB %
Root MUST	53.0	26.8	30.0	64.8
Epistemic MUST	46.0	73.2	70.0	31.4
Indeterminate	1.0	0.0	0.0	3.8
Totals	100.0	100.0	100.0	100.0

Table 3 shows that the distribution of MUST senses in Scots is the reverse of that in StE. In Scots Epistemic MUST (expressing Prediction) predominates; in StE it is Root Must (expressing Obligation). These figures are confirmed by the Edinburgh corpus. Miller (1982d) found that MUST was mainly Epistemic: 79 out of 85 occurrences (or 92.9 per cent) in the private school data, and 65 out of 71 occurrences (or 91.5 per cent) in the state school data. GSc examples of Root MUST include:

BL ST 1418 You *must* wait for the photo, Doctor.
SB AL 5156 (Phil): You havenae been sayin anything tae hur, huv ye? See if ye huv . . .

(Alan): No, I haven't, if you *must* know.
TH MW 8054 Still, we *mustn't* dwell on these things, *must* we?

TrSc examples of Root MUST, realised as *maun*, include:

JS BM 10603 Weill, Mistress Edward, ye'll ken fine, yer guid man bein a
Bailie himsell, that I *maun* gaird aye my tongue weill in maitters that affect the
Toun.
JS ME 10622 Ye *maun* sit doun, Bailie, and I'll licht a wheen mair caunles, for
the gloamin's weirin on.
JS ME 10918 (Mistress Edward): Yer Grace, I'm shair he *maun* cheynge his
claes?
(King): (his nose in his stoup) Eh?
(Mistress Edward): I'm shair he canna sit doun like that?

GSc examples of Epistemic MUST include:

LE JE 228 The neighbours *must* think yer a right nosey bugger.
SB PH 4973 Ye *must*'ve seen them musicals.
TH MW 7598 She *must*'ve realised she'd get her arse scorched.

TrSc examples of Epistemic MUST include:

JS LO 10804 Shairly, Bailie, as a pillar o the Kirk, ye *maun* be sair grieved that
the King can hae freinds [sic] amang the papists?
JS ME 10879 I canna richt mak oot, wi the wind blawin at the links, but
Nicholl *maun* hae tummlet in a moss-hole. He's thick wi glaur.
JS MO 12697 (Bothwell): What guid will that dae if he ance slips through my
fingers?
(Morton): Ye canna haud him in yer pouer aye! There *maun* be some respect for
the Croun!

Miller further argues (1982b and 1982d) that there is no Root MUST in
the spoken Scots of his informants — the StE meanings of Obligation and
Necessity being expressed in Scots by HAVE TO, HAVE *got* TO, GOT TO,
and NEED. When the corpus of dramatic texts is compared with Miller and
Brown's findings on the one hand and StE on the other, it is tempting to
conclude that the dramatic texts go some way towards representing the
situation in Scots speech, but perhaps the failure to exclude Root meanings
completely may be due once again to the influence of written StE. The status
of GSc as a decidedly Scottish style is, however, in no way diminished by the
copresence of StE variants.

PERMISSION

A third example concerns the modal verb of Permission which is shown in
Table 4. The source of Permission varies, ranging from one of the speakers

Table 4
TrSc and GSc — The Expression of Permission — Occurrences and
Percentages

	TrSc N	GSc N	TrSc %	GSc %
MAY	8	1	53.3	3.7
CAN	7	20	46.7	74.0
GET TO	0	6	0.0	22.3
Totals	15	27	100.0	100.0

present, to absent individuals, and finally to regulations and other impersonal but binding authorities. Permission GET TO is recorded by Miller
(1982b) in the Edinburgh data and, dispite his uncertainty about its
currency in other dialects (I can certainly say Northern Ireland), is identified
as a clear feature of spoken Scots, and this is reflected in its frequency
distribution both within the paradigm occupied by Permission modal verbs,
and between TrSc and GSc. At the same time, GSc avoids MAY, which,
according to CGEL (§4.53) is more formal and less common as a Permission
modal than CAN. In Miller's investigation of Edinburgh speech, MAY is
extremely rare ('either completely absent or peripheral', 1982c). The only
GSc example of Permission MAY is formulaic of politeness:

SL JA 9218 . . . hi Lucille . . . that's a very nice outfit, if I *may* so so.

The eight TrSc examples of Permission MAY include

JS BM 10610 The Provost's at Leith for the horse-racin, and it's a maitter that
the Toun Gaird couldna settle. It micht, I *may* tell ye, mean a cry at the Cross
for the haill Toun to rise.
JS KI 11419 Rise up aff yer knees, man, and end this mockery! Ye hae come to
gar me gie ye back yer grun! But ye *may* threaten till ye're blue i' the face! I
winna heed ye!
JS MV 12367 (King): Is it a bairn?
(Melville): Yer Grace, ye *may* lippen for an heir in the coorse o the comin year.

GSc examples of Permission CAN include:

BL ST 1138 When I've got nae hair left, *can* I still come in for a chin-wag?
SB LU 5757 Sure you *can* get your Dad's MG the night, handsome?
SL PH 10563 You *can* work right up till your eighth month, you know.

The seven TrSc examples of Permission CAN include:

JS MV 11671 *Can* we come in? What daes he say?
JS KI 11755 Afore a man *can* claim authority in speeritual maitters he maun hae ae that thing yer Moderator hasna! He maun hae the pouer by Divine Richt to enforce his decrees!
JS BW 11957 My Lord Lennox *canna* leave us yet.

Finally, the six examples of GET TO meaning Permission (GET TO can also mean Obligation) include:

TH PH 6888 Listen, . . . tails you *get to* talk to her first . . . heads, I do . . .
SL SP 8154 Jesus . . . did you *get to* have a look?
SL PH 8658 We used to draw lots to see who would *get to* wander past his desk and casually flick it with the end of a palette knife.

The evidence of Table 4 reinforces the very strong TrSc conformity to, as well as the simplification of, the norms of formal, written StE, and its equally strong avoidance of spoken norms, unlike GSc, in which the situation in actual speech is reflected.

DARE and NEED

A further difference between the TrSc and GSc subcorpora concerns the categorization of the marginal modals, DARE and NEED. These behave differently in each subcorpus and in StE. According to CGEL (§3.42) DARE and NEED can be constructed either as main verbs or as modal verbs, but the former is more common. As modal verbs they are restricted to nonassertive contexts (i.e. negative and interrogative contexts). In TrSc both verbs function universally as full central modal verbs, as in the following examples:

JS BM 10792 (Logie): Are ye for the King or Bothwell? (Bailie Morison): How *daur* ye ask me that, ye brazen scoondrell!
JS AT 10862 (Logie): There's as muckle gowd in Papist Spain as there is in Protestant England.
(Atholl): But he *daurna* touch the Spanish gowd!
JS MA 11165 We fin oot that a man's a fause-hairtit traitor, thick as a thief wi ane that has time and again tried to take the life o the King, but *daur* we bring him to his trial? Na, na, his friends at Coort wad stop us!

Examples of NEED include:

JS LO 10792 Come come nou, Bailie, ye *needna* tak it ill.
JS KI 11391 Na, na, ye hypocrites, ye *needna* kneel!
JS OC 11557 Yer Grace, they *needna* ken ye were threatent!

In GSc, however, DARE only functions as a central modal in affirmative and rhetorical interrogative sentences, as in:

SB CU 5888 How *dare* you shoot your mouth off like that.
How *dare* you.
SL LU 10404 You *dare* say a word to him and I'll murder you!

compared with its function as a main verb in interrogative and negative sentences, as in:

TH SP 6231 'Don't you *dare* give this address if you get knocked down, d'you hear?'

NEED, however, functions as a central modal only in interrogatives and some negative sentences.

LE JO 174 Well, if it's that yer lookin fur, ye'd *needny* look any further than across the Atlantic.
TH CU 6277 Farrell, would you remove this carrier bag, please? I *needn't* ask if it's yours.
TH TE 6360 You *needn't* bother for my benefit . . . I'd just as soon not . . .

In affirmative sentences, NEED occurs as the main verb NEED TO, as in:

LE JO 381 Aw ye *need tae* dae is staun in the boozer an watch they married men footerin' aboot wi h'pennies, tryin tae scrape up the price o' a pint.
LE AG 755 Here Jean, A *need tae* go a place — where's the key?
BL ST 1405 Puggy, ye'll *need to* look after 'im!

NEED TO, as a main verb, also occurs in negative sentences:

SB PH 3929 Aw, Heck, ye *didnae need tae* go that faur. Ah know we wur gei'in ye the needle an that but ye *didnae need tae* go an throw twenty five bob away jist tae get yur ain back.
SB SP 4395 Ye *didnae need tae* shop us like that, did ye?
SP PH 4941 *Don't need tae* try a leg, dae ye?

In Miller's Edinburgh investigation, all occurrences of NEED are main verbs. GSc reflects the variation which is described by CGEL. TrSc, however, operates a simplified system which is not only furthest removed from actual speech practice but in which the norms of written StE are once again simplified and generalized.

NEGATION

A fifth difference concerns clausal negation. The negative forms used for marking clausal negation are set out in Table 5 in terms of the distribution of their occurrence in each play.

Table 5
Clausal Negative Forms and Plays — Occurrences and Total Frequencies (from Kirk, 1986:
Table 3.3)

Text	JS	LE	BL	SB	TH	SL	Total
Total words	23000	8000	17000	18000	16000	19000	101000
	N	N	N	N	N	N	N
no	27	54	78	47	0	4	210
not	0	1	12	15	52	65	145
nut	0	0	0	2	0	0	2
urnae	0	0	0	1	0	0	1
-n't	0	34	155	171	202	221	783
-nae	0	35	106	70	0	0	211
-na	291	0	0	0	0	0	291
-ny	0	5	0	0	0	0	5
Totals N	318	129	351	306	254	290	1648
frequency per 1000 words	13.82	16.12	20.64	17.00	15.87	15.26	16.31

The two occurrences of *nut*, as emphatic negator, are:

SB PH 3585 (Spanky): Show him where the Gerry grenade went right up yur
. . .
(Phil): Indeed I wull *nut*!
SB SP 4425 (Phil) Ah knew you'd turn oan us, ya whore. Ah bet it wis you that
showed Hitler ma folio.
(Spanky) It wis *nut*!
(Alan): It was me, if you must know, and I didn't do it deliberately.

And the example of *urnae*, claimed by Macafee (1983: 50) to be West Central
Scots, and a blend of AM + ARE + NEG (the word boundaries in writing
are far from standardized) is:

SB PH 4703 (Phil): Ah wis wonderin if ye'd . . . er . . .
(Lucille): Wonderin if Ah'd whit?
(Phil): If ye'd . . . er . . . um . . . like tae . . . er . . . (in a rush) If ye'd like
tae go tae the Staffie wi' me?
(Just then a face appears at the window, a dirty bloodstained rag around its
forehead. Lucille drops everything and rushes out screaming.)
(Phil): (puzzled) Ah realise Ah'm *urnae* Dinsdale Landrover but . . . (sees
Hector) Godalmighty!!!!

Table 5 shows that the TrSc system of negation is also simplified,
comprising one contracted and one uncontracted negative form. Each is

associated with its own range of functions: the contracted form occurring in declaratives, and the uncontracted form occurring in interrogatives. In three of the GSc texts (LE, BL and SB), a mixed system is operated, consisting of both the standard and the Scots forms, neither exclusively Scots (as in TrSc) nor exclusively StE (as in the other two texts TH and SL). Actual speech practice in Scots, as recorded by Miller (1982a) is shown to consist of mixed systems (-*n't* forms as well as -*nae* forms, *no* forms as well as *not* forms), except for speakers of Scottish StE who generally eschew the Scots choices. The standardized GSc texts are thus as unrealistic for current speech as TrSc.

STRUCTURAL COMPLEXITY

As a final comparison, two different markers of structural complexity associated with each style are now considered. Even the illustrative examples given above are sufficient to reveal the incompleteness of many of the GSc utterances as well as their phrasal structures and their paratactic coordination. In TrSc, by contrast, utterances are constructed in complete sentences, with a higher frequency of clausal embedding and subordination. A further and more conveniently quantifiable marker of clausal and propositional complexity, however, is the presence and frequency of modal auxiliary verbs. This frequency (per 1,000 words) is shown in Kirk (1986: Table 5.3) to be 31.78 for TrSc and 20.98 for GSc, suggesting the presence of a much greater semantic complexity in the TrSc (almost half as much again as in GSc). These figures provide further evidence for the general differences between TrSc and GSc, as between a written style which is intentionally formal and literary, and a written style which is intentionally informal and realistic.

These seven syntactic and semantic criteria have uncovered stylistic features of TrSc and GSc and shown how they differ in their speech implications. TrSc has demonstrably been crafted into a written *standard* Scots. As Murison says:

> A standard language is of necessity a somewhat artifical construct, because one of its functions is to serve for writing, which lacks the spontaneity and looseness of ordinary speech and demands an exactness and consistency not to be expected in conversation. (Murison, 1977: 7).

McLellan is quoted by Campbell (1986) as considering his literary Scots to be 'proper' Scots and Murison also talks in prescriptive terms. Such arbitrarily codified use of Scots as a literary vehicle certainly yields powerful evidence of its status; by the criteria of the Stewart (1968) typology, however, literariness is not sufficient in itself to elevate a 'dialect' into a 'language'. The style of the Glasgow plays is shown to be different from both TrSc and

StE. Expressed negatively, their language does not have a regular or simplified system and thus does not match up to the norms of TrSc or what might be expected of a written, standardized language, as indeed Murison (1977: 56) claims, somewhat dismissively. Expressed positively, GSc has a mixed syntactic system. Indeed the decision to represent variation (especially in LE, BL and SB) reveals a greater awareness of the reality not only of local dialect, but of conversational speech as a register of the language within which individual speakers have their own styles, and even of the range of styles which a single individual has on different occasions. Where McLellan closed the variable speech patterns down, the Glasgow dramatists have opened them up and made greater use of larger and more complex syntactic and semantic paradigms. [5]

Whatever the degree of speech realism may be, as *dramatic texts* both styles remain inherently and inextricably styles of the written language. In its assimilation towards speech, GSc suffers from external editorial and publishing interference while TrSc is constrained by authorial policies of selectivity and simplification. As Morgan (1983: 204) says of the 'Traverse Plays' edition of *Paisley Patterns* (Byrne, 1982a-c), 'one could read the printed text of the three plays and be only very intermittently aware that the characters are speaking Glaswegian or West of Scotland patois'. In view of Byrne's open acknowledgement of the influence of his London agent, Margaret Ramsay, confirmed by the extensively revised typescripts in her files, and the apparent influence also of his publishers, it is *An Me Wi Ma Bad Leg Tae* and *Benny Lynch* which emerge as probably the most authentic of the five GSc texts (on the grounds of the amount as well as the consistency of syntactic non-standardness). The Connolly text has the further advantages that it has never been published and that it has an exclusively domestic setting in which the characters are either relations or neighbours.

Moreover, the principal internal differences between TrSc and GSc amount to differences of exponence in individual syntactic and semantic paradigms, or systemic heterogeneity (or diversity), which is also shared with StE. [6] At the same time, the syntactic and semantic functions inherent in these syntactic forms are identical, so that TrSc and GSc also share with StE a homogeneity of dialect. [7]

GSc appears most distinctive from both TrSc and StE in its semantics (the relationship between lexical categories and their meanings — whether mono- or polysemeous — and between meanings and their exponence, the diversity of which carries stylistic significance). GSc has its own, more complex system of semantic structures as, for instance, the comparison of Possessive HAVE and HAVE *got* (above) indicates. [8] There is a tendency, which is realistic for speech, for modal meanings to be ambiguous between semantic categories, in contrast with TrSc where the categories of meaning are always quite unambiguous, no doubt the result of carefully considered authorial planning. Despite such differences, however, the semantic systems are overwhelmingly shared by TrSc, GSc and StE and the structure of semantic agreement is shown quite emphatically by the very high degree of distributional agreement between the most frequent senses of the modal verbs, expressed as percentages of sense distributions within individual modal verbs, and represented in Table 6.

In the light of increasing research on the nature of the syntax of speech among presumed speakers of StE, it is becoming clearer not only that the grammar of speech is very different from that of writing but what the nature of the differences is. CGEL matches up well with the observation made by Miller (1984) that speech and writing have their own separate grammars. Some GSc features, thought to be regional nonstandardisms may yet prove to be general characteristics of speech, available in all dialects. On the basis of an exhaustive study of primary and modal auxiliary verbs in Scots, I have been able to demonstrate afresh the general similarities as well as the kind and degree of differences of dialect, register and style between TrSc and GSc and between them and StE. The admixture of systems in GSc facilitates an increase in the range of stylistic values (as between working-class and middle-class characters, or between narration and phatic exchange). Its realism is finally confirmed by the operation of such patterns in spoken dialects elsewhere, for instance in the speech of state school children in Edinburgh, or of working-class adolescents in Reading (cf. Miller, 1982a-d and Cheshire, 1982).

None of these patterns of similarities and differences indicate that there are differences in terms of the abstract or typological categorization or classification of their syntactic and semantic features. In other words, there is no autonomy, for TrSc, GSc and StE all share the same 'grammar', and so the

Table 6
TrSc and GSc — Central Modal Verbs — Most Common Senses — Percentage Distribution (Inter-corpus Comparisons) (from Kirk, 1986: Table 5.22)[9]

	Lund %	GSc %	TrSc %	LOB %
Epistemic WOULD	82.5	49.0	75.6	58.0
Epistemic WILL	57.5	59.5	66.9	71.4
Root Possibility and Ability CAN	95.0	81.9	70.1	88.7
Root Possibility and Ability Could	90.9	82.4	88.2	90.0
Epistemic MIGHT	78.5	88.9	65.7	60.0

same identity. All are subject-verb-object dialects, in which the sentence has the same set of constituents and the same principles and patterns of ordering and embedding these constituents. Comparisons with CGEL and other studies of English syntax reinforce the general applicability of the abstract categories of the auxiliary verbs. Not one of these patterns is qualified to substantiate the claim, made by popular as well as academic commentators, and reviewed disbelievingly by Aitken (1981b) on external grounds, for the autonomy of Scots.

NOTES

1 Citation references consist of three elements: a two-letter abbreviation for the play, a two-letter reference to the character, and the line number in the machine-readable corpus. The abbreviated character references are: AG Agnes (LE), AL Alan (PP), AT Atholl (JS), BM Bailie Morison (JS), BW Bothwell (JS), CU Curry (PP), HE Hector (PP), JA Jack (PP), JE Jean (LE), JO John (LE), KI King (JS), LO Logie (JS), LU Lucille (PP), MA Maitland (JS), ME Mistress Edward (JS), MO Morton (JS), MV Melville (JS), MW Miss Walkinshaw (PP), OC Ochiltree (JS), PH Phil (PP), SA Sadie (PP), SP Spanky (PP), ST Stoorie (BL), TE Terry (PP). The speeches of the Queen, Sir Robert Bowes and the Stranger in JS are excluded.
2 Spellings are sometimes ambivalent, e.g. *wur* and *wull* sometimes represent unstressed cliticized forms 'we were' or 'we will', sometimes stressed isolate forms 'were' or 'will' alone.
3 See Brown and Millar (1978), Millar and Brown (1979), Miller (1982a-d and 1984).
4 Lund and LOB figures are from Coates (1983: 32).
5 The GSc texts are also realistic in other ways not present in TrSc, and these include the presence of what Bolinger (1957) calls 'verbalised intonation' (specifically the tag particle *eh*) and the representation of some prosodic features, of hesitation phenomena, of incomplete and even interrupted sentences, of simultaneous (actually unison) speaking, and so on, as many of the illustrative examples above show. The informality of GSc is also represented in terms of its discourse, including what is described by reviewers as pantomime-like 'patter' and 'banter' — the abuseful humour which abounds throughout these texts, much of it face-threatening, and which is only just tolerated within the intimacy of the family circle in *An Me Wi Ma Bad Leg Tae*, or on account of the mateyness which exists both among Benny Lynch's helpers and supporters, and among the adolescent boys who work in the Slab Room. The GSc dramatists' attempt to equate the text convincingly with speech is undoubtedly the greater *linguistic* achievement.
6 There are a number of differences from StE in the auxiliary form paradigm, including the generalization of *in't* (but not *ain't* forms, common in England and in the United States, and found in the GSc subcorpus in imitations of American speakers), and also the extension of the paradigm to include the Perfective BE

after Verb-*ing* construction. In *Paisley Patterns* this has a stylistic function in the characterization of Glasgow Catholics (as distinct from Glasgow Protestants), especially the character Phil (as in: TH PH 6896 You're just *after sayin* heads), but it is used by other characters too.

There is, however, no evidence for a number of other paradigm differences which have been recorded in speech, such as the Permission GET + Gerund construction (e.g. *do I get keeping it?* commonly heard also in Northern Ireland) (cf. Miller, 1982b), or the double modal construction or the infinitive use of central modal verbs (e.g. *I won't can afford it* and *I used to could do it*, both of which I hear myself uttering regularly) (cf. Brown and Millar, 1978: 174; Macafee, 1983: 50; Kirk, 1986: 338 ff.).

None of these differences detract from the contention that the auxiliary verb systems in Scots and StE are not significantly different, or from the existence of a common core between the two.

7   I have examined in detail the criteria by which the syntactic function of auxiliary verbs in TrSc and GSc is established (Kirk, 1986: Ch. 3). All the features proposed by CGEL (§3.40) for StE are found relevant, so that on this basis the structural homogeneity of Scots and StE is fully reaffirmed. Such features common to both dialects include forms (there are no special third person forms in -*s* and only finite forms), word-order (in the placement of negatives, quantifiers and adverbs), subject-operator agreement (especially concord and including its pattern of variation), and certain 'meanings' (such as the abnormal time reference embedded within certain modals, especially COULD, MIGHT, SHOULD and WOULD).

8   Similar results are obtained for Obligation and Necessity, including the relationship between Root HAVE TO and Root HAVE *got* TO, and the use of WANT TO in the second person.

9   Lund and LOB figures are based on Coates (1983).

FIFTEEN

Language and modern life: notes from Glasgow[1]

Caroline Macafee

It was Jack Aitken who first stirred my interest in Glasgow dialect when I was a student. He drew our attention to the language of writers like Tom Leonard and to Macaulay's (1977) sociolinguistic work. It was he also who later put me in the position of having to find out more about Glaswegian (cf. Macafee, 1983), which could only end in accosting perfect strangers with a microphone and asking them impertinent questions, thus risking an ulcer. This paper represents the first flowers of that research, and I offer this somewhat mixed bouquet in recognition of my debt.

In the winter of 1984–85, with the help of a sabbatical from the University of Glasgow, I made about 40 hours of tape recordings in the East End of Glasgow, interviewing people of all ages, mainly in groups of acquaintances, met for other purposes on neutral territory, such as youth clubs, pensioners' clubs and mother-and-toddler groups.

The East End is typical of the heartlands of Britain's old industrial cities. Harrison (1983) defines the 'inner-city' phenomenon in terms of three characteristics:

(i) the former prosperity of these areas was based on traditional heavy industries. They have experienced the shedding of labour and the take-over of local firms by large, often multinational companies (eight out of the ten biggest employers in the Glasgow Eastern Area Renewal district are multinationals), so that

> what determines their prosperity or misery is an impersonal calculus of profit or rationalization pursued regardless of social costs (1983: 23);

(ii) there is a legacy of bad housing, partly Victorian working-class housing reaching the end of its useful life, and partly modern council housing of poor design;

(iii) the population contains a high proportion of unskilled, and indeed deskilled, manual workers. In Glasgow, the inner-city population represents a residue of the 'overspill' process with the aged and disabled over-represented.

In doing the fieldwork I had the advantage of living in the area. I found McIlvanney's characterization of Glasgow life, in *The Papers of Tony Veitch*, very much to the point:

> You never knew where the next invasion of your privateness was coming from. (1983: 5).

Working-class Glaswegians accept a surprising degree of invasion of privacy, but as McIlvanney also observes, 'They hate to be had' (1983: 50):

> in Glasgow, openness is the only safe-conduct pass. Try to steal a march and they'll ambush you from every close. . . . Come on honestly and their tolerance can be great. (*ibid*)

Bearing in mind McIlvanney's strictures, my own fears as a green fieldworker and the impulses of common decency, I felt it necessary, if I wanted to record anything like natural speech, to put people on the historical witness stand, rather than try to manipulate them in an impersonal way. My ethical responsibilities were expressed to me by one elderly lady: 'Well, mind an say everythin nice, hen.'

I approached my witnesses with a word-list based on written sources, discussions with initial local contacts (themselves too sophisticated to use as informants) and preliminary recordings with the oldest and youngest groups. In the interviews I mainly asked whether each individual a) knew b) had used the word in question, in the sense in question.[2] Group interviews were less than ideal for the elicitation of this type of information. On the other hand, the word list did provide a good focus for discussion in the more successful interviews. (Much analysis remains to be done on the tapes). Here I am concerned with the findings from the word-list questionnaire. There were about a hundred items, and it was not always completed. In some cases it was spun out over a series of recording sessions with shifting membership of the group. The pool of informants who answered substantial parts of the questionnaire is shown in Table 1. Flawed as they are, I believe these findings are consistent enough to be of some interest, particularly in conjunction with the remarks the exercise stimulated (quoted from the transcribed tapes).

Tables 2–8 illustrate typical patterns, particularly the fading out of traditional terms through the age groups at different rates. The frequent gap between knowledge and use, e.g. *hippen, knock* (tables 3, 4), is very suggestive. There tends to be a higher proportion of speakers who have heard

Table 1

Pool of informants for lexical questionnaire

Age	Females					Males			
10+	PB	PB	PB	PB	PB	PB	PB		
	−F					CB	CB	CB	CB
						CC	CC		
16+	CB					PB	PB		
	PC					PF			
	PS	PS	PS			CS	CS	CS	
	CD	CD	CD			CD			
26+	PB	PB				CB			
	CC	CC				PS	PS		
	CF	CF	CF			CS	CS		
	CB					−D			
	CD								
46+	PB	PB	PB			PB	PB	PB	PB
	CB					CC			
	CC					PC			
	PS					PS	PS	PS	
	PD	PD				CD			
66+	PB	PB				PB	PB		
	CB					CC	CC		
	CC								
	PC	PC	PC						
	PS								
	CD								

Key: P − Protestant   C − Catholic   − − not ascertained

B − Bridgeton   F − Barrowfield   C − Calton

D − Dennistoun   S − Surrounding districts

but not used the item (K), following the generation who used it (U), and thereafter a decline in knowledge of it. Although the question on use is a difficult one (image being asked if you ever actually used the terms *antimacassar*, *puce*, or *nutty slack*), most people tried seriously to answer it. (When not mercilessly winding you up, Glaswegians are almost pathologically honest). This gap suggests that disuse in practice is an important mechanism for the putative vocabulary loss. Other items which show similar results are: *sody-heidit*, *synd(d)*, *well (females)*, *jawbox*, *pen(d)*,

Table 2
Claimed use of *two bob* 'two shillings' = 10p

	Females		Males	
	%	N	%	N
10+	100	6	100	7
16+	50	8	100	6
26+	75	8	100	6
46+	50	8	60	10
66+	22	9	33	3

Fractions are expressed as percentages for ease of comparison, but it will be observed that the numbers (N) involved are quite small, and the figures should therefore be examined for very broad trends only. The same applies to Tables 3–9.

brace, waggity-wa, sugarallie, hunch cuddy hunch. In some cases quite marked sex differences can be observed, e.g. *kinderspiel, tossing school* and *toller* (tables 6–8). *Fernietickles* is another word known more to females. Claimed use of items is often slightly higher for males.

Some items are innovating, e.g. *swedger* (table 9) and *jeggie* (short for *jeginger*, itself *eggie-language* for *ginger* 'soft drink'). Not all older items are disappearing, despite material change, e.g. *two bob* (table 2). In the latter, the question on usage refers to current usage, and it would seem that older people are more likely to avoid the terminology of the old money.

Table 3
Claimed knowledge and use of *hippen* 'nappy'

Age	Females				Males			
	K	U	?	N	K	U	?	N
10+	0	0		5	0	0		7
16+	0	0		8	20	0		5
26+	25	0		8	0	20		5
46+	43	57		7	30	60		10
66+	0	83		6	0	100		4

Key: K – knowledge of item; U – knowledge and current or former use of item; ? – data incomplete or unclear. Where the figures do not add up to 100%, the residue are those who neither use nor know the item.

Table 4
Claimed knowledge and use of *knock* 'clock'

Age	Females				Males			
	K	U	?	N	K	U	?	N
10+	20	0		5	43	0		7
16+	12.5	12.5		8	40	40		5
26+	62.5	25		8	25	50		4
46+	43	57		7	0	90	10	10
66+	29	71		7	0	100		4

Is it possible to make some historical generalization about what is happening? A lady in her sixties put it thus:

> as Ah say, the more — the more your education goes on, the more ye lose the old words that ye used tae just gather from all yer friends — playmates. An the more you're educated, the more the right word's instilled intae yer mind an ye just use the right word.

The advance of the superposed Standard form of English at the expense of traditional Scots clearly continues, but this is not the whole story. The process is not a homogeneous one, and the change is not uniformly in the direction of the Standard.

Table 5
Claimed knowledge and use of *kinderspiel* (an evening entertainment for children, of the kind associated with the Temperance movement. The word is StE, but is an uncommon item, and is included here for its local historical interest).

Age	Females				Males			
	K	U	?	N	K	U	?	N
10+	0	0		5	0	0		8
16+	0	0		8	0	0		5
26+	0	0		8	0	0		5
46+	0	14		7	10	0		10
66+	0	67		6	50	0		4

Table 6
Claimed knowledge and use of *poky hat* 'ice-cream cone'

Age	Females				Males			
	K	U	?	N	K	U	?	N
10+	40	60		5	50	37.5		8
16+	25	75		8	0	100		5
26+	12.5	87.5		8	0	100		5
46+	0	100		7	10	90		10
66+	33	67		6	0	100		4

Both local innovations and borrowings help to maintain a non-standard element. Kirk (1981) reports a levelling of Scots grammar towards other non-standard British usage, and Thelander (1980) finds regional (as opposed to highly local) dialects crystallizing in Sweden. In this we can detect the influence of improved communications, both individual travel, and the broadcast media. As Dillard (1985: 208) puts it with reference to the USA:

> An electronic medium like radio simply made available to the non-erudite, even to the illiterate, user of English the same kind of shared communication and non-local vocabulary which had long been available to the reader of poetry, philosophy or philology.

Table 7
Claimed knowledge and use of *tossing school* (group gathered to play pitch and toss

Age	Females				Males			
	K	U	?	N	K	U	?	N
10+	20	0		5	0	0		8
16+	0	0		8	0	20		5
26+	12.5	25		8	0	60		5
46+	43	57		7	0	100		10
66+	12.5	87.5		8	0	100		4

Table 8
Claimed knowledge and use of *toller* (man who handles the bets at a *tossing school*)

Age	Females				Males			
	K	U	?	N	K	U	?	N
10+	0	0		4	0	0		8
16+	0	0		8	0	0		5
26+	12.5	0		8	0	20		5
46+	14	14		7	20	70		10
66+	12.5	0	25	8	0	75		4

Change in the direction of StE is not usually seen as requiring very serious explanation. Given sufficient exposure, the working-class presumably recognize the inherent superiority, or at any rate, greater utility of StE. Rather, the problem for sociolinguists has been to explain why the working-class *don't* move unanimously in that direction. Labov in New York (1972) and Milroy in Belfast (1980) have understood the maintenance of the vernacular in terms of values of solidarity (as opposed to those of status which support the spread of the Standard). Middle-class outsiders can find it difficult to identify with this solidarity. Butters (1984) rightly takes Labov to task for making the vernacular synonymous with the language of tightly bonded teenage gangs of boys. The danger to be avoided is that of romanticizing an anti-social and immature sector of the community.

Table 9
Claimed knowledge and use of *swedger* 'sweetie'

Age	Females				Males			
	K	U	?	N	K	U	?	N
10+	0	100		5	0	100		8
16+	37.5	62.5		8	40	60		5
26+	50	0		8	0	20		5
46+	29	0		7	0	0		9
66+	17	0		6	25	0		4

What is lacking in these explanations is a historical dimension. Any available linguistic difference would *do* as a badge of solidarity, whereas we know that it is the inheritance of shared traditions and mores which confers a sense of identity. This is particularly apparent in lexis — words encode, evaluate and transmit specific aspects of the past as experienced by the dead generations.[3]

In my interviews, I was struck by the number of comments from informants to the effect that they used to say a certain word, but not now, the bulk of such remarks coming from those in their forties and over. The following is typical:

> We're aw merr kinna modernized noo, we cry it the 'fire brigade', aye. (A lady in her eighties, on the subject of the *butts*)

So these are not just differences in the language of succeeding generations, but something more complex: different generations passing, at whatever age they happened to be, from one historical period to another. This is the transition from the quasi-village life of the tenements, best described (with reference to Salford) by Roberts (1971), who calls it the Edwardian period, to the period of modernity. This transition was complex and multi-faceted, and affected communities and individuals at different times. Modernity came very late to Glasgow in some areas, for instance housing and the secularization of society. Housing is a theme which comes over very strongly in my interviews in relation to words like *brace* 'mantelpiece', *closet* 'w.c.', *jawbox, scullery, kitchen* 'living room', *lobby, knock* 'clock'. As one gentleman put it, discussing *syn(d)*:

> Ah mean, even me, Ah don't use that type a language now, ye know. An Ah think if ye found most people i ma age at sixty odds — [sixty]-seven years of age, wouldnae use that. Yet, when they were in their — teenagers — runnin about this area, they would use it. Or they — they did use it. Until they moved out the arear [*sic*] or goat a better house in this arear or somethin, that they don't — they're easily converted, people, ye know.

A lady in her sixties identifies leaving home as a turning-point:

> When Ah was helpin ma mother, Ah would say tae er, 'Where's ma peenie?' But since Ah married an had children an latterly, Ah would just say 'apron'. Ah think Ah'm a wee bit further up in the world, ye see, we don't refer tae aw thae old . . .

In the course of their lives, then, individuals apparently stopped using some words. On the other hand, for no obvious reason, some words survive, e.g. *well* 'tap', *two bob*.

These are straws in the wind, but they tend to confirm Thelander's (1980) view that the stigma which attaches to words and renders them obsolescent is not the stigma of being working-class — which is no stigma at all — but the stigma of being old-fashioned.

Another type of comment very striking on my tapes comes from grandparents, who have to accept the indignity of correction from sons and daughters, and even grandchildren themselves, when they use the words that were at one time the only ones in their mouths.

> Naw, it's is bloody auld man sayin, 'Bobby, don't you say that,' — don't — don't. Jawboax is a — Christ, it's a nice word. It was, aye, it was a jawboax, it was somethin tae dae — in the auld days there used tae be a community — bloody — an then all of a sudden, ye goat yer — Ah don't know, what it is. Jawboax. (A grandfather)

> Ah still caw it a knoack. An mines always laughs at me. Ma faimly always laugh at me when Ah say, 'Gie me ower the knoack.' (A grandmother)

Even younger people find this:

> You're no teachin the wean a very good lesson, are ye? The wean'll go tae school an tell the teacher it's a knoack. An she'll think ye cannae talk right. (A young mother responding to a young father who claims to use the word *knoack* for 'clock')

> A: An Ah used tae call it 'ginger', but the weans checked me.
> B: Ah know. They check ye an tell ye it's 'juice'.
> C: The first thingwy Ah heard 'juice' was actually in England. Ye know, they called it 'juice' doon there. Then Ah come in here, the weans were callin it 'juice'. (. . .) His Ma was killin ersel at Desmond, 'Ah want juice!' (Young mothers in a day nursery.)

This generation gap is partly the result of the slum clearances and general mobility which have scattered families far and wide, so that the grandchildren and the in-law side may not be Glaswegian.

> But as Ah say, we're no — we're no in wi the young kids, truthfully, Caroline, we're no — is it Caroline? We're no in wi the — we're no in wi the young kiddies. Ah mean, we're only — we're seein them wance a fortnight. (. . .) Well, Ah only see mine wance every foartnight. Ah go tae wan wan week an Ah go tae wan the other week, an Ah only see them every foart — (A grandfather).

But it is partly also the result of modern values.

At this point it becomes necessary to attempt some interpretation of 'modernity', not just to appeal to it as an unanalysed concept. This will necessarily be brief, personal and unconvincing. My own feeling is that two aspects of modern capitalism stand out as engines of change since the First World War. The first is corporatism, and particularly the access of large companies to risk-free taxpayers' money via central or local government contracts. The classical exposition is Cawson (1982). The mass housing and road-building operations which have devastated cities like Glasgow are prime cases, but the process is not necessarily corrupt. It is rationalized as being for the good of the economy, and even — through the ethos of new professional groups — as being for the good of society. Goodman (1972), for instance, offers a harsh critique of town planning.

The second force for change is consumerism, very forcefully described by Haug (1971). Mass production and planned obsolescence have given us a culture of innovation. Viewed in this light, it can be appreciated that modernism devalues the past — everything that is free or home-made, already standing and not requiring to be knocked down and rebuilt is *not worth it*. At worst, it might be said that our culture has an animus towards the past because it is free and therefore unprofitable, and towards the future because it exacts free gifts of nurturance, health and education from us.

The role of the mass media then is not only (perhaps not even primarily) the exposure of the working-class to a quantity of Standard English speech. Rather, it is the dissemination of modern culture, with its devaluation of the old. My impression is that the Scottish working-class went into modernity as the middle-class went into the Union. They saw it as progress for themselves, but begin to be disillusioned.

In linguistic terms, the effect of modern life, thus understood, is to shift the balance within the vernacular between traditional dialect and slang in favour of the latter, while shifting the whole system in the direction of StE as the *lingua franca* of consumerism and the corporate economy. This is not something to be regarded with equanimity (though it must of course be studied with objectivity). Slang is fascinating, but the traditional dialect forms are an accretion of centuries. Still — we must avoid sentimentality — they are valuable not in themselves, but as symbols, signifying that the people *have* a past, and that it is not a shameful one.

QUESTIONNAIRE

Questions about knowledge and usage were asked about the prompt items.

A. *Money*

1. How much is a *bob*? Would you still use it? *Ten bob. Two bob*
2. How much is a *tanner*?
3. How much is a *tishy, tisharoon*?[4]
4. Can you tell me any expression for money in general? What is *gelt*?
5. What do you call it when you get something for nothing? *Buckshee*.

B. *Games and entertainment*

1. What did/do you play at?
2. What is *hunch cuddy hunch*?
3. What are *elastics*? Any other names? *Chinks*.[5]
4. What is *chickie mellie*?
5. What is *ring/bing bang skoosh*?
6. What is *five stanes*?
7. What did/do you say if you want to stop a game for a rest? *Keys. Baurlay*.
8. Did/do you ever go out dressed up at Halloween? What are the people doing it called? *Guisers. Galoshans*.
9. What is a *kinderspiel*?
10. What is a *tossing school*? What are the people running it called? *Tollers*.
11. The shows — what things did/do you like? What is a *stookiedoll*?
12. What does it mean to *stooky* somebody?[6]

C. *Food*

1. What do you call a sweetie? *Swedger*.[7]
2. What do you call chewing gum? *Chinex*.[8]
3. What do you call lemonade? *Ginger. Jeggie*.
4. What do you call a cone? *Poky hat*.
5. What do you call liquorice? *Sugarallie*
6. What other kinds of sweeties did/do you eat?
7. What did/do you eat made from peas? *Pea Leap*.[9]
8. What do you call a match? *Scratch. Spunk*.

D. *Clothes*

1. What do you call it when you're all dressed up? *Dolled up. Brammed up. In your paraffin*.
2. What do you call an apron? *Peenie. Daidlie. Thibbet*.[10]

E. *Household*

1. What do you call an uneven bit in a table cloth when it's spread out? *Lirk*.[11]
2. What do you call the square of cloth that you wrap around a baby's bum? *Hippen*.[12]
3. What do you call a clock? *Knock. Waggity-wa*.
4. What do you call the shelf above the fire? *Brace*.
5. What do you call the toilet? *Closet. Cludgie*.
6. What do you call the place where you leave the rubbish to be collected? *Midden. Midgie*.
7. Did you ever have/see a metal tool for mending shoes on? What's it called? *Tackety jock*.
8. What do you call an old style block of houses? *Tenement. Laun(d)*. What's a *buggy laun(d)*?
9. What do you call an arched passage between blocks of houses? *Pen(d)*.
10. What do you call the sink? *Jawbox*.
11. What do you call the tap? *Well. Wall*.
12. What do you say for rinsing out, e.g. a cup? *Syn(d)*.

F. *General*

1. What do you call somebody's place, e.g. 'We'll go to ma . . .'? *Bit. Cane*.[13]
2. What does *send for the butts* mean?
3. What do you call freckles? *Fernietickles*.

4. What does it mean to *take the spur* at something?[14]
5. What does *turn it up* mean?[15] When would you use it?
6. What do you call a lie? *Dinghy*.[16]
7. What does *going out for cadgies* mean?[17]
8. What do you say for 'have a look' at something? *Clock. Have a shuftie.*
9. What do you call it if somebody blushes? *Beamer. Riddie. Brassie.*
10. What do you call something that's nasty? *Mingin. Clingin. Gingin. Boggin. Bowfin. Honkin.*
11. What do you call something that's really good? *Brill(iant). Magic.*
12. What does *gallus* mean?
13. How do you tell somebody to hurry up? *Get a jildi on.*

G. *People*

1. What do you call somebody who is thick? *Balloon. Sody-heidit.*
2. What does a person who is a *minesweeper* do?[18]
3. What kind of person is a *bampot*? Is there any difference between a *bampot* and a *bamstick*?
4. What kind of person is a *chanty wrassler*?
5. What kind of person is a *ned*?
6. What kind of person is a *keelie*?
7. What kind of person is a *bachle/bauchle*?
8. What kind of person is a *bun*?
9. What kind of person is a *guppy*?[19]
10. What kind of person is a *gitter*?
11. What kind of person is a *boot*?
12. What kind of person is a *mingmong*?[20]

H. *Animals*

1. What is a *bubblyjock*?
2. What is a *netterie*?[21]
3. What does it mean to *put the hems on* somebody?

I. *Language*

1. What do you call the bones of the body? *Skelington*. Would that be used seriously?
2. Would you say *occifer* instead of *officer*? Would that be used seriously?
3. Describe a *sherricking*.
4. Give examples of *patter*.
5. Give examples of rhyming slang.

J. *Attitudes*

1. What do you think of the language of young/old people? Do you notice any differences?
2. What do you think of the way men/women boys/girls speak? Do you notice any differences?

NOTES

1 I have benefited from the comments of participants at the Languages of Scotland Conference (Aberdeen, July 26–29, 1985) and the Linguistics and

Politics Conference (Lancaster, April 1–3, 1986), who heard earlier versions of this paper.

2   Interviewing in groups, not all informants have the opportunity to give an unprompted response. The results are therefore treated as if all were prompted.

3   It is unfortunate that a sense of historical identity is often associated with xenophobic right-wing attitudes in the working-class but this makes it all the more important to advance on and recover this territory.

4   *Tisharoon*: cf. Partridge (1937, 1984) *tusheroon*, 'half a crown'.

5   *Chinks* = *Chinese ropes*. Also called *American ropes* — a string of (coloured) elastic bands.

6   *Stooky*: synonyms elicited include *banjo*, *stiffen*, *gub*, *chin*, *stick wan oan somebody*, *scud them*, *heider them*, *hook im*.

7   *Swedger*: cf. SND *swage* v., *swauger* n. 'a long satisfying drink of liquor'.

8   *Chinex*: not confirmed. Probably *chiclets*. (Source: school teacher).

9   *Pea leap*: confirmed, but more usually *pea loop*. Cf. *loop the loop* = soup. (Source: tape recordings held in the People's Palace).

10   *Thibbet*: known to a very few elderly informants. (Source: LAS vol. I).

11   *Lirk*: unknown to my informants. (*Source*: SND).

12   *Hippen*: 'Ah used them when — when Ah goat married first. Used hippens, but they don't use hippens now, they use Pampers!' (70 year old man).

13   *Cane*: confirmed — underworld slang known to a few Barrowfield informants. (Source: McGhee, *Cut and Run*, 1963).

14   *Take the spur*: also *take the needle*, 'become annoyed'.

15   *Turn it up*: 'stop it', 'shut up'. Cf. Partridge (1937, 1984) *turn it up (at that)*, permission to knock off — naval slang, from the action of making fast a rope.

16   *Dinghy*:confirmed — (to throw somebody a) *rubber dinghy* or *rubber ear* is to ignore them, or refuse to take them seriously (with the possible implication that they are lying). In the latter case, the phrase can be shortened to *dinghy* and accompanied by a flick of the ear. (Source: school teacher).

17   *Cadgies*: not confirmed. (Source: *Cut and Run*).

18   *Minesweeper*: not confirmed. Supposedly somebody who lifts others' drinks. (Source: *Cut and Run*).

19   *Guppy*: false item included as a control. Sometimes led to a discussion of *baggy meenies*.

20   *Mingmong*: a nickname used by Bridgeton youngsters, developing into a general insult. From *mingin*.

21   *Netterie*: 'spider' not known to my informants. (Source: LAS vol. I).

SIXTEEN

Three Translations by Douglas Young

J Derrick McClure

The art of poetic translation is fraught with profound difficulties both theoretical and practical; but a fundamental fact is that during the process an implicit claim is being made for the target language: the status of being a fit vehicle for a literary text which will be — not equivalent, for such a concept is not even meaningful — but comparable, in factual, intellectual and emotional content, to the original poem. That is, a translator's work is always offered as a demonstration that the expressive power of his language is adequate to encompass what has been achieved by the original poem in the source language. To the extent that a translation, as a poem, approaches the stature of the original, it is both a worthy tribute to that and a vindication of the language in which it is written. Conversely, if it fails signally to do this, it is both a mockery of the original poem and a proclamation of the weakness of the translator's linguistic resources. If the translation is into a language already extensively developed for all branches of literature the weakness can only be the translator's own; however, the target language may itself be deficient in some respects — it may be excessively culture-bound (no doubt it would be *possible* to render a courtly romance from mediaeval Japan into Buchan Doric, but the result would be beyond literary credibility) or may simply lack the necessary vocabulary (no sort of equivalent could be found in Lakotah for the military terminology used by John Barbour) — and a translator working in a less comprehensively developed language, such as Scots, runs the risk of making the defects of his medium painfully obvious. Translation of literary works of acknowledged merit is a method often used for the aggrandizement of languages in process of development; but as the stakes are high, so are the risks.

Douglas Young, a more important figure in recent Scots letters than the sparseness of his published poetic corpus might suggest, faced this challenge by translating into Scots poems from many languages and periods. In what follows, his versions of three contrasting poems — Sorley MacLean's *Ban-Ghaidheal*, Dante's *Mentre io pensava la mia frale vita* and Valéry's *Le Cimetière Marin* — will be examined for their fidelity to the originals and their success as contributions to the literary development of Scots.

In the Gaelic poetry of Sorley MacLean, Young was translating the work of a compatriot, co-idealist and personal friend; each man was intentionally contributing to the revival of a language which had declined catastrophically in the previous hundred years (Gaelic had suffered the more serious demographic loss, Scots the graver literary degeneracy), and each, though thoroughly versed in the very different literary traditions of his own tongue, wrote in the context not only of those but of the general culture of their contemporary Western world. These factors combined to make Young's task as translator relatively easy: the profound differences between the cultural gap to be bridged was minimized by the poetic and personal affinities between the two poets. The resulting poem, *Hielant Woman*, albeit a fine piece of Scots writing, is therefore not particularly experimental or innovative. Young has not ventured into uncharted linguistic territory here: his vocabulary contains no archaic or recondite words, and only one which seems, without reference to the Gaelic, to be inappropriate in its context: *sleek* 'alluvial mud' is not what comes seeping through the sooty thatch of a peasant hovel. Comparison with the original shows, too, that Young has lost not only the denotative meaning of a word but also a pointedly relevant overtone: the verb from which *snighe* is derived, used of water oozing in drops, can also be applied to the shedding of tears. This word apart, however, Young's poem is a valid essay in an established style of Scots writing; and it is also a convincing re-creation of MacLean's sombre *Ban-Ghaidheal*. The metre and rhyme-scheme of the Scots poem are comparable to those of the Gaelic (because of the differing nature of Scots and Gaelic prosody, *comparable* is all that can be hoped for); and Young's occasional use of sound-patterning other than end-rhymes is in accordance with the literary traditions of both languages: alliteration and vowel harmony in classical Gaelic poetry, though not in this particular poem, are regularly developed to levels of intricacy and technical virtuosity rarely attained in Scots. For the sake of a sound pattern Young at times alters the meaning of the original lines; in the second stanza *measan* 'fruit' is changed to *corn* and *searbh* 'bitter', with all its overtones, to *saut*, for alliteration; and in the third a phrase which means 'the basket for her food' becomes 'her wechtit creel', thus gaining a reverse-rhyme with *westland* but losing much of the ironic point of MacLean's line.

Despite the close resemblances between the two poems, however, Young's poetic statement is in two respects more extreme than MacLean's: the challenge to Christ is more fundamental, and a greater emphasis is placed on the helpless suffering of the woman. MacLean, by placing *Tu* in a stressed position and addressing Christ as *Iudhaich mhóir* (*mór* is 'big', but also 'great, noble, imposing') combines a tone of respect with the characteristic boldness of his challenge: he is arguing with the Deity as an opponent, but not calling His status into question. Young's *unco*, though its basic sense of 'unknown' would effectively suggest the remoteness of Christ from the scene described, suggests 'strange' or 'terrifying' — a negative word replaces McLean's positive one — and there is a doubt implied in 'Ye that they *caa* Ae Son o God' which the Gaelic word *abair*, 'say' or 'affirm', does not carry. This becomes more overt in 'Wi King o Glory fowk roose ye weel', where MacLean simply repeats *ri 'n abair*. Young, unlike MacLean, is questioning not only Christ's actions but also His divine nature. In keeping with this is the underlining of the irony in the word *caomh* 'kindly', by translating *labhair* as *threeps aye* instead of simply *says* and making 'her puir saul is eternallie tint' into a principal clause instead of a noun phrase.

'Thon trauchlit woman' is thrown at once into much sharper focus than in the grammar of MacLean's line, and *trauchlit* suggests a more helpless, unequal, exhausting struggle than *ri strì*. This is emphasized by a repetition of the word, corresponding to nothing in the original, in a later stanza. The sequences of adjectives (a traditional Gaelic device) with which MacLean ends his second stanza, *chrùibte, bhochd, thruaigh* — in his own translation, 'bent, poor, wretched' — is significantly altered by Young. *Crùibte* suggests more than 'bent': the verb from which it is derived means 'crouch', 'creep' or 'shrink', and a related adjective means 'cripple'. *Bochd* in its immediate context must convey something more definite than 'poor', and it can imply decrepitude or ill-health: by its ultimate etymology it means 'broken'. *Truagh* suggests an unspecified state of misery. The first impression of physical weakness is thus gradually merged in a suggestion of generalized suffering. Young in effect reverses the sequence: a head could be *laigh-bouit* without necessarily being *crùibte*; but *dwaiblie* and (still more) *sick* convey a picture, perhaps even falsely exaggerated, of physical debility. The charge of exaggeration becomes difficult to deny in the line 'pleud its rigg on her clear face': the application of *clais* 'furrow' to facial wrinkles is an accepted usage, not restricted to poetry; but *rigg*, suggesting a whole strip of ploughed land, can describe a worn face only by a fairly extreme hyperbole. One more detail of a different kind serves, more successfully, to underwrite the woman's oppression: 'the laird', for two hundred years the villain of Highland social history, does not appear in person in the Gaelic poem, Young having substituted an identifiable human enemy for MacLean's metonymy *an tùr* 'the castle'.

These relatively minor changes notwithstanding, the effect of *Heilant Woman* is to demonstrate that a contemporary Gaelic poem can be rendered into Scots with no fundamental alteration either to the target language itself or to the sense of the original. When Young moves for his inspiration from the twentieth century to the end of the thirteenth, the effect is, predictably, very different. 'Ae time that I our flownrie life appraisit' is written in a register wholly unlike that of *Heilant Woman*: archaic spellings, rare and recondite words, and rhetorical inversions of syntax appear in abundance.

Since the most immediately obvious effect of this is to impart a quasi-mediaeval tone to the poem, the procedure might be seen as fundamentally misleading: Dante wrote at the very outset of the literary development of the Italian language, and his style in his time was the reverse of archaic — as fresh and innovative as it could be. But Young's use of an old-fashioned register has wider implications than this. In one sense, the purpose and method of both Young and Dante were the same: both were aiming, from motives as much political as literary, to devise a national language based on vernacular speech which would compete with the dominant *lingua franca* (Latin or English). But whereas Dante was starting completely afresh, Young's intention was not only to develop the contemporary language but to reinforce its connection with earlier and richer stages in its development. Dante had nothing comparable to the great corpus of mediaeval Scots poetry, or Jamieson's *Dictionary*, to draw on; the fact that Young had is not only a convenience to him but a major point which his poetic practice is intended to emphasize. His translation is not simply a Middle Scots pastiche in the manner of Lewis Spence, but a demonstration of the vivifying effect which the language and technique of the Makars can have on contemporary Scots poetic method.

The result is a carefully contrived, and impressively successful, 'learned' register. Words such as *appraise, duration, firmament, fantasy, faculty, ponder* or *phantom*, which — whatever the spelling — would look odd in the context of a vernacular Scots poem, appear with no discordant effect here. In a few instances, a common word in the original is replaced by a much more *recherché* one in the translation: *appraisit* for *pensava*, *waement* for *pianger*, *grame* for *tristizia*. Young's use of quasi-MSc spellings for some of these words is more interesting than it at first appears. Not all of them are authentic MSc words: *appraisit* and *duratioun*, for example, were extremely rare, in English or Scots, before the seventeenth century: before the period, that is, when Scots virtually ceased to develop in its scholarly and erudite register. Superficially, Young is merely taking words from present-day English and giving them a speciously archaic and Scottish appearance. But because the forms thus concocted are both consistent with the language of the poem and in tune with its mediaeval origin, the effect is rather of discovering in Scots words which it could have acquired for itself, not necessarily mediated through English, during its period of full autonomy. *Conturbatioun* is a word of still more doubtful authenticity: it does not appear in the DOST and has very few attestations, none of them Scottish, in the OED; and, incidentally, it does not translate any word in Dante's poem. But not only is it the *kind* of word that abounds in certain registers of Middle Scots poetry, and acceptable for that reason: it instantly recalls *Timor mortis conturbat me*, and what could be more appropriate? In *dubie* poetic licence is carried to questionable lengths: a word for which the sole attestation in DOST or Jamieson is in a text-book of grammar, where it denotes words that can be declined as masculine or feminine, is glossed by Young as 'obscure' and made to stand for Daute's *dubitoso*, meaning (in this context) 'strange and frightening'. Also present in abundance are archaisms in the simplest sense: words which poets of earlier ages used freely but which have ceased to be common currency. Such are *bruit, forvay, grame, whaurin* and *owerhail*, which here does not mean 'overtake', as sometimes in modern texts, but has the DOST-attested sense of 'conquer' or 'subdue'. The seemingly bathetic *verra bonnie* which concludes the poem becomes less disappointing if *verra* is taken not as a mere intensifier but in its original and literal sense of *truly*.

Young's choice of lexical items is most interesting. Though remarkably faithful to his original, his words have been carefully chosen to alter the overall impression in a consistent direction, and one very much in accordance with Scottish tradition: to increase the eldritch quality of Dante's vision. *Scolorito* is intensified to *deid-wan*. *Crucciati* in the line corresponding to line 13 of the translation suggests a state of anguish or intense suffering, but Young replaces it by *brayn-wud*; and the phantoms so described *skraugh* — not merely *dicea*. 'Cam stravaigin traikit', in which either of the two senses of the last word, 'lost' or 'ailing', could be intended with equal aptness, is substituted for the unemphatic *andar per via*. *Frazit* is not a literal translation of *smarrito*: Dante's word connotes the doubt and confusion resulting from the loss of something — a road, literal or metaphorical, to follow, a direction or purpose, one's mental equilibrium. Young's probable source for his word is a single entry in Jamieson, s.v. *frais'd*, where it is defined as 'greatly surprised, having a wild staring look', and derived, rightly or wrongly, from a Teutonic root denoting terror. The sense of delirium or nightmare, not yet overtly present in the original, is potently suggested by Young. Present, too, is an echo of the homophonous noun *phrase*, which means, among other things, a deluded or misled state: *smarrito*, in fact.

Frequently, Young takes advantage of the seven centuries of literary history separating himself and Dante by drawing on the etymological and literary echoes of the words he is using, replacing Dante's pellucid language by a register weighty with nuances and resonances. *Flownrie* corresponds in position to Dante's *frale*, a rare and poetic form of the adjective *fragile*, and is fortuitously similar to it in sound: it is perhaps for this reason that Young used Soutar's idiosyncratic *flownrie* rather than the more common *flownie*. But — Young's gloss of it as 'fragile' notwithstanding — it is not a simple translation. *Flows* or *flowins* are small quantities of light, particulate material; and Young's use of the derived adjective, by a striking metaphor not present in the original, compares life to chaff or thistledown. The connotations of *flownrie*, indeed, combine those of *frale* with those of *leggiero* in the next line. Here Young writes *brief and bruckil*, a neat alliterative pair in which the second word, though literally meaning simply 'fragile', was regularly applied in the time of the Makars and later t the world or life: ideally appropriate overtones for this context.

By rendering *io presi tanto smarrimento* as 'I was dumbfounert fairly', Young alters the impression from one of an emotional state to one almost of a physical sensation: his use of a passive construction makes his persona more of a helpless victim than Dante's, and has verb his overtones of physical violence where Dante's abstract noun carries no such implications. This is achieved at the cost of Dante's elegant circumlocution and his repetition of a key word, but the greater force of the Scots line is undeniable. By contrast, in *vilmente gravati* Dante, for once, insists on actual bodily distress: his adverb connotes moral condemnation rather than physical repugnance, but *gravati* can only mean 'weighed down'. Neither *forfairn*, which literally means something more like 'gone astray' than the sense intended by Young of 'exhausted', nor even *drowie*, an adjective apparently coined by Young from *drow*, a fainting fit or an attack of illness, evokes the precise sensation of eyelids drooping with weariness. *Drowie*, however, enables Young to emulate Dante in rhyming two words with powerful negative overtones: *smagati* suggests 'knocked over', literally or otherwise, and *dowie*, though perhaps a less violent word than the Italian, shares its implications of both emotional dejection and physical debility.

Sheylit, meaning 'with the face twisted as by grief or pain', is not a literal translation of *disciolte*; but the sense of the original is subtly combined with that of Young's word by a sort of trans-linguistic pun: another form of the Scots word is *shevelit*, which suggests — though it is not related to — the French-derived *dishevelled* which conveys the meaning of the Italian. In Dante's marvellous *Che di tristizia saettavan foco*, Young has been faced with a difficulty which not even his ingenuity could resolve completely: no period in the history of Scots furnishes an equivalent to *saettare*, a verb derived from the noun *saetta* 'arrow'. Young's word *flauchter* combines the literal meaning of 'flutter' (like a bird) or 'flicker' (like a flame) with overtones of an excited, high-strung state and echoes of the noun *flaucht* meaning a flash of lightning — the latter association is reinforced by the adverb *fierilie* — and his 'Whas een wi grame flauchterit maist fierilie' is an impressive line; but Dante's central metaphor of archery is lost without trace.

Since Young is following Dante's metrical patterns, the greater length of Italian as compared to Scots words presents him with the difficulty of finding the requisite number of syllables for each line: a problem which in most cases is ingeniously resolved. *Sairlie*, supplied in the third line, provides an alliteration to match Dante's internal rhymes. Three lines further on, the emphasis on *mora* which Dante achieves by placing it at the end of a line is suggested by the repetition of *maun dee*; and the heavy imperative force of *converra* by the synonymous *siccar* and *shairlie* which frame Young's line. In

'The starns atour the firmament sae lither', nothing but *starns* is actually present in the original; but the 'padding' retains the appropriate register — though the word *lither*, used of the sky 'when clouds undulate' according to Jamieson, could be criticized on the grounds that in a 'nebulously opaque' sky — Young's gloss — the stars would not be visible at all.

Even admitting such minor flaws, this translation is a remarkable achievement, in which a highly synthetic Scots is most convincingly vindicated as a medium for re-creating a mediaeval poem. A still more ambitious venture, the largest and most enterprising of all Young's published translations except for his Aristophanean plays, is *The Kirkyaird by the Sea*. The boldness of Young's assay here is not due only to the scale and complexity of Valéry's poem, but to the absence of any analogue for French symbolist poetry, unlike the work of Dante or MacLean, in the Scots literary tradition. The type of poetry represented by *Le Cimetière Marin*, in which highly evocative images combine with intricate patterns of verbal overtones to give a suggestive, ambivalent, but immensely complex effect is foreign to the more direct and sharp-edged statements which have always characterized Scots poetry. Young's valiant attempt to render Valéry's masterpiece in Scots, partly for this reason, is not an unqualified success.

Linguistically *The Kirkyaird by the Sea* lacks the consistency of the MacLean and Dante translations: the language is an erratic mixture of Scots and English, old and new. In several passages, indeed, it is simply English with a more or less thin Scots overlay: in Stanzas 13 and 14, for example, except for the alliteration on *dernit deid* and the potency of the words *tash* and *drowie* it is hard to see that anything is gained by the few forms which dutifully keep the language from being plain English; and the attempt to rhyme *yird* with *interred* even seems to call for a Anglified pronunciation! Archaisms are not self-justifying in a translation from a modern poem, but could be accepted if used according to a recognizable pattern: here, however, such spellings as *diamant* and *fruct*, and such words as *guerdon, musardrie, thesaur, gesserant* and *fullyeries*, are too thinly scattered through the poem to give any impression other than that of random selection. Recondite words do not harm if the meaning, once ascertained, fits the context, or if the phonaesthetic force is poetically appropriate: *snurler* for *rongeur*, for instance, is admirably chosen: but not all of the lexical rarities in this poem are apt or even sensible: the meaning of Valéry's *le songe est savoir* could be discussed at length, but Young's rendering of it as 'the dream is savendie' merely replaces an intriguing grammatical ambiguity with the momentary curiosity aroused by an odd and doubtfully authentic word. (Galt uses the form *sauvendie* — or at any rate he makes the Leddy of Grippy use it among her many idiosyncratic forms — and apart from this the only recorded precedent for Young's form is a mention, with no literary attestation, in Jamieson.) Confusion is further confounded by the fact that the next word is *savendle*, which is unrelated in meaning.

Several words seem, as translations, to be simply off the mark; and not (as in the translations previously discussed) in accordance with any definite principle: *perjink* for *juste*, *thowlessness* for *oisiveté*, *makin me chief* for *m'apprivoise*, *arrogance* for *dédain*: even *riggin-side* and *brod* are just too redolent of thatch and wood to be altogether suitable for *toit* and *table* when the 'roof' and 'table' referred to are the sea and the surface of the earth. In a few cases the effect achieved can only be described as coarsening: *quhidders* is more violent than *palpite* and *tumult* than *rumeur*, *paupières mouillées* conveys a far more delicate image than *greetan een*, and by rendering *Comme le fruit se fond en jouissance* by 'As a fruct dwynes awa at a bite' Young ruins the ethereally refined sensuality of Valéry's line by introducing not only the inappropriate connotations of his verb — *dwyne* suggests withering or declining from age or illness — but the jarringly physical *bite* (to say nothing of the super-abundance of plosive consonants in the Scots line compared to their virtual absence in the French). And, most unusually for this linguistically inventive and exuberant poet, once or twice a phrase seems oddly feeble and unimpressive: 'Secrets that blin' has scarcely the force of *secrets éblouissants*, all the resources of Scots could surely have provided a more worthily emotive translation of *morne* than *dull*, and even 'gane intil the fleurs' is semantically weaker, as well as metrically less regular, than *passé dans les fleurs*.

Exigences of rhyme, or desire to maintain an alliterative pattern ('turnan to tumult o thir shores' — *changement des rives en rumeur*) may serve to explain some of these infelicities, but hardly to justify them; and not all of them can claim even this excuse. The verdict must be that Young's Scots, though rich and powerful, was simply not equipped to recreate the unique and elusive combination of intellect, imagination and sensuality that characterize Valéry's poem.

Certainly the translation is not without its merits. The invented compounds which Young introduces are often ingenious and striking: 'lyke-wauk-kimmer', 'water-flads'; 'my sea-stravaigan glance', 'this bane-rife grund', 'the golloch-scartit drouth', 'licht-bumbazeit blads'. If the choice of words enforced by a rhyme-scheme is sometimes inept, on other occasions the challenge is triumphantly met: *les anges curieux* becoming 'angels gleg tae speir', *un creux toujours futur* becoming 'a chasm never rent'. A register approaching the colloquial is used to good effect in 'Wha kensna them, wha scunnersna at them, The tuim beld skull, the ever-girnan chap!', and intensifies the startling effect of Valéry's line in 'C'wa, my grand bitch! gar misbelievers skail!' But on the whole *The Kirkyaird by the Sea* reads like an exercise in somewhat misplaced scholarly ingenuity rather than an inspired poetic translation. Perhaps the sparkling Mediterranean cannot be precisely evoked in the language of harsher climes, perhaps in a poem so dependent on the emotive force and power of imaginative suggestion of words a translation using words with equally strong, but different, overtones is bound to be false, or perhaps Young was simply unable to do what another poet might have done more successfully: if the last, he must at least be given credit for a remarkable technical achievement.

Poetic translation serves as a measure of the potential, and the limitations, of a language; and Young's work, which contains the widest range of translations in the *oeuvre* of any single writer in recent Scots poetry, is particularly interesting for this purpose. Despite a lack of uniform success, he has unquestionably demonstrated the presence of unsuspected resources in the Scots tongue.

FRAE THE GAELIC O SORLEY MACLEAN

HIELANT WOMAN

Hae ye seen her, ye unco Jew,
ye that they caa Ae Son o God?
Thon trauchlit woman i the far vine-yaird,
saw ye the likes o her on your road?

A creelfu o corn upo her spaul,
swyte on her brou, saut swyte on her cheek,
a yirthen pat on the tap o her heid,
her laigh-bouit heid, dwaiblie and sick.

Ye haena seen her, ye son o the vricht,
wi "King o Glory" fowk roose ye weel,
on the staney westland machars thonder
swytan under her wechtit creel.

This spring o the year is by and gane
and twenty springs afore it spent,
sin she's hikeit creels o cauld wrack
for her bairns' meat and the laird's rent.

Twenty hairsts hae dwineit awa,
she's tint her simmer's gowden grace,
while the sair trauchle o the black wark
pleud its rigg on her clear face.

Her puir saul is eternallie tint,
as threeps aye your kindly Kirk;
and endless wark has brocht her corp
to the graff's peace, lown and derk.

Her time gaed by like black sleek
throu an auld thaikit hous-rig seepan;
she bruikit aye sair black wark,
and gray the nicht is her lang sleepan.

Douglas Young (1943)
Auntran Blads Glasgow: McLellan (p 18)

HIGHLAND WOMAN

Has Thou seen her, great Jew,
who art called the One Son of God?
Hast Thou, on Thy way, seen the like of her
labouring in the distant vineyard?

The load of fruits on her back,
a bitter sweat on brow and cheek;
and the clay basin heavy on the back
of her bent, poor, wretched head.

Thou hast not seen her, Son of the carpenter,
who art called the King of Glory,
among the rugged western shores
in the sweat of her food's creel

This spring and last
and every twenty springs from the beginning
she has carried the cold seaweed
for her children's food and the castle's reward.

And every twenty autumns that have gone
she has lost the golden summer of her bloom;
and the black-labour has ploughed the furrow
across the white smoothness of her forehead.

And Thy gentle Church has spoken
of the lost state of her miserable soul;
and the unremitting toil has lowered
her body to a black peace in a grave.

And her time has gone like a black slush
seeping through the thatch of a poor dwelling
the hard black-labour was her inheritance;
grey is her sleep tonight.

BAN-GHAIDHEAL

Am faca Tu i, Iudhaich mhóir,
ri 'n abrar Aon Mhac Dhé?
Am fac' Thu a coltas air Do thriall
ri stri an fhion-lios chéin?

An cuallach mheasan air a druium,
fallus searbh air mala is gruaidh;
's a' mhios chreadha trom air cùl
a cinn chrùibte, bhochd, thruaigh.

Chan fhaca Tu i, Mhic an t-saoir,
ri 'n abrar Righ na Glòir,
am measg nan cladach carrach siar,
fo fhallus cliabh a lòin.

An t-earrach so agus so chaidh
's gach fichead earrach bho 'n tùs
tharruing ise an fheamainn fhuar
chum biadh a cloinn is duais an tùir.

Is gach fichead foghar tha air triall
chaill i samhradh buidh nam blàth;
is threabh an dubh chosnadh an clais
tarsuinn minead ghil a clàir.

Agus labhair T' Eaglais chaomh
mu staid chaillte a h-anama thruaigh;
agus leag an cosnadh dian
a crop gu sàmchair dhuibh an uaigh.

Is thriall a tím mar shnighe dubh
a' drùdhadh tughaidh fàrdaich bochd:
mheal ise an dubh chosnadh cruaidh;
is glas a cadal suain an nochd.

D MacAulay ed. (1976)
Nua-Bhàrdachd Ghàidhlig Edinburgh: Southside (p. 105)

FRAE THE SECOND CANZONE O DANTE'S "VITA NUOVA."

'MENTRE IO PENSAVA LA MIA FRALE VITA . . .'

Ae time that I our flownrie life appraisit
and saw hou brief and bruckil its duration,
i ma hert, whaurin he wones, Luve sabbit sairlie,
and wi Luve's sabban then my saul was frazit,
sae that I sychit and spak in conturbatioun:
'Siccar my luve maun dee, maun dee fu shairly'.
At thocht o that I was dumbfoundert fairlie,
I steekit my een, that were forfairn and drowie,
and my hale spreit was dowie,
ilk facultie disjeskit and forwandert.
Syne as I ponderit,
frae trowth and kennan furth forvayt unwarelie,
phantouns o brayn-wud weemen drave at me,
and skraugh, 'Yoursel maun dee. Ay, ye maun dee'.

Then saw I monie a dubie ferly, glaikit
wi slidder phantasies I gaed amang.
I kenna in whatna rowm I seemit to be,
whaur sheylit weemen cam stravaigan, traikit
wi makan waefu mane and greetan lang,
whas een wi grame flaughterit maist fierilie.
Howdlins a mirk owrehailt the sun's bricht blee,
the starns atour the firmament sae lither
waementit ilk til ither;
I saw the birds fleean i the lyft down drap,
the hale yird quok and lap.
Syne cam a deid-wan chiel, spak hairsilie:
'Hae ye na heard the bruit o it frae onie?
Deid is your leddie, that was verra bonny'.

Douglas Young (1943)
Auntran Blads Glasgow: McLellan (p 43)

Mentr'io pensava la mia frale vita,
e vedea 'l suo durar com'è leggiero,
piansemi Amor nel core, ove dimora;
per che l'anima mia fu sì smarrita,
che sospirando dicea nel pensero:
— Ben converrà che la mia donna mora. —
Io presi tanto smarrimento allora,
    . . .   . . .
che di tristizia saettavan foco.
Poi mi parve vedere a poco a poco
turbar lo sole e apparir la stella,
e pianger elli ed ella;
cader li augelli volando per l'are,
e la terra tremare;
ed omo apparve scolorito e fioco,
dicendomi: — Che fai? non sai novella?
Morta è la donna tua, ch'era sì bella. —

Dante Alighieri *Vita Nuova*,
a cura di Domenico De Robertis, Milano-Napoli,
Ricciardi, 1980

THE KIRKYAIRD BY THE SEA

Frae the French a Paul Valéry

This lown riggin-side, whaur whyte doos gang,
quhidders amang the pines, the graves amang;
thonder perjink midday compounds frae fires
the sea, the sea, that's aye begun anew.
Braw guerdon eftir musardry to view
canny and lang the verra Gods' lown lires.

Wi what pure wark fine fuddrie-leams consume
monie an unseen diamant frae the spume.
Hou lown a peace is kendlit keethanlie.
When the sun liggs abune the abysm o swaws,
pure craturs o an everbydan cause,
time skinkles and the dream is savendie.

As a fruct dwynes awa at a bite,
turnan its absence til a delyte
intil a mou whaur its form smoors,
I am braithan here my future fume,
and the luift sings to the saul gane tuim
the turnin to tumult o thir shores.

C'wa, my grand bitch! gar misbelievers skail!
When I'm my lane smilean I tell my tale
o ferlie sheep lang I hae herdit here,
the whyte flock o thir my laigh lown lairs.
Keep aff the doos wi their auld-farrant airs,
and thowless dreams, and angels gleg to speir.

Aince here, the future is but indolence.
The golloch-scartit drouth liggs here intense.
Aathing brunt up, forduin, taen intil air.
intil ane essence stark ayont our thocht. . . .
Life becomes merchless, fou wi want o ocht,
wershness is douce, the spreit is clear and rare.

The wind wins up! . . . I maun ettle to live!
The merchless air apens and steeks my breve.
Abune the craigs swaw-pouther daurs be sprayed.
Flee awa nou, ye licht-bumbazeit blads.
Brak, brak, ye swaws. Brak wi blyth water-flads
this lown riggin-side whaur reivan jibsails gaed!

Explicit feliciter a.d. xxi. Kal. Sept. MCMXLV.
Douglas Young (1948)
A Braird o Thristles Glasgow: McLellan (pp 41–45)

LE CIMETIÈRE MARIN

Ce toit tranquille, où marchent des colombes,
Entre les pins palpite, entre les tombes;
Midi le juste y compose de feux
La mer, la mer, toujours recommencée!
O récompense après une pensée
Qu'un long regard sur le calme des dieux!

Quel pur travail de fins éclairs consume
Maint diamant d'imperceptible écume,
Et quelle paix semble se concevoir!
Quand sur l'abîme un soleil se repose,
Ouvrages purs d'une éternelle cause,
Le Temps scintille et le Songe est savoir.

Comme le fruit se fond en jouissance,
Comme en délice il change son absence
Dans une bouche où sa forme se meurt,
Je hume ici ma future fumée,
Et le ciel chante à l'âme consumée
Le changement des rives en rumeur.

Chienne splendide, écarte l'idolâtre!
Quand solitaire au sourire de pâtre,
Je pais longtemps, moutons mystérieux,
Le blanc troupeau de mes tranquilles tombes,
Éloignes-en les prudentes colombes,
Les songes vains, les anges curieux!

Ici venu, l'avenir est paresse.
L'insecte net gratte la sécheresse;
Tout est brûlé, défait, reçu dans l'air
A je ne sais quelle sévère essence . . .
La vie est vaste, étant ivre d'absence,
Et l'amertume est douce, et l'esprit clair.

Le vent se léve! . . . Il faut tenter de vivre!
L'air immense ouvre et referme mon livre,
La vague en poudre ose jaillir des rocs!
Envolez-vous, pages tout éblouies!
Rompez, vagues! Rompez d'eaux réjouies
Ce toit tranquille où picoraient des focs!

Paul Valéry, ed. G D Martin (1971)
with kind permission of Edinburgh University Press.

SEVENTEEN

The Sib and the Fremd

Community Life in the Dictionaries

Margaret A Mackay

Scotland's national dictionaries provide a veritable encyclopedia of the lives of the Scottish people from mediaeval times to the present day. One area which they illuminate is that relating to community life, the structures and practices which form part of the cultural heritage of Scottish society. Some have survived through time, others have altered over the years or passed from use. In certain cases, oral testimony, recounting personal experience or inherited tradition, can offer additional detail and particular examples which complement the sources on which the dictionary entries are based and point to practices which have characterized Scottish society in the Northern Isles, the Highlands and Islands and the Lowlands and which may have parallels in cultures elsewhere.

The bonds which link individuals in intersecting networks of kinship, friendship, acquaintance and shared interest are themselves intangible, operating quietly in everyday encounters. But turning points in the human life span, times of celebration and crisis, and particular periods in the cycle of the calendar or the agricultural year have traditionally provided the occasions for the outward manifestation of these links in group actions and activities which can be observed and described more readily. These illustrate the nature of the society in the organization and interaction of its elements: household, family, neighbourhood and community, both kin and non-kin, the *sib* and the *fremd*.

Both DOST and SND cite several meanings for *nichbour* or *neibour* from a person living near or next door, one of a number living near one another, a fellow inhabitant of one's community or a member of one nearby. In an extended use and as a plural it may be applied to one's fellow creatures, or to other persons, while the *guid nichbouris* (DOST) were the elves or fairy folk. *Nichbourhede* or *neibourhood* refers both to a physical entity, a community of people living in a certain place or in close proximity, and to friendly relations, feelings and conduct. These may have been expressed spontaneously in co-operation, interdependence, responsibility and reciprocity or in a formal undertaking. To *kepe*, *hald*, *schaw* or *use gude nichbourheid* was to observe agreed rules for carrying out common duties and obligations among tenants of an estate, phrases which might be written into leases.

In the small community one was likely to be in regular contact with kin and non-kin alike and these elements of society are given a particular focus in Scotland by the fact that Scots *friend* and Gaelic *càirde* can mean either a person well disposed to another or a relative, blood relation (DOST: s.v. *frend(e, freynd, freind*; SND: s.v. *friend*; Dwelly, 1901–11: s.v. *càirde, càirdeas*). The latter of these is intended when a Shetlander says of wedding and funeral preparations that 'A neighbour wis as good as a freend',[1] and in the Gaelic proverb 'Is fhearr eòlas math na droch chàirdeas', (Good acquaintance is better than bad relationship) (Nicolson, 1881: 246). The sentiment expressed in 'Is fhearr coimhearsnach 'am fagus na bràthair fad o làimh', (Better a neighbour at hand than a brother far away) (Nicolson, 1881: 244) is echoed in the lore of small communities throughout Europe.

It was the immediate vicinity which provided those to whom one could turn for support and by whom it might be given unasked. This might be described in a variety of ways. In Shetland, for example, the term *leek* (ON *lík*) was given not only to a corpse, but also to a district whose inhabitants were responsible for attending to the funeral and burial rites of their neighbours, kin or non-kin. Jakobsen quotes the phrase 'to be within de lik [(līk) lik]', to be within the burial district, to be included among those invited to partake of the funeral repast (Jakobsen, 1928–32: s.v. *lík*, citing Edmondston's gloss, 'the persons in a district invited to the funeral of one of their number' (Edmondston, 1866: s.v. *lík*)).

In a letter of 5 November 1881, the Shetland historian and antiquarian Laurence Williamson wrote that the *leek* referred both to the district and to certain individuals within it:

> The division of the parish into quarters is well known. Every quarter was also a 'lik', and it was obligatory on a man from every house therein to help to bury the dead of that district. Besides the men of the district collectively were named 'da lik'.
>
> (Johnson, 1971: 112)

Jessie M E Saxby supplied further details on the subject for the *Orkney and Shetland Miscellany of the Viking Club*:

> All the men within a certain radius were expected, nay, bound, to attend a funeral and help carry. No invitation was issued. If anyone within the leek

absented himself it was taken as a mortal offence. No person outside the leek would attend without a special invitation, which was called the 'moinboo'.

(Saxby, 1908: 273)

None of these sources gives any indication of the period at which the word, concept and practice went into decline, but J J Laurenson of Fetlar attested in 1980 that they were current in that island community until the time of his grandfather, mid-nineteenth century, and he defined the word in this way:

> Well, what the leek means, you see, what the leek means is a part of the district where there was enof o men ta carry out the carrying of the dead person to the graveyard. An if they were thought to be enof, than that would do. But in the event of a long way to go, or stormy waether an that, then they would bid others, outside the leek, the other leek, if they would kindly come to the funeral, to assist. If it was a heavy bier perhaps to be carried. Then they would say when they come home from the funeral, 'Wel, it wad ha' been a bad day.' 'Yes, but we had some people outside the leek', you see. The leek was just the district . . . sufficient to do the carrying of the boadie.[2]

He also enumerated eight Fetlar *leeks* corresponding to *scattalds* in the island, hill pastures or common grazings associated with groups of townships or neighbourhood units (Smith, 1984). The total number of Fetlar *scattalds* has varied from thirteen to ten since the beginning of the eighteenth century (Fenton, 1978: 37–8; Knox, 1985: 207–9), but Mr Laurenson explained that at least one of the *leeks* he knew of incorporated two *scattalds*. It was located furthest from the parish graveyard and would require more men than the others to carry the coffin. From Orkney comes evidence that men of districts called *urislands* or *eyrislands* (ON *eyrir* ounce of silver, though Firth suggests an association with ON *erfi* funeral feast), each with its own chapel in pre-Reformation times, were similarly required to attend the funerals of those who died within the district and help bear the corpse to burial (Clouston, 1918 and 1927: xx; Firth, 1922: 88; Marwick, 1929: 201–2). Fetlar's *leeks* also appear to have had pre-Reformation chapel sites (Cant, 1976: 48) and when the local chapel graveyard came to be superseded by a parish graveyard used by all, the earlier mourning practice continued to be enacted.

Studies of Norwegian rural society offer parallels to neighbourhood groups such as this, formed to fulfil certain festive or work functions, or to respond to particular needs and situations.

> For these purposes the farms in the neighbourhood formed groups varying in size. The smallest was the *grannelag*. This consisted of the nearest neighbours, and often it did not extend beyond the inhabitants of the multiple farm. The main object of the *grannelag* was to provide mutual help and support and it

operated in any eventuality that went beyond daily needs. The people within the *grannelag* met together voluntarily when they knew that help was needed When a baby was born, the women from the *grannelag* would help, watching over the baby in turn until the child was christened. When someone died, members of the *grannelag* helped to make the coffin, carry the corpse to the graveyard and on arrival there dig the grave.

(Frimmanslund 1956: 70)

J J Laurenson's use of the verb *bid* in his account and Jessie M E Saxby's *moinboo* (ON *mann-boð*: a banquet; a message) are examples of the language of funeral and wedding protocol. While the *mort-bell* and the *funeral letter* were used at certain times and in certain places, the word-of-mouth funeral invitation delivered by a messenger was a widespread and significant custom. The *Statistical Account* for Campsie Parish in the County of Stirling records that this was termed 'bidding to the burial' (Vol XV, 372) and both DOST and SND give *bid* as the verb 'to invite'. SND cites *bid* and *bidding* (*g*) as the General Scots words for an invitation. A *fiddler's bid* was and is a late invitation to a wedding. 'Bidding the folk' comes from Orkney, while in Sheltand *bid on* 'bid' is an invitation. *Innbø* is a welcome, *innbø* 'to welcome' (Norw. *inn-bod*; Faer. *innbjoða*), used in the phrase *innbø de fremd*, to welcome the guest/stranger (Jakobsen 1928–32: s.v. *innbø*). The same word appears in the name of the rural Norwegian invitation groups for funerals and weddings. This was the *bedlag*, the members of which were *bedt*, i.e. invited, and were drawn from a circle of neighbouring farms (Frimannslund, 1956: 70). In Wales, a *gwahoddwr*, bidder, brought the wedding invitation, a *rhybuddiwr*, announcer, the funeral invitation (Owen, 1959: 159; Tibbott, 1986: 43).

While Edmonston and Jakobsen both refer to invitations, Saxby suggests that while no invitation was issued to those within the *leek*, no one outside the *leek* would attend without having received a *moinboo*. This apparent discrepancy may lie in the subtle difference between an announcement or intimation and an invitation: those within the *leek* would be alerted to the death and would respond appropriately. In Orkney funeral invitations were given by 'wird o' mooth' and 'for one to absent himself from a funeral, after being invited, was considered most disrespectful, and was often the cause of ill-feeling between families' (Firth, 1922: 86). For a Scots-Canadian community the same pertained. 'The advent of death must be announced at once to the whole family connexion. To neglect any member was a sign of ostracism and the message must be received before the victim was "on the boards" ' (Macphail, 1977: 109). In Shetland this was *strikid on a dil* 'laid out on a board' (Johnson, 1971: 112). Breton practice was much the same (Hélias, 1978: 108).

The author of the Statistical Account for the Parish of Tongue in the County of Sutherland reported in the 1790's that 'none, even of the common people, attend without a particular invitation' (Vol. III, 525). In Gaelic-speaking Scotland the *baile* or township corresponded to the *leek* in terms of funeral protocol. The township households would be alerted and a messenger or messengers dispatched with a funeral invitation, *fios tòrraidh* or *fiathachadh tiodhlagaidh*, issued orally, to those beyond in the *càirdeas fios tòrraidh*, 'the relationship of the funeral invitation' (Mackay, 1984: 9). This practice helped keep honed the detailed genealogical expertise of the township, though the formula to regulate funeral invitations extended beyond ties of kin alone to *Càirdeas is comain is eòlas*, 'relationship, obligation and acquaintanceship' (Dwelly, 1901–11: s.v. *càirdeas*).

A Scots proverb runs 'Better a fremit friend than a friend fremit' (Henderson, 1832: 24), i.e. better a stranger for a friend than a friend estranged. The word *fremd*, *fremit*, 'strange', 'unfamiliar', 'foreign', 'not related by kinship or otherwise', was widely used in Scots and Norn to distinguish those who were not blood relations from those who were. It is often found in conjunction with *sib*, 'related by blood, descent, marriage', 'familiar', 'close', 'bound by affection or familiarity', either as adjective or noun. The phrase could be used to describe the composition of various kinds of groups, general and particular. For example, a company of harvest workers might be called 'the sib and the fremit', the relatives of a farmer and his hired hands (Spence, 1900: 217). As a collective *fremd* could refer not only to outsiders or strangers — *out amang the fremd, to try the fremd* — but also to individuals within one's own community but beyond one's own family or immediate circle.

Wedding celebrations focus more than any other on the two groups these words describe, those from which the new household will be created. Shetland tradition provides an instance of the incorporation of the concept of *the fremd* into the wedding ritual itself. In the Cunningsburgh district, as in several other parts of the island group (Flett, 1964: 73–74; Cooke, 1986: 85–86, 131), the bride's move from one family group into another was portrayed symbolically in a women's dance at the start of the festivities, before she danced with the groom. Along with the bride and her nearest female kin one 'fremd wife', i.e. unrelated woman, participated in this dance, the mother of the groom, and the following verse was sung as an accompaniment to the steps.

Noo mun I lave fai-ther an mi-ther

An noo mun I lave sis-ter an bri-ther,

Noo mun I lave kith an kin

An fol-low the back o a fremd man's sin [son][3]

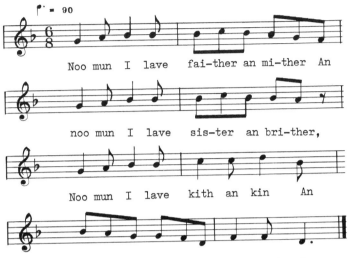

Noo mun I lave fai-ther an mi-ther An

noo mun I lave sis-ter an bri-ther,

Noo mun I lave kith an kin An

fol-low the back o a fremd man's sin.

The significance of the dance has been described in this way by Mrs Laura Malcolmson of Cunningsburgh, who sang the verse as well:

> At the auld Bridal Dance they always sang that as a last verse . . . they sang it, the company. Before they startit and danced they hed their cake an wine an their tea or whatever, their meal, an then this wis the first dance on the floor. That wis the eight ladies, the bride and the bride's maid, her mother an his mother . . . she wis the only fremd wife, but sho wis welcomin in her new daughter to her family. An then the nearest kin, the nearest kin, and they danced this dance you see, kind of a liltin step an dance.[4]

When a newly-married couple were setting up home, or a newcomer arrived in a locality, or sickness or death struck a household, voluntary assistance in getting a piece of essential work done expeditiously might be forthcoming from members of the community. Communal work took a variety of forms, shared, exchanged, voluntary and charitable. For example, *to neibour* or *to neibour wi* meant to co-operate with someone close by, especially in agricultural tasks such as ploughing. The earliest SND reference to this usage is taken from the *Statistical Account* for the Parish of Glenbervie in the County of Kincardine (Vol. XI, 451), but its use is widely distributed in Lowland Scotland in the nineteenth and twentieth centuries. Irish *meitheal* (O'Dowd, 1981) and Norwegian *grannelag, bytesarbeid* and *dugnad*

(Frimannslund, 1956: 72–4; Norddølum 1980: 103–4) offer useful models against which to define the Scottish experience of mutual labour and the ways in which this could be organized and carried out, group to group, group to individual, or person to person.

In Perthshire and areas to the east and north-east the term *love-darg* was applied to work offered gratuitously at times of particular need, ploughing, preparing a garden, building or repairing a house, barn or byre, casting or carting peats, lifting potatoes or other harvest work. Jamieson glossed *love-darg* as 'a piece of work or service done not for hire but merely from affection' (Jamieson, 1825: s.v. *darg*). The earliest SND citation of the term dates from 1761, but DOST offers instances from the fifteenth century onwards of the use of the second element, *darg, dark, dawark* (OE *dæȝweorc*), a day's work, particularly harvest work, or a quantity (of turf peats, or hay) representing a day's work. Nineteenth and twentieth century Scots sources show the continued use of the word into modern times, in some cases with the word *day* prefixed (*the day's darg*), and meaning in some contexts work by the day or simply work or toil in general. *Love-darg* is one of the few combinations with *luve* or *luf* in the dictionaries which does not have to do with romantic love. Another, cited in DOST, also refers to the concept of neighbour: *trew nichtboure lufe*, love of one's neighbour (in the 1572 *Satirical Poems of the Time of the Reformation*).

Though still recalled in connection with efforts of communal work freely given today, the word is rarely used now as organised forms of the activity have passed from the scene. However, participation in *love-dargs* is still remembered, often by retired agricultural workers whose employers sent them on occasion to perform *love-darg* tasks. Mr Dave West of Crieff described the practice in this way:

> Oh, the love-darg. This is if, mebbe if a farmer comes intae a farm, you know. Mebbe you're here . . . a farmer comes intae a farm an he falls behind wi his work. An if he's neighbourly at all, mebbe you'll get sent. 'You take your horses an ploo an plough to Mr So-and-so for a day.' That's what they called a love-darg.[5]

The word *love-darg* continues to be known and used in contemporary Scotland, however, in a different context, though one which is in accord with its original meaning. In this case, it has been kept in regular use by the Dundee-based publication *The People's Friend* and its readers, who participate in an annual fund-raising appeal, associated with handwork competitions, in aid of children's hospitals and homes and care of the elderly. Established in 1885, the appeal was christened the Love Darg, 'work done for love', in 1895, a time when the practice in the agricultural community would have been widely known. Originally work in which the male members of the community predominated, today's *love-darg*, like many other communal activities associated with textile processing, is women's work. The mass media have helped to extend the concept of neighbourhood and community beyond the bounds of the immediate vicinity, and the present day use of *love-darg* is a good example of Scots kept current by the popular press.

These are but a small gathering of the many examples of the interplay between society and language provided by Scotland's dictionaries, and they illustrate only one facet of the resource which these repositories provide for the Scottish nation and for all those with an interest in its life and history. The Scottish community may be found in them in a further way, for in many respects the national dictionaries present excellent examples of communal work, the editors working with the items excerpted from texts by numbers of readers. Community effort plays a part too in the fund-raising projects which ensure that such lexicographical riches continue to be produced and made widely available. The debt which we owe to such editors, and their teams, can never be measured.

NOTES

1   L Malcolmson, sound recording by M A Mackay SA1980/122/A1, School of Scottish Studies Archives.
2   J J Laurenson, sound recording by M A Mackay SA1980/124/A1, School of Scottish Studies Archives.
3   Music transcription courtesy of Dr A J Bruford.
4   L Malcolmson, sound recording by M A Mackay SA1980/123/A2, School of Scottish Studies Archives.
5   D West, sound recording by G West (Scottish Ethnology Honours undergraduate), School of Scottish Studies Archives, 1986.

EIGHTEEN

Eighteenth-century Scots food terminology

Iseabail Macleod

Much — though not enough — has been written about the elimination of the Scots element in the language of Lowland Scotland in the seventeenth and eighteenth centuries. Though most formal writing was heavily anglicized, it is clear that the people, even the upper classes, still spoke Scots, and there is evidence of this in many non-literary sources (see MacQueen, 1957). Cookery books and other household material provide an interesting example, especially since they also to some extent reflect usage at different social levels. On the one hand their language is informal, dealing with everyday situations. It is in one sense women's language and thus, given the social conditions of the time, some distance from the central arena of public life where the strongest anglicizing influences were at work. In another sense this is specialized language, that of a craft or trade, having its own vocabulary as used by its practitioners and less subject to external change.

Cookery books appear rather late in Scotland, the earliest known published work being *Mrs McLintock's Receipts for Cookery and Pastry-Work*, published in Glasgow in 1736. Nothing is known of the author, but the style of writing suggests that she was a cook writing for other cooks, and the recipes contain a considerably higher number of Scotticisms than one would find in a literary text of the time. The recipes on p. 6 are good examples (Fig. 1).

There is an earlier manuscript collection of recipes, *Lady Castlehill's Receipt Book*, gathered together by Martha Lockhart, Lady Castlehill in 1712 and 1713 for her upper-class household or rather, by the time of the collection, two households. Born in 1668, she was a daughter of Sir John Lockhart, Lord Castlehill, a Lord of Session. In 1694 she inherited the family estates, including the house of Cambusnethan, near Wishaw in Lanarkshire (birthplace of a later Lockhart, Sir Walter Scott's son-in-law and biographer). Her second husband was Sir John Sinclair of Stevenson in East Lothian, who

XV. *To make Sugar Cakes.*

Take 7 Eggs, take away the Whites of two of them, take a lib. of Candy-broad Sugar, beat and fearch it, beat it up with your Eggs, till they be thick ; take three Quarters of a lib. of Flour, and 3 Ounces of Cordecidron, 3 Ounces of Orange-peil, a Grate of a Lemon ; mix all together, put it in your Pans, and fend it to the Oven.

XVI. *To make French Bread.*

Take half a Peck of Flour, 4 Whites of Eggs, beat them till they drop like Water, take a Mutch-kin of fweet Barm, let the reft of your Liquor be warm fweet Milk, it muft be pretty fwak in the Leaven ; when it is wrought, part it in 10 Pieces, and work it up in the Shape of Oat-loaves, cut it in the Sides, and job it on the Top, and fend it to the Oven.

Fig. 1

inherited that estate in 1713. The *Receipt Book*[1] is contained in the Bogle family papers in the Mitchell Library in Glasgow and has indications of being a collection of ideas from friends and other sources, some of them English. Given this background it is not surprising that the Scots element in the vocabulary is lower than in Mrs McLintock; Scotticisms do however creep in, sometimes rather unexpectedly, e.g. (in a recipe for orange cream): 'beat all those very weel togither'; in her occasional use of *ane*: 'To boile ane Eele'; in fact there is more Scots in the structure words than in the vocabulary in general.

Later in the eighteenth century there were a number of cookery books written by professional cooks who ran cookery schools in Edinburgh. The earliest of these is *A New and easy Method of Cookery* by Mrs Elizabeth Cleland; first published in 1755, it was 'chiefly intended for the benefit of the young ladies who attend her school'. The title is an indication of the book's straightforward approach and this is reflected in the language, not only in the Scots words she uses, e.g. *ashet, hough, rasps* for raspberries, but also in her use of Scots measures, e.g. *chopin, mutchkin.*

Hannah Robertson's *The young ladies school of arts*, published in Edinburgh in 1766, has fewer Scots words, although some Scottish measures are used. As the title suggests, it embraces more than cookery, although the arts are all household ones. The section on decoration includes a reference to '. . . all sorts of gum-flowers, breast-flowers, garlands, pongs . . .', the last being a Scots word for a kind of artifical flower or rosette.

Another Edinburgh cookery school was run by Mrs Susanna MacIver, in Peebles Wynd, where she also sold prepared foods, and later in Stevenlaw's Close. Her *Cookery and Pastry* (1773) has a higher level of Scotticism than Mrs Robertson's, with many Scottish recipes, such as 'Parton Pie', 'A good Scots haggies', as well as those noted below. She was joined and later succeeded by Mrs Frazer, whose *The Practice of Cookery* (1791) is based heavily on Mrs MacIver, but is more comprehensive. It still has a reasonable number of Scots words and usages, including *butcher meat, rasp, nips* (for turnips). This is in sharp contrast to a manuscript collection of recipes of the same period by Anne Susanna Hope (1786), no doubt influenced by the English connections of the Scottish aristocracy by the end of the eighteenth century. The first impression is of an entirely English text, but there are one or two Scots words, such as *candit* (orange) and, especially towards the end of the MS, Scots measures (*drop, mutchkin, choppen*); see also note to *grate* below.

Other cookery books were aimed specifically at the upper-class household, with a predictable reduction in the number of Scotticisms. For example, Thomas Houldston (or Huddleston) on *A New Method of Cookery*, published in Dumfries about 1760, states in his preface, '. . . Things wholly new and useful, which are daily the Practice of every Nobleman's and Gentleman's Kitchen . . .' Likewise George Dalrymple in 1781 published 'The practice of modern cookery; adapted to families of distinction, as well as to those of the middling ranks of life . . .'

The language of these contrasts with an anonymous collection 'printed for Francis Douglas' in Aberdeen, 1750. As in Mrs McLintock, the level of Scotticisms is high, and indeed there is some evidence of influence from her recipes (or perhaps both were influenced by an earlier source which has not survived). Plagiarism was no more absent from cookery books of the eighteenth century than it is today.

Apart from cookery books as such, a good source of food vocabulary is to be found in the household books of the time. Two of the best known are *Lady Grisell Baillie's Household Book* (1692–1733) and the *Ochtertyre House Booke of Accomps* (1737–1739) and their language can be compared with contemporary recipe collections, i.e. Lady Castlehill and Mrs McLintock. The Baillies' household was an upper-class one, latterly with strong connections with England. Both their fathers had suffered for their opposition to Charles II. Lady Grisell's father, Sir Patrick Hume of Polwarth (later earl of Marchmont), was fed by his daughter while he hid in the family vaults before escaping to Holland, and Robert Baillie of Jerviswoode was executed in 1684. But his son George, by the time of his marriage to Grisell Hume in 1692, had been enabled by the Revolution of 1688 to enter public life as a member of the Convention Parliament. He continued in this capacity in the United Parliament in London after the Treaty of Union in 1707 and this entailed long residences for the family in London, leaving behind their Scottish home at Mellerstain in Berwickshire. One would expect this life style to have an influence on the language but there are in fact Scots words in plenty, though sporadically, in the accounts, even in those sections which deal with London periods, e.g. in 1716: 'For 1/4lb. orange pill 1/4lb. cordicitron [£]0 1 6'. Scots measures are frequently used, e.g. *furlit, forpit, fou, muchkin*.

The Murrays of Ochtertyre were a family of landed gentry who, in contrast to the Baillies, spent most of their time in two country houses, Ochtertyre near Crieff and Fowlls (or Fowlis) in the foothills of the Sidlaws near Dundee. Life in the country is reflected in the vocabulary, not only in the Scots words themselves, but in the use of local produce, for example (3 January 1737) 'Dinner sheephead broth', (19 February 1737) 'Dinner cockie leekie fowlls in it' (SND's first quotation for *cockie leekie*), (22 February 1737) 'Puddings and hagas for servants'. Fish figures prominently in the diet of the household, mostly with Scots names or spellings: *sparlings* 'sprat' *salmond, partons* 'crabs', *bufft harrings* 'salt herring steeped in water and then cooked on an open fire'. Some spellings are indicative of Scots pronunciation: *sweet breeds*.

Research into food vocabulary can also be pursued in contemporary medical textbooks; several eighteenth-century medical books for the layman have an interesting emphasis on diet (echoed in today's attitudes to health). Many are written in a rather formal style, with a resultant reduction in the Scots element; but Scots words do occur. There is thus a considerable body of material to be investigated. There follows a brief comparison of a selection of words in five of the cookery books discussed above; these are accompanied by notes drawn on the whole from the main lexicographical sources, SND, DOST and OED and by comments, where relevant, on their use at the persent time.

word (noun)	Castlehill	McLintock	Cleland	MacIver	Frazer
carvie	+	+	−	+	−
cordecidron	−	+	−	−	−
diet loaf	+	+	+	+	+
gigot	−	−	+	+	+
grate	−	+	+	+	+
haggis	−	−	−	+	−
hookbone	−	+	−	+	+
muirfowl	−	+	+	+	+
rizzar	−	+	−	−	−
sweet	+	+	+	+	+

carvie, carvey or *carvey seed* caraway, from French *carvi*, is recorded in Scots from the sixteenth century; it appears to have been widely used in large quantities, latterly especially as a flavouring for bread, cake and cheese, but it was also used in savoury dishes. It became popular in the nineteenth century as a confection, the sugar-coated seed being known as a *carvey* or *carvey sweetie*. SND quotes from Susan Ferrier (1824) 'Pretty — What makes her pretty? — wi' a face like a sooket carvy' The word does not occur in the main body of Lady Castlehill's MS, where there are several mentions of 'caraway', but in the recipes added at the end, after the index (perhaps at a later date).

cordecidron lemon peel, again from French, *écorce de citron*, recorded in Scots from the early seventeenth century and not mentioned in OED. It apparently died out in the early eighteenth century. SND's last (indeed only) quotation is from Foulis of Ravelston (1704) (see Hallen, 1894); Mrs McLintock's use of it seems to have been missed; probably the book was excerpted after the editing of C. The word is also used by Lady Grisell Baillie (*cordicitron*).

diet loaf a light sponge cake. Lady Castlehill, Mrs McLintock and Mrs Cleland all predate SND's first quotation (from Boswell's *Tour to the Hebrides* 1773); the word is recorded up to the end of the nineteenth century and there is no trace in English. The reason for the name is not clear; all 'receipts' are clearly cakes rather than loaves and the connection with 'diet' is obscure, whether in the modern English sense or in the Scots one of a meal.

gigot a leg of mutton or lamb, is often quoted as an example of the French influence of the Auld Alliance, but the evidence fails to bear this out. The earliest Scots reference (*geigget*) is from *Rob Stene's Dream* in the late sixteenth century, and thus postdates the Auld Alliance. Also throughout most of its history the word is shared with English, until in the nineteenth century it became obsolete except in dialect. The figurative use of *gigot sleeve* for leg-of-mutton sleeve is also recorded in English in the nineteenth century.

grate material grated, as in 'the grate of two lemons'. This meaning does not seem to occur in English, although the word is used as a noun meaning a grater up to the seventeenth century. Mrs McLintock's recipe for 'Lemon Bisket' is the only source given by SND, but it does occur later, e.g. in the MS collection of Anne Susanna Hope (1786) and in Meg Dods *The Cook and Housewife's Manual* (1826).

haggis, that symbol of Scottish cuisine, was in fact originally English. It was widely made in England until the early eighteenth century and still is in the North. OED quotes Smollett (*Humphrey Clinker* in 1781): 'I am not yet Scotchman enough to relish their singed sheep's-head and haggice', which suggests that by Mrs MacIver's day it was already considered Scottish (as indeed does her own recipe, 'A good Scots Haggies'). Presumably its later prominence was at least in part influenced by Burns.

hookbone the hip-bone; English *huckbone* was used up to the seventeenth century, thereafter only in dialects; in ME *hoke-bone*, of obscure origin, though probably from the same Germanic root as *hook*. The modern spelling *beukbone* or (*-bane*) appears in the *Foulis Account Book* in 1703 (see Hallen, 1894): 'For a heuck bone of beif.' These forms are obviously influenced by *heuk/hook* and there are also *heuch-/heugh* forms, presumably by analogy with *hough*. The word is still used by some butchers in eastern Scotland for a cut of beef for frying from the hip; in western areas it is known as *Pope's eye* and it corresponds to English *rump steak*.

muir fowl or *moor fowl* Scots name for the red grouse, recorded since the sixteenth century. Mrs Cleland (p. 100) has a recipe 'To roast Growse, or what is called Moor-fowl'.

rizzar the redcurrent, or with qualifying word, the black- or white currant. Mrs McLintock has recipes for *geils* of 'red Rizers', 'white Rizers', and 'black Rizers'. It is probably a later form of *raser (berry)*, itself a variant of *Russer berré*, which may be compared with *russell*, occurring in Carmichael's *Proverbs* in 1734, all from French meaning red or redness.

sweet of butter, meaning fresh, not salted, is frequently used by many of these sources; the last English quotation in OED for this meaning is 1591; its use with cream or milk to mean fresh, untreated, not sour, does not seem to appear in standard English, though this may be due to gaps in the record.

	Castlehill	McLintock	Cleland	MacIver	Frazer
verbs					
cast	−	+	−	+	+
pilk	−	+	−	−	−
skink	−	+	−	−	−

cast to beat (eggs etc); OED quotes only from Jamieson, who also notes the meaning of dropping eggs into water as a means of divination.

pilk to pick out or off, shell (peas); in Mrs McLintock, to top and tail (gooseberries). Thus to remove something; hence it also means to pilfer.

skink to pour, especially from one container to another. Used in OSc to mean make (someone) a present of; to pour (wine); compare MDu *schenken, schinken*, with both meanings (as also Modern German: *schenken* to give a present; *einschenken* to pour out). *Skinking* easily poured, hence thinly diluted, appears in Burns' 'To a Haggis':

> Auld Scotland wants nae skinking ware,
> That jaups in luggies.

	Castlehill	McLintock	Cleland	MacIver	Frazer
measures					
Sc specified	−	−	+	+	+
Eng specified	−	−	+	+	−
chopin	+	+	+	+	+
drop	+	+	−	+	−
forpet	−	+	−	+	−
mutchkin	+	+	+	+	+

Scots measures present a particular problem in elucidation, owing not only to lack of early standardization — there was very little until the Act of Parliament of 1824 which introduced Imperial measure — but also to confusion with English measures, especially in the eighteenth century when economic and social contacts were increasing.

chop(p)in or *choppen* a liquid measure of capacity of half a Scots pint, about 1½ imperial pints (52 cubic inches or 852 ml). It also occurred in the form *chapin* and was used up to about the beginning of this century. It was used in English, but rarely after the seventeenth century; from French *chopine*, a similar measure, itself connected with German *Schoppen*, still used in southern German for a glass of beer or wine.

drop or *drap*, also *drop wecht*, a very small weight of 1/16 of a Scots ounce (about 29.7 grains or 1.92 grams). It was frequently used of metals and of fabrics, especially silk; the *Foulis Account Book* exemplifies both: 1672 '. . . halfe drop of silk.' 1700 '. . . a silver possit dish weighing 31 unce 12 drap.' It also has examples used of food: 1701 '. . . for 3 drap Silesia lettuce.' Culinary uses as noted above are not included in SND. This use of *drop* seems to have become obsolete by the end of eighteenth century. (In the MS of Anne Susanna Hope we find (p 49) '18 drops of Ambergris', but this may simply indicate a small quantity).

forpet(t) or *forpit* was originally a dry capacity measure, a 'fourt pairt' (one fourth) of a peck, first recorded in the early seventeenth century; Mrs McLintock uses it for flour (p. 5). (The Scots peck was 553.6 cubic inches (9.07 litres) for wheat, pease and beans, or 807.6 cubic inches (13.23 litres) for barley and oats.) Later the term was used for a weight, based on the imputed bushel of 56 pounds, and was used thus, at least in Edinburgh, until very recently. Its value depended on the commodity, being $3\frac{1}{2}$ pounds for potatoes and $1\frac{3}{4}$ pounds for oatmeal. (The equivalent measure *lippie* has also been used in this way in recent times, at least in Fife.)

mutchkin a capacity measure for liquids and for powdered or granulated solids, equal to a quarter of a Scots pints, about 3/4 of an Imperial pint (26.05 cubic inches or 426.9 ml). It was commonly used as a measure for alcohol, especially spirits and was sometimes loosely used to mean an Imperial pint.

The above comparisons give some small indication of a language in a process of change, but a change which was neither uniform not total. The Scots element, while diminishing, remained in books aimed at the middle classes, but disappeared more rapidly from those written by or for the upper classes.

This short article makes no claims to be an in-depth, exhaustive study but is rather an exploratory foray to test what might be done in a corner of this fascinating field. Writers on food and domestic matters have commented, though often obliquely, on the language of food. F Marian McNeill (1929), Marion Lochhead (1948) and to a lesser extent, H G Graham (1899) draw food vocabulary to our attention, and the editors of the household books also present data, in the case of James Colville in some detail in the introduction to his glossary for the Ochtertyre book (Colville, 1907). There remains a great deal more to be done.

NOTE

1   A selection was published recently (see Whyte, 1976).

NINETEEN

Measurement by the Hand in Lowland Scots A study of Four Scandinavian Loanwords

Karl Inge Sandred

Counting, measuring and weighing, so necessary in commerce, medicine and cooking, no doubt began without any special instruments. According to Kisch (1965), counting was the starting point for all commerce (even if the ability to count appears to have developed slowly among primitive people), and measuring was the next step in evaluating goods and experiences. The original procedure in measuring was to compare the size of a part of one's body like the foot or the cubit with objects in the surrounding world (Kisch 1965:1). *Finger* and *cubit* are found among linear measurements in Old Babylonian cuneiform inscriptions, dated 1900–1500 BC (Friberg 1984:78 ff.). In Greek we find, for instance, δάκτυλος 'finger's breadth', πῆχυς 'ell' and πούς 'foot' and in Latin similarly *cubitus*, *ulna* for 'ell' and *pes* 'foot' as measures of length. In OE there were the corresponding measures *eln* and *fot* and the more unusual *sceaftmund*, which was a term for the distance from the end of the extended thumb to the opposite side of the hand, similar in sense to the OE and ME *spann* 'the distance from the tip of the thumb to the tip of the little finger when the hand is fully extended' (OED s.v. *span* sb. 1).

Kisch says further that primitive weighing was not necessarily done with instruments. Taking one object in each hand to assess their relative weights was enough for a rough judgement as late as the eighteenth century in certain branches of commerce (Kisch 1965:1). Unlike counting and measuring, weighing could not very well take even its most primitive standard units direct from the human body. But the human hand was the natural instrument for rough cubic measurement of smaller quantities of grain, meal, salt and the like.

The present short article will draw attention to four words which are used to express cubic measurements by the hand in Lowland Scots and which, moreover, are of Scandinavian origin. This type of measurement is also evidenced in Latin, where we find *manipulus* and *pugillus* for 'a handful'.

The Swedish scholar Sam Owen Jansson has collected and explained a great number of old Swedish terms for standards used in measuring and weighing. He stresses the richness of this type of terminology, often unknown today outside a small group of experts, and the difficulties in knowing exactly what the terms implied, for their meanings changed both with time and place and also depending on what was measured (Jansson 1950: 3).

Obvious sources for the study of terms of this kind in Scots are SND and DOST. In addition to these we now also have CSD, which has provided information for the part of the alphabet not yet treated by DOST. The search in the Scandinavian languages has been based on the dictionaries which are available for the different countries.

The Scottish words to be discussed here are *gowpen, luif, nief* and *starn*. The quantities thus measured were of an imprecise character by modern standards. Still these terms must have been in everyday use by numerous generations as rough cubic measures.

(i) *gowpen*, n.   (1) 'both hands held together in the form of a bowl'
(2) 'as much as can be held in both hands when placed together'

These two senses are well evidenced in Scottish and northern English. SND quotes as its earliest example of sense (1):

> An' weel it's kent his winsome Lady
> Has ay her heapit goupins ready
> (1791 Learmont, *Poems*)

Sense (2), evidenced in SND by 'Oure Fore-fathers thought they would all get Gold in Goupins' from 1705, is found much earlier. DOST quotes, as its first example:

> With ane grit gowpene of the gowk fart
> (c. 1470–80 Henryson, *Poems*)

In DOST we find, as a variant for the same measure, *gowping* from 1583. *Goupen* has also been used as a verb, 'to scoop up or ladle out with the two hands placed together', evidenced in SND from 1804.

Besides its occurrence in Scots, *gowpen* is known to EDD, in both senses, from northern English (Northumberland, Cumberland, Westmorland, Lancashire and Yorkshire) and, as a measure, as far south as Lincolnshire. In OED, which classes *gowpen* as Scottish and dialectal, it is recorded from

c. 1325, when ME *goupynes* glosses *les galeyns* (OF *galein* 'Zweihandvoll', Tobler and Lommatzsch, 1915-). This is also the earliest example quoted in MED (s.v. *goupen*, dated c. 1300). In all the early examples given in OED and MED it serves as a measure.

The oldest Scandinavian evidence for this word is naturally found in Old Icelandic, where *gaupn* f. occurs both in the literal sense and as a measure. Cleasby and Vigfusson (1957) give it in the phrases *sjá, horfa, lúta, líta í gaupnir sér* 'to cover one's face with the palms', i.e. both hands held together, from saga texts, and Fritzner (1883—96) quotes *gaupnir silfrs, moldar* 'hands full of silver, earth'. The meaning would seem to be simply 'the hollow of the hand' (note the plural form in the examples), as it is correctly given in Fritzner.

Torp (1915—19) quotes *gaupn* from Norwegian dialects (also *gaukn, gaufn, göuftn* f.), where the meaning is 'the hollow of the hand', and sometimes 'of both hands held together'. For the measure 'as much as can be held in both hands held together' Torp gives *gauping* and *gjøping* f. A Norwegian verb *gaupna* (or *gaupa*) 'to scoop with the hand' also exists.

This word is not at all limited to West Scandinavian. It is also well evidenced in Sweden, as OSw *göpn* f. 'the hollow of the hand' and 'a handful', illustrated by Söderwall (1884—1918) with the following early example:

> bättre är en fuller neffwi i handhom, än twa fulla göpnar i wanom [= in sola exspectatione][4] one fistful in the hands is better than the mere prospect of two handfuls
>
> (late 15th-century translation of H. Suso)

SAOB knows ModSw *göpen* as a term both for one hand formed as a hollow and both hands held together similarly (from 1604 onwards), and about the amount that can be held by one or both hands, especially common in old recipes (evidenced from 1555 to 1894). According to the more recent information in Jansson (1950: 27), it was used in cooking recipes both in the Middle Ages and later, but is rarely used nowadays. There is also a Swedish verb *göpna* 'to scoop with the hand or hands', but according to SAOB this is hardly used any more (1929).

A great many dialect forms are recorded from all over Sweden. In Rietz (1867) we find *gäpn, göppen, gökken, göfn, göfft, gauken* and the like, referring to 'the hollow of the hand', sometimes 'of the two hands held together', often used as a measure. As variant forms of the noun, SAOB gives ModSw (dialectal) *göpe, göpa*, which are explained as due to analogy with ModSw *näve, näva* 'fist, fistful'.

The Danish counterpart is found in older periods as ODan *gøben* 'a handful' (Kalkar, 1881—1918) and survives as ModDan *gøvn* (with several variant forms) 'the hollow of the hand' or 'of both hands held together' and, as a measure, 'as much as can be held in both hands together' (ODS). There is also a corresponding Danish verb *gøvne* 'to take a handful, scoop with the hand, enclose with a hand or both hands'.

As regards Danish dialects, Feilberg know the word *gjøbning* 'as much as can be held in the hollow formed by both hands' from Jutland, which is to be compared with the corresponding *-ing* derivative in Norwegian dialects (Torp), mentioned above.

The phonological development in ME of the OScand diphthong *au* is considered to be a good test of Scandinavian origin. In England OScand *au* was represented by ME *ou, au*, to be compared with the corresponding OE diphthong *ea*, which is represented by ME *ē* (Björkman, 1900–02: 68). ME *ou, au* are explained as substitutes for the Scandinavian diphthong (Luick, 1914–40: § 384: 2). In the larger part of the East Scandinavian area *au* had been monophthongized to *ö* by 1100 (Wessén, 1945: § 10).

Thus, *gowpen* is undoubtedly of Scandinavian origin. Additional evidence in favour of this conclusion is offered by the dialect distribution in the Danelaw area of England. In view of the evidence provided by the Scandinavian languages, it seems plausible that the original sense was 'the single hand hollowed' (this is also the suggestion of OED), the sense 'double handful' being first expressed by the plural, which seems to be the prevailing form when the word is found in Old West Scandinavian.

(ii)   *luif*, n. 'the palm of the hand, the hand outspread and upturned'

SND gives examples of this word, found in Scottish and northern English dialects:

> To be burnt . . . with a hot iron with the town's mark, being the letter L for Lanark, on the right hand on the luiff thereof
>
> (1714 Davidson, *Lanark*)

It is found as a measure in *lüiff-foo, loof(f)u, liv-fu* 'a handful'.

Earlier Scots evidence is found in DOST (s.v. *lufe* n. 2), starting with Henryson:

> I sall of it [the fox's pelt] mak mittenis to my lufis
> (*c*. 1470–80 Henryson, *Fables*)

In the following example, quoted in DOST, it serves as a measurement:

> [A wine pedlar] lets any man taste it that desires, giving them their loof full
> (1665 Lauder, *Journals*)

OED (s.v. *loof*) and MED (s.v. *lōve* n. 3) know this word from the early fourteenth century, OED classing it as Scottish and Northern dial. OED also gives *loof-ful* as Scots for 'a handful' (with examples from 1540 and 1728). The dialect situation as described in EDD shows *loof* 'the palm of the hand, the open hand' as Scots, Northern English (Northumberland, Cumberland, Yorkshire) and Northamptonshire. EDD quotes *loof-fu* 'a handful' only from Scots.

The dictionaries agree in explaining this word as Scandinavian, and if we turn to Scandinavia, we find OIcel *lófi* m. 'the hollow of the hand, the palm' (Cleasby and Vigfusson, Fritzner) in the West and, in East Scandinavian, OSw *love, handlove* m. in the same sense (Söderwall). In Modern Standard Swedish *(hand)love* has changed its meaning from 'the palm of the hand' to 'wrist', which is evidenced in SAOB from 1740 (s.v. *handlove*). ODan *lov(e)* is similarly found in the sense 'the palm of the hand', but also 'handful' (Kalkar). Under *handlove* (-*lue*) Kalkar quotes:

fersk' oc salt vande, som Gud self slutter ind uti sin haande-lue (fresh and salt water, which God himself encloses in the palm of his hand)
(1661 *Hexaemeron*)

However, in ModDan this sense is archaic outside dialects, according to ODS (s.v. *haandlove*).

Only in Danish have I found evidence of Scandinavian use of the word as a measuring term, i.e. ODan *lov(e)* 'handful' (above). But this does not mean that it could not have been more widely spread. The rival term, ModSw *handfull* 'handful', is well evidenced from 1645 onwards (SAOB). OIcel *lófi* is found as a linear measure in the sense 'a handbreadth' (Cleasby and Vigfusson).

The loss of -*e* in final position in Middle English led to devoicing of the fricative (occurring in the north in the thirteenth century) and variation in the paradigm (*lof: loves*), so that such loanwords can show forms with both voiced and voiceless fricatives (Jordan, 1934: § 217, Thorson, 1936: § 26).

(iii) *nieve*, n. 'The fist, the clenched hand'

This common Scots word is evidenced in SND and combined with *full* in *nieve(a)fu, neafful*, etc. 'a handful, a fistful' from 1785, which is also found in the transferred sense 'a small quantity, something of small and little value', even 'a small person'.

The earliest Scots evidence, which is found in DOST (s.v. *neve*), is from the fourteenth century:

Newys that stalwart war & squar
That wont to spayn gret speris war
(1375 Barbour, *Bruce*)

Dost gives *neve* also as a measurement of the stature etc. of horses, 'the breadth of a fist', e.g.

They have a sort of little horses called shelties . . . some will be but 9, others 10, nieves or hand-breadths high
(1701 Brand, *Orkney & Shetland*)

In OED *nieve* 'a clenched hand, a fist' is classed as current in Northern English dialects and in Scots, otherwise archaic, the earliest English evidence being from c. 1300 *Havelok* (also in MED). MED adds the sense 'a handful' (s.v. *neve* n.2) c. 1475, evidenced in the gloss *neffe: pugnus, pugillus, pugilla*. OED gives *nieveful* (Scottish and northern dial.) from c. 1375 to 1863. The dialect distribution in England is obviously important in proving the origin. As well as in Scots, *nieve* is evidenced in EDD (s.v. *neive*) in Northern English and the East Midlands (Northumberland, Durham, Cumberland, Westmorland, Yorkshire, Lancashire, Derbyshire, Nottinghamshire and Lincolnshire). *Nievefu(l)* is found in Scots and in Northumberland, Yorkshire and Lancashire.

The dictionaries are in full agreement about the Scandinavian origin. We find the word in both East and West Scandinavian. OIcel *hnefi* m. 'fist' is found in the laws as well as in sagas (Cleasby and Vigfusson, Fritzner). OSw *nävi* m. (from **hnefan-*) is well evidenced in the same sense, but also as a term for measuring, i.e. 'a fistful'. The latter use is illustrated in one of the examples quoted under *gowpen* above, and in e.g. *aff enom näwa fullom mz iordh* 'of a fistful of earth' from a text dated 1430–50 (Söderwall). ModSw *näve* is still commonly used in both senses (SAOB). The corresponding ODan *næve, nøve* seems to be used similarly (Kalkar). Moreover, ModDan *nævefuld* 'a handful' is well evidenced both in Standard Danish and in dialects (ODS, Feilberg).

The OScand root vowel, short -*e*-, will have been lengthened in ME disyllabic forms (Luick § 391, Jordan § 25). The loss of -*e* in final position in ME led to devoicing of the fricative and variation within the paradigm (*nef: neves*), so that forms with both voiced and voiceless fricatives could occur, to be compared with *luif* above (Jordan § 217, Thorson § 26). Analogy generally settled such variation in one or the other direction.

   (iv)   *starn*, n. (1) 'a star', 'anything resembling a star'
                     (2) 'a grain, a particle, a small amount of anything'

This Scots word is evidenced in SND. Additional information is to be found in CSD, which gives *starn* 'a star' from the late fourteenth century. SND suggests very plausibly that the sense 'a small amount of anything' developed from the star-like arrangement of some granulated substance such as meal, sugar, salt when it was gathered together between the tips of the four fingers and the thumb, i.e. a pinch. The earliest evidence of *starn* in this figurative sense, according to CSD, is 18th century. SND quotes as its earliest example:

> We hae scarce ae starn
> O' fardel strae laid by 'gain Yeel
> (1801 Beattie, *Tales*)

OED knows *stern, starn* 'star' from c. 1200 (*The Ormulum*) but classes it as 'now only Scottish'. That it was used earlier south of the Scottish border is also clear from EDD, which gives evidence for it in the sense 'star' from Northern English (Northumberland), as well as from Scots.

EDD lists *starn* 'a single grain, a particle, the least possible quantity' as a separate word with examples from Scots ('No a starn meal' is quoted from Jamieson), Northern English (Northumberland, Lancashire and Lincolnshire). The Scots form is frequently *starnie*, e.g. 'a starnie sugar for oor tea' (1917 SND), according to CSD recorded from the late nineteenth century.

Starn is commonly held to be the Scandinavian word for 'star'. Cf. OIcel *stjarna*, OSw *stiœrna*, ODan *stiœrnœ* f., in which the PrScand -*e*- has undergone 'breaking' i.e. diphthongization. According to Björkman (292 f.), Scandinavian loanwords such as ME *ker* 'marshy ground', *sterne* 'star' and *terne* 'tarn, lake' (ModSw *kärr, stjärna, tjärn*) offer no evidence as to whether this 'breaking' had taken place at the time of their importation. Ekwall, however, thinks that they represent an archaic form of Scandinavian (1930: 21). As regards the ModE form *starn*, it shows the regular development of *er* to *ar* before a consonant (Jordan § 270, Thorson §§ 2, 15).

In this case the occurrence in West Germanic of MLG *stern(e)* and OHG *sterno* is to be noted, but Björkman (220 f.) and Thorson (p. 80) class ME *sterne*, ModE *starn* as Scandinavian, correctly it seems, because of its dialect distribution.

The Scandinavian evidence for the use of this item in the sense 'a small amount of anything' is very slender. According to Blöndal (1920–24, s.v. *stjarna*) it occurs in Modern Icelandic about liquids, as in *eiga e-a stjörnu af víni* 'a drop of wine' But as this use is very rare in Scots (SND, CSD), it seems plausible that the Scots use of this item as a measuring term is the result of an independent semantic development.

CONCLUSION

Both phonological evidence and the dialect distribution in the old Danelaw area plus Northumberland serve as indications of the Scandinavian origin of the items under notice here. Of the Scandinavian counter-parts of *starn*, only the ModIcel word has been found as a term for measuring small quantities, although it differs from the Scots in being used about liquids. It seems that we must reckon with the possibility that we have here two independent semantic developments in the two language areas.

It seems apt to conclude this paper with a note on how some of the more important predecessors in the study of Scandinavian influence on the English language have dealt with these lexical items. The most important of them, Erik Björkman, included all four items in his discussion of Scandinavian loan-words in Middle English: *gowpen* in the phonological survey, where the selection is based on difference between the Scandinavian and English sound-systems, *loof, nieve* and *starn* among the examples of words 'the Scandinavian origin of which is tolerably certain', where he paid great attention to their distribution in ModE dialects (Björkman 1900–02:70, 217, 220 f.). In a later study, by Thorson, we find *gowpen* among 'provable loans' (which largely correspond to Björkman's phonological section), *loof, niefe* and *starn* among 'probable loans' (Thorson 1936: 30 f., 68, 71, 80). The tests Björkman and Thorson apply are phonological and distributional. The former are in their opinion the most reliable. The next most important test is the distribution in the dialects, and next to this comes the question whether the item is found in other Germanic languages than English and Scandinavian.

These are the criteria anyone investigating Scandinavian lexical items in English still has to apply, and what has come to light about the items under notice here after Björkman and Thorson does not invalidate their conclusions and bears especially strong testimony to Björkman's standards and procedure, as Thorson emphasized (1936:1).

Recent corroborative evidence for the dialect distribution in England for two of our items can be found in Orton's (1962–71) material. In vol. 1 of the *Basic Material* of SED we find *gowpen*, both in the sense 'double handful' and 'handful' in Northumberland, Cumberland and Westmorland (VII. 8.10), which shows that this item has been receding in English dialects since its distribution was recorded in EDD, as described above. A similar trend can be noted for the item *nieve* 'fist'. Orton and Wright (1974:110, Map 59) give *nieve* as a lexical variant for 'fist' in the northern counties, but only as far south as Lancashire and northern and western Yorkshire. EDD, as shown above, knew it also from the East Midlands. In no case does SED give *luif* for 'palm of the hand' (VI.7.5) or *starn* for 'pinch' (VII.8.6).

It has been considered outside the scope of the present investigation to examine the distribution today of these items within Scotland itself. It is clear from LAS (vol. 1) that *gowpen* has a wide distribution. It was one of the answers received for 'quarter of a peck' from Aberdeen in the north to Roxburgh in the south. LAS also provides the information that *lu(i)ffie, liffie* is found as a term for 'a stroke with the tawse' from Aberdeen to Kirkcudbright, and *nievie* was received as an answer for 'shooting a marble' in Kirkcudbright.

Although they are now mainly of historical interest, there are also two early dissertations on the Scandinavian element in English and Lowland Scots: Flom (1900), which is limited to the Scandinavian loanwords he had found in Lowland Scots literature, and Xandry (1914), which receives some recognition for its statistics by Thorson, although it takes its information on the dialect distribution in ModE mechanically from EDD.

The question why these Scots words for measurement by the hand are of Scandinavian origin can probably only be answered in a wider context, for they are not the only Scandinavian terms for measuring found in Scots. Another example is *firlot*, OSc (Latinized) *ferthelota* 'the fourth part of a *boll*' (cf. OIcel *fjórði* 'fourth' and *hlotr* 'lot, portion'). A *boll*, also possibly Scandinavian (OED, CSD), which varied according to commodity and locality, is to be compared with the Old West Scandinavian measuring term *bolli* m. (Cleasby and Vigfusson, Fritzner).

An investigation including these and other items had to be considered beyond the scope of the present study. I can only hope that my friend, whose own scholarly works and generous personal advice have been a constant source of inspiration in my Scots studies, will be indulgent with this omission in my modest tribute to him.

BIBLIOGRAPHY

Agutter, A (forthcoming) 'Standardisation and restandardisation in Older Scots'.

Aitken A J (1954) 'Sources of the vocabulary of Older Scots' (unpublished).

Aitken, A J (1957) 'A sixteenth century Scottish devotional anthology', review of J A W Bennett ed., *Devotional Pieces in Verse and Prose* (1955), *Scottish Historical Review* 36, 147–50.

Aitken, A J (1964a) Review of C Elliott ed., *Robert Henryson, Poems* (1963), *Studia Neophilologica* 36, 344–6.

Aitken, A J (1964b) 'Completing the record of Scots', *Scottish Studies* 8, 129–40.

Aitken, A J (1969) Review of C Elliott ed., *Robert Henryson, Poems* (revised edition), *Studia Neophilologica* 41, 427–8.

Aitken, A J (1971a) 'Variation and variety in written Middle Scots' in Aitken *et al.* eds. (1971), 177–209.

Aitken, A J (1971b) 'Historical dictionaries and the computer' in R A Wisbey ed., *The Computer in Literary and Linguistic Research* Cambridge University Press, 3–17.

Aitken, A J, A McIntosh and H Palsson eds. (1971) *Edinburgh Studies in English and Scots* London: Longman.

Aitken, A J (1973a) 'Sense-analysis for a historical dictionary' in H Scholler and J Reidy eds., *Zeitschrift fur Dialektologie und Linguistik* Beiheft, Neue Folge no. 9, 5–16.

Aitken, A J (1973b) 'Definitions and citations in a period dictionary', in R I McDavid and A R Duckert eds., *Lexicography in English, New York Academy of Sciences*, vol. 211, 259–65.

Aitken, A J, R W Bailey and N Hamilton-Smith eds. (1973) *The Computer and Literary Studies* Edinburgh University Press.

Aitken A J (1976) 'The Scots language and the teacher of English' in *Scottish Literature in the Secondary School*, 48–55.

Aitken, A J (1977a) 'How to pronounce Older Scots' in Aitken *et al.* (1977), 1–21.

Aitken, A J (1977b) 'Textual problems and the Dictionary of the Older Scottish Tongue' in R W Bailey, ed., *Dictionaries of English: Prospects for the Record of our Language* Ann Arbor: The University of Chicago Press.

Aitken, A J *et al.* eds. (1977) *Bards and Makars* Glasgow University Press.

Aitken, A J (1978) 'Oral narrative style in Middle Scots' in J-J Blanchot and C Graf eds., *Actes du 2e Colloque de Langue et de Littérature Ecossaises (Moyen Age et Renaissance)*, University of Strasbourg, 98–112.

Aitken, A J (1979) 'Scottish speech: a historical view, with special reference to the Standard English of Scotland' in Aitken and McArthur eds. (1979), 85–119.

Aitken, A J and T McArthur eds. (1979) *Languages of Scotland* Edinburgh: Chambers.

Aitken, A J (1980a) 'On some deficiencies in our Scottish dictionaries' in W Pijnenburg and F de Tollenaere eds., *Proceedings of the Second International Round Table Conference on Historical Lexicography*, Dordrecht: Foris Publications, 33–56.

Aitken, A J (1980b) 'New Scots: The problems' in McClure *et al.*, 45–63.

Aitken, A J (1981a) 'The Scottish Vowel-length Rule' in M Benskin and M L Samuels eds., *So meny people longages and tonges: Philological Essays in Scots and Mediaeval English presented to Angus McIntosh* Edinburgh, 1981, 131–57.

Aitken, A J (1981b) 'The Good Old Scots Tongue: Does Scots have an identity?' in Haugen *et al.* eds., 72–90.

Aitken, A J (1981c) 'DOST: How we make it and what's in it' in Lyall and Riddy eds., 33–51. Also *Dictionaries* 4 (1982), 42–64.

Aitken, A J (1982) 'Bad Scots: Some superstitions about Scots speech', *Scottish Language* 1, 30–44.

Aitken, A J (1983) 'The language of Older Scots poetry' in McClure ed. (1983a) 18–49.

Aitken A J (1984a) 'Scottish accents and dialects' in Trudgill ed. (1984), 94–114.

Aitken, A J (1984b) 'Scots and English in Scotland' in Trudgill ed. (1984), 517–32.

Aitken, A J (1985) 'The pronunciation entries for the CSD', *Dictionaries* 7, 133–50.

Aitken, A J (forthcoming a) 'The extinction of Scotland in popular dictionaries of English?' in the Proceedings of the Dictionary Society of North America's Symposium on English Lexicography, University of Michigan Press.

Aitken, A J (forthcoming b) 'The period dictionaries' in R W Burchfield, ed. *Studies in Lexicography* Oxford University Press.

Arngart, O (1942, 1955) *The Proverbs of Alfred I, II* Acta Reg. Societatis Humaniorum Litterarum Lundensis XXXII, 1–2.

Atchley, E G C F (1904) 'The Parish Records of the Church of All Saints, Bristol', *Transactions of the Bristol and Gloucestershire Archaeological Society* 27, 221–74.

Bawcutt, P (1981) 'The text and interpretation of Dunbar', *Medium Ævum* 50, 88–100.

Bawcutt, P (1983) 'The art of flyting', *Scottish Literary Journal* 10:2, 5–24.

Baxter, J W (1952) *William Dunbar* Edinburgh.

Beattie, J (1779, 1787) *Scoticisms* Edinburgh.

Bennett, J A W ed. (1955) *Devotional Pieces in Verse and Prose* Edinburgh and London: The Scottish Text Society.

Björkman, E (1900–02) *Scandinavian Loan-Words in Middle English* Halle: Studien zur englischen Philologie hrsg von L. Morsbach 7, 11.

Black, D (1985) 'Scots and English', *Chapman* 8:4, 11–14.

Blake, N F (1981) *Non-standard Language in English Literature* London: André Deutsch.

Bliss, A J (1951) 'Notes on the Auchinleck Manuscript', *Speculum* XXVI, 652–8.

Bliss, A J ed. (1966) *Sir Orfeo* second ed., Oxford University Press.

Blöndal, S (1920–24) *Islandsk-dansk ordbog* Reykjavik.

Bold, A (1974) Interview 'Bryden meets Bold', *Scots Review* 8, 9–16.

Bolinger, D (1957) *Interrogative Structures of American English: The Direct Question* University of Alabama Press, Publications of the American Dialect Society 28.

Bonar, A A ed. (1891) *Letters of Samuel Rutherford* Edinburgh: Oliphant Anderson and Ferrier.

Borrow, George (1851) *Lavengro: The Scholar, the Gypsy, the Priest* London: John Murray (1931).

Borrowman, L S (1979) 'Scots in education', *Chapman* 5:5–6, 51–4.

Bradley, H (1916) 'Shakespeare's English' in *Shakespeare's England. An Account of the Life and Manners of his Age* vol. II, Oxford University Press.

Brainlearn (1986) An authoring System for IBM-PC, Lund: Studentlitteratur.

Brown, B ed. (1927) *The Southern Passion* Early English Texts Society, Old Series 169.

Brown, K and M Millar (1978) 'Auxiliary verbs in Edinburgh speech', *Work in Progress* 11, Department of Linguistics, University of Edinburgh, 146–84. Also *Transactions of the Philological Society* (1980) 81–133.

Brown, P H (1891) *Early Travellers in Scotland* Edinburgh.

Brown, T (1845) *A Dictionary of the Scottish Language* London.

Bryden, Bill (1975) *Benny Lynch* Edinburgh: Southside.

Buchanan, James (1757) *Linguae Britannicae vera Pronunciatio* London.

Buthlay, K (1982) *Hugh MacDiarmid (C M Grieve)* Edinburgh: Scottish Academic Press, Scottish Writers Series 2.

Butters, R (1984) 'When is English "Black English Vernacular"?', *Journal of English Linguistics* 17, 29–36.

Byrne, John (1980) 'Threads' in *A Decade's Drama: Six Scottish Plays* Todmorden: Woodhouse Books, 145–91.

Byrne, John (1981) *The Slab Boys* Glasgow: Scottish Society of Playwrights.

Byrne, John (1982a) *The Slab Boys* Edinburgh: The Salamander Press, The Traverse Plays 2.

Byrne, John (1982b) *Cuttin' a Rug* Edinburgh: The Salamander Press, The Traverse Plays 3.

Byrne, John (1982c) *Still Life* Edinburgh: The Salamander Press, The Traverse Plays 4.

Campbell, D (1986) 'A sense of community — Robert McLellan: An appreciation', *Chapman* 43–4, 35–41.

Cant, R G (1976) *The Medieval Churches and Chapels of Shetland* Lerwick: Shetland Archaeological and Historical Society (reprint with emendations of 1975 publication).

Carnie, R H (1976) 'Scottish Presbyterian Eloquence and *Old Mortality*', *Scottish Literary Journal* 3:2, 51–61.

Cawson, A (1982) *Corporatism and Welfare. Social Policy and State Intervention in Britain* London: Heinemann.

Chambers, R (1826) *Popular Rhymes of Scotland* Edinburgh: Chambers.

Cheshire, J (1982) *Variation in an English Dialect* Cambridge University Press.

Cleasby R and G Vigfusson (1957) *An Icelandic-English Dictionary* second ed. with a supplement by W Craigie, Oxford University Press.

Cleishbotham the Younger [pseud.] (1851) *A Handbook of the Scottish Language*.

Cleland, Elizabeth (1755) *A New and Easy Method of Cookery* Edinburgh.

Clouston, J S (1918) 'The old chapels of Orkney', *Scottish Historical Review* 15, 89–105, 221–40.

Clouston, J S (1927) *The Orkney Parishes* Kirkwall: W R Mackintosh.

Coates, J (1983) *The Semantics of Auxiliary Verbs* London: Croom Helm.

Cockburn, Henry (1856) *Memorials of his Time* Edinburgh: Adam and Charles Black.

A Collection of the most approved receipts (1750) Aberdeen: Francis Douglas.

Colville, J ed. (1907) *Ochtertyre House Book of Accomps 1737–1739* Edinburgh: Scottish History Society.

The Concise Scots Dictionary (1985) ed.-in-chief M Robinson, Aberdeen University Press. (CSD).

Connolly, Billy [first performed 1976] *An me wi ma Bad Leg tae* unpublished MS, Borderline Theatre Company, Irvine.

Cooke, P. (1986) *The Fiddle Tradition of the Shetland Isles* Cambridge University Press.

Craigie, W A ed. (1919, 1927) *The Maitland Folio Manuscript* 2 vols., Edinburgh and London: The Scottish Text Society.

Daiches, D (1957) *Two Worlds. An Edinburgh Jewish Childhood* London: Macmillan.

Dalrymple, George (1781) *The Practice of Modern Cookery* Edinburgh.

De Robertis, D, ed. (1980) *Dante Alighieri, Vita Nuova* Milan, Naples: Riccardo Ricciardi Editore.

Devitt, A J (1982) 'Standardizing Written English: The influence of genre, audience, and medium, on Scots-English usage', unpublished PhD Thesis, University of Michigan.

Dieth, E. (1932) *A Grammar of the Buchan Dialect (Aberdeenshire)*, vol. I, *Phonology-Accidence* Cambridge University Press.

Dillard, J L (1985) *Towards a Social History of American English* The Hague: Mouton.

A Dictionary of the Older Scottish Tongue vols. 1–5 (19378) eds. W Craigie, A J Aitken *et al.* (see pp. vii), Aberdeen University Press. (DOST).

Dods, Meg (1826) *The Cook and Housewife's Manual* Edinburgh.

Duncan, D (1965) *Thomas Ruddiman. A Study in Scottish Scholarship of the Early Eighteenth Century* Edinburgh: Oliver and Boyd.

Dwelly, E (1901–11) *The Illustrated Gaelic-English Dictionary* Glasgow: Alex. MacLaren and Sons.

Edmondston, T. (1866) *An Etymological Glossary of the Shetland and Orkney Dialect* Edinburgh: Adam and Charles Black.

Ekwall, E. (1930) 'How long did the Scandinavian language survive in England?' in *A Grammatical Miscellany Offered to Otto Jesperson* Copenhagen, 17–30.

Elliott, C ed. (1963) *Robert Henryson, Poems* Oxford University Press.

The English Dialect Dictionary 6 vols (1896–1905) ed. J Wright, Oxford (EDD).

Erdman, D V and E G Fogel eds. (1966) *Evidence for Authorship: Essays on Problems of Distribution* Ithaca, New York.

Feilberg, H F (1886–1914) *Bidrag til en Ordbog over jyske Almuesmål* Copenhagen: Universitets-Jubilæets danske Samfund.

Fenton, A (1976) *Scottish Country Life* Edinburgh: John Donald.

Fenton, A (1978) *The Northern Isles: Orkney and Shetland* Edinburgh: John Donald.

Firth, J (1922) *Reminiscences of an Orkney Parish* Stromness: John Rae.

Flett, J F and T M (1964) *Traditional Dancing in Scotland* London: Routledge and Kegan Paul.

Flom, G T (1900) *Scandinavian Influence on Southern Lowland Scotch* PhD thesis, Columbia University, New York.

Fox, D (1956) 'The Poetry of William Dunbar', unpublished PhD, Yale.

Fox, D (1977) 'Manuscripts and prints of Scots poetry in the sixteenth century' in Aitken *et al.* eds. (1977), 156–71.

Fox, D ed. (1981) *The Poems of Robert Henryson* Oxford University Press.

Fox, D and W Ringler eds. (1980) *The Bannatyne Manuscript, Facsimile* London.

Frazer, Mrs. (1791) *The Practice of cookery, pastry, pickling, preserving* Edinburgh.

Frazer, J G (1890, 1930) *The Golden Bough* London: Macmillan.

Friberg, J (1984) 'Numbers and measures in the earliest written records', *Scientific Amercian* 250:2.

Frimannslund, R (1956) 'The old Norwegian peasant community: Farm community and neighbourhood community', *The Scandinavian Economic History Review* 4, 62–81.

Fritzner, J (1883–96) *Ordbog over det gamle norske sprog* 3 vols., Kristiania. Reprinted Oslo: T Juul Møller Forlag (1954). F Hødnebø, *Rettelser og tillegg* Oslo: Universitetsforlaget (1972).

Geddie, W (1912) *A Bibliography of Middle Scots Poets* Edinburgh and London: Scottish Text Society.

Gibb, A D, revised A G M Duncan (1982) *Students' Glossary of Scottish Legal Terms* second ed. Edinburgh: W Green & Son.

Girvan, R ed. (1939) *Ratis Raving and Other Early Scots Poems on Morals* Edinburgh and London: Scottish Text Society, Third Series 11.

Glauser, B (1974) *The Scottish-English Linguistic Border* Bern: Francke.

Goodman, R (1972) *After the Planners* Harmondsworth: Penguin.

Görlach, M (1976) *An East Midland Revision of the South English Legendary* Heidelberg: Julius Groos, Middle English Texts 4.

Görlach, M (1985) 'Scots and Low German: the social history of two minority languages' in Görlach ed., 19–36.

Görlach, M ed. (1985) *Focus on: Scotland* Amsterdam: John Benjamins.

Graham, H G (1899) *The Social Life of Scotland in the Eighteenth Century* London.

Grant, N (1982) *The Crisis of Scottish Education* Edinburgh: The Saltire Society, Saltire Pamphlets, new series 2.

Gray, D ed. (1985) *The Oxford Book of Late Medieval Verse and Prose* Oxford University Press.

Gregor, W (1866) *The Dialect of Banffshire* London.

Hall, R A Jr (1961) *Sound and Spelling in English* Philadelphia: Chilton.

Hallen, Rev A W Cornelius ed. (1894) *The Account Book of Sir John Foulis of Ravelston 1671–1707* Edinburgh: Scottish History Society.

Harris, J (1985) *Phonological Variation and Change: Studies in Hiberno-English* Cambridge University Press.

Harrison, P (1983) *Inside the Inner City. Life under the Cutting Edge* Harmondsworth: Penguin.

Haug, W (1971, 1986) *Critique of Commodity Aesthetics. Appearance, Sexuality and Advertising in Capitalist Society* Oxford: Polity.

Haugen, E, J D McClure and D Thomson, eds. (1981) *Minority Languages Today* Edinburgh University Press.

Hélias, P J, trans. J Guicharnaud (1978) *The Horse of Pride* New Haven: Yale University Press.

Henderson, A (1832) *Scottish Proverbs* Edinburgh: Oliver & Boyd.

Henderson, T F (1912) *The Ballad in Literature* Cambridge University Press.

Heslinga, M W (1979) *The Irish Border as a Cultural Divide. A Contribution to the Study of Regionalism in the British Isles* Assen: Van Gorcum.

Hill, G B ed. (1905) *Samuel Johnson, Lives of the English Poets* 3 vols., Oxford University Press.

Hill, G B ed., revised L F Powell (1934) *Boswell's Life of Johnson* 6 vols., Oxford University Press.
Houdlston [Huddleston], Thomas (1753) *A new method of cookery* Edinburgh.
Hudson, A (1983) 'Observations on a northener's vocabulary' in E G Stanley and D Gray eds., *Five Hundred Years of Words and Sounds*, 74–83.
Hume, David (1752) 'Scotticisms', appendix to *Political Discourses* Edinburgh: A Kincaid and A Donaldson.
Jakobsen, J (1928–32) *An Etymological Dictionary of the Norn Language in Shetland* London: David Nutt.
Jamieson, J (1808, 1825) *An Etymological Dictionary of the Scottish Language* 2 vols., Edinburgh.
Jamieson, J (1877) *Jamieson's Dictionary of the Scottish Language*, abridged J Johnstone and revised J Longmuir, London: William P Nimmo.
Jansson, S O (1950) *Svensk måttordbok. Svenska måttstermer före metersystemet* Stockholm: Nordiska museet.
Johansson, S, G N Leech and H Goodluck (1978) *Manual of Information to Accompany the Lancaster-Oslo/Bergan Corpus of British English, for Use with Digital Computers* Department of English, University of Oslo.
Johnson, L G (1971) *Laurence Williamson of Mid Yell* Lerwick: The Shetland Times.
Johnson, Samuel (1755) *A Dictionary of the English Language* London.
Johnston, P A (1985) 'The rise and fall of the Morningside/Kelvinside accent' in Görlach ed., 37–56.
Jordan, R (1934) *Handbuch der mittelenglishen Grammatik*, vol. I, second ed. Heidelberg: Carl Winter's Universitätsbuchhandlung.
Kalkar, O (1881–1918) *Ordbog til det ældre danske Sprog* Copenhagen: Universitetsubilœets danske Samfund.
Kay, B (1986) *Scots. The Mither Tongue* Edinburgh: Mainstream.
Ker, N R (1931) 'The scribes of the *Trinity Homilies*', *Medium Ævum* I, 138–40.
Kerling, J (1979) *Chaucer in Early English Dictionaries. The Old-Word Tradition in English Lexicography down to 1721 and Speght's Chaucer Glossaries* Leiden University Press.
Kerr, R D ed. (1980) *A Glossary of Mining Terms used in Fife.*
Kinsley, J ed. (1958) *William Dunbar. Poems.* Oxford University Press.
Kinsley, J ed. (1979) *The Poems of William Dunbar* Oxford University Press.
Kirk, J M (1981) 'On Scottish non-standard English', *Nottingham Linguistic Circular* 10:2, 155–78.
Kirk, J M (1986) 'Aspects of the Grammar in a Corpus of Dramatic Texts in Scots', unpublished PhD Thesis, University of Sheffield.
Kisch, D (1965) *Scales and Weights: A Historical Outline* New Haven and London: Yale University Press.
Knox, S A (1985) *The Making of the Shetland Landscape* Edinburgh: John Donald.
Kohler, K J (1967) 'Aspects of Middle Scots phonemics and graphemics: the phonological implications of the sign ⟨i⟩', *Transactions of the Philological Society*, 32–61.
Kratzmann, G (1980) *Anglo-Scottish Literary Relations* Cambridge University Press.
Krull, A F (1901) *Jacobus Koelman. Eene Kerkhistorische studie* Sneek: J Campen.
Labov, W (1972, 1977) *Language in the Inner City. Studies in the Black English Vernacular* Oxford: Blackwell.

A Language for Life (1975) [The Bullock Report, 1974] London: HMSO.

Lass, R ed. (1969) *Approaches to English Historical Linguistics* New York: Holt, Rinehart and Winston.

Lass, R (1976) *English Phonology and Phonological Theory* Cambridge University Press.

Law, A (1965) *Education in Edinburgh in the Eighteenth Century* University of London Press.

Leith, D (1983) *A Social History of English* London: Routledge and Kegan Paul.

Lévi-Strauss, C, tr. J and D Weightman (1973) *From Honey to Ashes* London: Cape.

L'Isle, William (1638) *Divers Ancient Monvments in the Saxon Tongue* London: Francis Eglesfield.

Lochhead, M (1948) *The Scots Household in the Eighteenth Century* Edinburgh.

Longman Dictionary of the English Language (1984) London: Longman.

Lorimer, William L, tr. (1983) *The New Testament in Scots* Edinburgh: Southside.

Low, D A ed. (1975) *Critical Essays on Robert Burns* London.

Low, J T (1974) 'The Scots language: The contemporary situation' in McClure ed., 17–27.

Low, J T (1980) 'A Scots language policy for education' in McClure *et al.*, 67–95.

Low, J T (1983) 'Mid twentieth century drama in Lowland Scots' in McClure ed., (1983a), 70–94.

Luick, K (1914–40) *Historische Grammatik der englischen Sprache* Leipzig: C H Tauchnitz.

Lyall, R J and F Riddy, eds. (1981) *Proceedings of the Third International Conference on Scottish Language and Literature (Medieval and Renaissance)* Stirling and Glasgow: Department of Scottish Literature, University of Glasgow.

Lyall, R J ed. (1985) *William Lamb, Ane Resonying of ane Scottis and Inglis Merchand Betuix Rowand and Lionis* Aberdeen University Press.

Macafee, C. (1981) 'Nationalism and the Scots Renaissance now', *English World-Wide* 2:1, 29–38.

Macafee C (1982) 'Glasgow dialect in literature', *Scottish Language* 1, 45–53.

Macafee, C (1983) *Glasgow* Amsterdam: John Benjamins, Varieties of English Around the World, Text Series 3.

MacAulay, D ed. (1976) *Nua-Bhàrdachd Ghàidhlig* Edinburgh: Southside.

Macaulay, R K S (1974) 'Linguistic insecurity' in McClure ed., 35–43.

Macaulay, R K S (1977) *Language, Social Class, and Education. A Glasgow Study* Edinburgh University Press.

McClure, J D (1974) 'Modern Scots prose-writing' in McClure ed. (1974).

McClure, J D ed. [1974] *The Scots Language in Education* Aberdeen: Association for Scottish Literary Studies, Occasional Papers 3.

McClure, J D (1979) 'Scots: Its range of users' in Aitken and McArthur, 26–48.

McClure, J D (1980) 'Developing Scots as a national language' in McClure *et al.*, 11–41.

McClure, J D *et al.* (1980) *The Scots Language: Planning for Modern Usage* Edinburgh: The Ramsay Head Press.

McClure, J D (1981a) 'Scottish, Inglis, Suddroun: Language labels and language attitudes' in Lyall and Riddy eds., 52–69.

McClure, J D (1981b) 'The synthesisers of Scots' in Haugen *et al.*, eds. (1981), 91–99.

McClure, J D ed. (1983a) *Scotland and the Lowland Tongue. Studies in the language and literature of Lowland Scotland presented to David A. Murison* Aberdeen University Press.

McClure, J D ed. (1983b) *Minority Languages in Central Scotland* Aberdeen: Association for Scottish Literary Studies.

McClure, J D (1985) 'The Pinkerton Syndrome', *Chapman* 8:4, 2–8.

McCrum, R, W Cran and R MacNeil (1986) *The Story of English* New York: Elisabeth Sifton Books-Viking.

McDiarmid, M P and J A C Stevenson eds. (1980–85) *Barbour's Bruce* 3 vols., Edinburgh and London: Scottish Text Society.

McGhee, Bill (1963) *Cut and Run* Ealing: Corgi (first published 1962).

McIlvanney, William (1983) *The Papers of Tony Veitch* London: Hodder and Stoughton.

McIntosh, A (1956) 'The analysis of written Middle English', *Transactions of the Philological Society*, 26–55.

McIntosh, A (1978a) 'The dialectology of Medieval Scots: some possible approaches to its study', *Scottish Literary Journal* Supplement 6, 38–43.

McIntosh, A (1978b) 'The Middle English poem *The four foes of mankind*', *Neuphilologische Mitteilungen* LXXIX, 137–44.

McIntosh, A (1979a) 'Language' in C MacLean ed., *The Crown and the Thistle: The Nature of Nationhood* Edinburgh: Scottish Academic Press. 144–48.

McIntosh A (1979b) 'Some notes on the language and textual transmission of the *Scottish Troy Book*', *Archivum Linguisticum*, New Series X, 1–19.

McIntosh, A et al (1986) *A Linguistic Atlas of Late Mediaeval English*, 4 vols., Aberdeen University Press. (LALME).

MacIver, Susanna (1773) *A new and experimental treatise on cookery, pastry etc* Edinburgh.

Mackay, M A (1984) 'Kinship and Community in Northern Districts of Argyll', unpublished SSRC Report (copies lodged in British Library and National Library of Scotland).

Mackenzie, W M (1932) *The Poems of William Dunbar* London: Faber and Faber.

McLellan, Robert, *Jamie the Saxt* eds. I Campbell and R D S Jack (1970) London: Calder and Boyars.

McLintock, Mrs. (1736) *Receipts for Cookery and Pastry-Work* Glasgow. Reprint ed. I. Macleod (1986) Aberdeen University Press.

McMillan, J (1982) Interview 'John Byrne', *Scottish Theatre News* June 1982, 2–6.

McNeill, F M (1929) *The Scots Kitchen: Its lore and recipes* Glasgow.

Macphail, A (1977) *The Master's Wife* Toronto: McClelland and Stewart Ltd. (first published 1939).

MacQueen, L E C (1957) 'The Last Stages of the Older Literary Language of Scotland' unpublished PhD thesis, University of Edinburgh.

Manly, J M and E Rickert eds. (1940) *The Text of the Canterbury Tales* Chicago.

Marwick, H (1929) *The Orkney Norn* Oxford University Press.

Mather, J Y (1980) 'The dialect of the Eastern Borders', *Scottish Literary Journal* Supplement 12, 30–42.

Mather J Y and H H Speitel eds. (1975–86) *The Linguistic Atlas of Scotland. Scots Section* 3 vols., London: Croom Helm. (LAS).

Meier, H H (1977) 'Scots is not alone: the Swiss and Low German analogues' in Aitken *et al.*, eds., 201–13.

Meier, H H (1985) 'Love, law and lucre: Images in Rutherfurd's letters' in M-J. Arn *et al.*, eds., *Historical and Editorial Studies in Medieval and Early Modern English for Johan Gerritsen* Groningen Wolters-Noordhoff.

Middle English Dictionary (1954–) eds. H Kurath and S M Kuhn, Ann Arbor: University of Michigan Press. (MED).

Millar, M and K Brown (1979) 'Tag questions in Edinburgh speech', *Linguistische Berichte* 66, 24–45.

Miller, J (1982a) 'Negatives in Scottish English', unpublished working paper, SSRC Grant 5152.

Miller, J (1982b) 'GET in a corpus of spoken Scottish English', unpublished working paper, SSRC Grant 5152.

Miller, J (1982c) 'The expression of Possibility and Permission in Scottish English', unpublished working paper, SSRC Grant 5152.

Miller, J (1982d) 'The expression of Obligation and Necessity in Scottish English', unpublished working paper, SSRC Grant 5152.

Miller, J (1984) 'Discourse patterns in spoken English', *Sheffield Working Papers in Language and Linguistics* 1, 10–39.

Milroy, L (1980) *Language and Social Networks* Oxford: Blackwell.

Morgan, E (1983) 'Glasgow speech in recent Scottish literature' in McClure ed. (1983a), 195–208.

Motherby, R (1828) *Taschen-Wörterbuch des Schottischen Dialekts*.

Murison, D (1971) 'The future of Scots' in D Glen ed., *Whither Scotland? A Prejudiced Look at the Future of a Nation* London: Victor Gollancz, 171–86.

Murison D (1977) *The Guid Scots Tongue* Edinburgh: Blackwood.

Murison, D (1978) 'The language of the ballads', *Scottish Literary Journal* Supplement 6, 54–64.

Murray, J A H (1873) *The Dialect of the Southern Counties of Scotland* London: The Philological Society.

Murray K M E (1977) *Caught in the Web of Words. James A H Murray and the Oxford English Dictionary* New Haven and London: Yale University Press.

Mustanoja T F ed. (1948) *The Good Wife Taught her Daughter . . .* Helsinki.

Mutschmann, H (1909) *A Phonogogy of the North-Eastern Scotch Dialect* Bonn: Bonner Studien zur englischen Philologie I.

Nicholson, A ed. (1881) *A collection of Gaelic Proverbs and Familiar Phrases based on MacIntosh's Collection* Edinburgh: Maclachlan and Stewart.

Norddølum, H (1980) 'The "Dugnad" in the pre-industrial peasant community', *Ethnologica Scandinavica* 102–12.

O'Dowd, A (1981) *Meitheal: A Study of Co-operative Labour in Rural Ireland* Dublin: Comhairle Bhéaloideas Eireann.

The Oxford English Dictionary and Supplements (originally *A New English Dictionary* (1884–1986) eds. J A H Murray *et al.*, Oxford. (OED).

Ordbog over det danske Sprog (1918–56) founded by V Dahlerup, Copenhagen: Det danske Sprog- og Litteraturselskab. (ODS).

Ordbok över svenska språaket utg. av Svenska akademien (1898–) Lund. (SAOB).

Orton, H and N Wright (1974) *A Word Geography of England* London, New York, San Francisco: Seminar Press.

Orton, H *et al.* (1962) *Survey of English Dialects. Introduction* Leeds: E J Arnold.
Orton, H *et al.* (1962–71) *Survey of English Dialects. The Basic Material* Leeds: E J Arnold.
Osselton, N E (1973) *The Dumb Linguists. A Study of the Earliest English and Dutch Dictionaries* Leiden University Press.
Owen, T M (1959) *Welsh Folk Customs* Cardiff: National Museum of Wales.
Parkinson, D (1983) 'Flyting and abuse in Scots Verse 1450–1580', unpublished PhD., Toronto.
Partridge, E (1937) revised P Beale (1984) *A Dictionary of Slang and Unconventional English* London: Routledge and Kegan Paul.
Pearsall, D and I C Cunningham eds. (1977) *The Auchinleck Manuscript* London: Scolar.
Penzl, H (1957) 'The evidence for phonemic change' in E Pulgram ed., *Studies Presented to Joshua Whatmough on his 60th Birthday* The Hague: Mouton, 193–208. Reprinted in Lass ed. (1969), 110–24.
Percy, Thomas (1765) *Reliques of Ancient English Poetry* ed. E Felber, Berlin: M M Arnold Schröer (1893). London: J M Dent & Co. Everyman's Library (n.d.).
Phillips, K C (1980) Review of Aitken and McArthur, eds. (1979), *Scottish Literary Journal* Supplement 12, 77–79.
[Picken, Ebenezer] (1818) *A Dictionary of the Scottish Language* Edinburgh: J Sawyers.
Pottle, F A ed. (1950) *Boswell's London Journal, 1762–1763* London: Heinemann.
Pottle, F A (1966) *James Boswell: The Earlier Years, 1740–1769* New York: McGraw-Hill.
Pottle, F A (1982) *Pride and Negligence: The History of the Boswell Papers* New York: McGraw-Hill.
Quirk, R, S Greenbaum, G Leech and J Svartvik (1985) *A Comprehensive Grammar of the English Language* London: Longman. (CGEL)
Ramsay, Allan (1721, 1728) *Poems* Edinburgh.
Reid, E (1978) 'Social and stylistic variation in the speech of children: Some evidence from Edinburgh' in P Trudgill, ed. *Sociolinguistic Patterns in British English* London: Edward Arnold, 158–71.
Rietz, J E (1867) *Ordbok öfver svenska allmogespråket* 2 vols. Lund. *Register och rättelser* by E Abrahamson, Uppsala: Kungl. Gustav Adolfs Akademien (1955).
Roberts, R (1971, 1983) *The Classic Slum. Salford Life in the First Quarter of the Century* Harmondsworth: Penguin.
Robertson, Hannah (1766) *The young ladies' school of arts* Edinburgh.
Robinson, M (1985) 'The Concise Scots Dictionary': A final report', *Dictionaries* 7, 112–33.
Rogers, C (1882) *History of the Chapel Royal of Scotland* Edinburgh: Grampian Club.
Rynell, A (1948) *The Rivalry of Scandinavian and Native Synonyms in Middle English* Lund Studies in English 13.
Ryskamp, C and F A Pottle eds. (1963) *Boswell: The Ominous Years, 1774–1776* London: Heinemann.
Samuels, M L and J J Smith (1981) 'The language of Gower', *Neuphilologische Mitteilungen* **82**, 295–304.
Sandred, K I (1983) *Good Scots or Bad Scots? Attitudes to Optional Lexical and*

Grammatical Usages in Edinburgh Stockholm: Almqvist and Wiksell, Studia Anglistica Upsaliensia 48.

Sandred, K I (1985) 'Overt and covert prestige: evaluative boundaries in a speech community' in Görlach ed. 69–86.

Saxby, J M E (1908) 'Shetland phrase and idiom', *Orkney and Shetland Miscellany of the Viking Club* 1, 267–74.

Scherpbier, H (1933) *Milton in Holland. A Study in the Literary Relations of England and Holland before 1730* Amsterdam: J H Paris.

Scott-Moncrieff, R ed. (1911) *The Household Book of Lady Grisell Baillie 1692–1733* Edinburgh: Scottish History Society.

Scottish English: The Language Children Bring to School (1980) [Falkirk]: Scottish Committee on Language Arts in the Primary School.

Scottish Literature in the Secondary School (1976) Scottish Central Committee on English, Edinburgh: HMSO.

The Scottish National Dictionary 10 vols. (1931–76) eds. W Grant and D D Murison, Edinburgh: Scottish National Dictionary Association. (SND).

Sheridan, Thomas (1762) *Course of Lectures on Elocution* London: W Strahan. Repr. New York: Benjamin Blom (1968).

Sinclair, J (1782) *Observations on the Scottish Dialect* London.

Sinclair, J ed. (1791–98) *The Statistical Account of Scotland* Edinburgh; William Creech.

Sisam, C (1951) 'The scribal tradition of the Lambeth Homilies', *Review of English Studies* 2:6, 105–113.

Skeat, W W ed. (1874) *A Duncan, Appendix Etymologiae* English Dialect Society.

Skeat W W ed. (1894) *The Bruce, compiled by Master John Barbour* 2 vols., Edinburgh and London: The Scottish Text Society.

Skeat, W W (1912) *English Dialects from the Eighth Century to the Present Day* Cambridge University Press.

Small, J ed. (1884–93) *The Poems of William Dunbar* 3 vols., Edinburgh and London: The Scottish Text Society.

Smith, B (1984) 'What is a scattald? Rural communities in Shetland, 1400–1900' in B E Crawford ed., *Essays in Shetland History* Lerwick: The Shetland Times.

Söderwall, K P (1884–1918) *Ordbok öfver svenska medeltide-språket*, Supplement (1925–73), Lund.

Speitel, H H (1978) 'The word-geography of the Borders' *Scottish Literary Journal* Supplement 6, 17–38.

Spence, J (1900) 'Folklore days and seasons', *Transactions of the Buchan Field Club* 5, 215–34.

Sprunger, K L (1982) *Dutch Puritanism. A History of English and Scottish Churches of the Netherlands in the Sixteenth and Seventeenth Centuries* Leiden: E J Brill.

Stanley E G and D Gray eds. (1983) *Five Hundred Years of Words and Sounds* Cambridge: Boydell & Brewer.

Stewart, W A (1968) 'A sociolinguistic typology for describing multilingualism' in J A Fishman ed., *Readings in the Sociology of Language* The Hague: Mouton, 531–45.

Svartvik, J and R Quirk (1980) *A Corpus of English Conversation* Lund: C W K Gleerup, Lund Studies in English 56.

Thelander, M (1980) 'De-dialectalisation in Sweden', Uppsala: Avdelningen för Forskning och Utbildning i Modern Svenska, University of Uppsala, Report 86.

Thorson, P (1936) *Anglo-Norse Studies. An Inquiry into the Scandinavian Elements of the Modern English Dialects* Amsterdam: Swets en Zeitlinger.

Tibbott, S M (1986) 'Liberality and Hospitality' in *Folk Life* 24, 32–51.

Tobler, A and E Lommatzsch (1915-), *Altfranzöschisches Wörterbuch* Berlin, Wiesbaden: Franz Steiner.

Tolkien, J R R (1934) 'Chaucer as a philologist: *The Reeve's Tale*', *Transactions of the Philological Society*, 1–70.

Tongue, R K (1974) *The English of Singapore and Malaysia* Singapore: Eastern Universities Press.

Toon, T (1983) *The Politics of Early Old English Sound Changes* New York: Academic Press.

Torp, A (1915–19) *Nynorsk etymologisk ordbok* Kristiania: Aschehoug & Co.

Trudgill, P ed. (1984) *Language in the British Isles* Cambridge University Press.

Valéry, Paul, ed. G D Martin (1971) *Le Cimetière Marin* Edinburgh University Press, Edinburgh Bilingual Library 1.

van Buuren, C ed. (1982) *The Buke of the Sevyne Sagis* Leiden University Press.

van Gennep, A (1947) *Manuel de Folklore Français Contemporain* Paris.

Venezky, R L (1967) 'The basis of English orthography', *Acta Linguistica Hafniensia* 10, 145–59.

Wallerstein, I (1984) 'Which historical present for which historical future?' *Cencrastus* 17, 3–5.

Wang, W S-Y and C-C Cheng (1970) 'Interpretation of phonological change: the Shuand-feng Chinese case' in *Papers from the 6th Regional Meeting of the Chicago Linguistic Society*, 552–59.

Warrack A (1911) *Chambers Scots Dictionary* Edinburgh: Chambers.

Wessén E (1945) *Svensk språkhistoria* vol. I *Ljudlära och ordböjningslära* second ed., Stockholm.

Wettstein, P (1942), *The Phonology of a Berwickshire Dialect* Bienne: Schüler S A.

Whyte H ed. (1976) *Lady Castlehill's Receipt Book. A Selection of 18th Century Scottish Fare* Glasgow.

Williamson, K (1982) 'Lowland Scots in education: An historical survey [Part I]', *Scottish Language* 1, 54–77.

Williamson, K (1983) 'Lowland Scots in education: An historical survey [Part II]', *Scottish Language* 2, 52–87.

Wimsatt, W K J and F A Pottle eds. (1960) *Boswell for the Defence, 1769–1774* London: Heinemann.

Xandry, G (1914) *Das skandinavische Element in den neuenglishen Dialekten* PhD thesis, Munster University, Neu-Isenburg.

Young, Douglas (1943) *Auntran Blads* Glasgow: McLellan.

Young, Douglas (1948) *A Braird o Thristles* Glasgow: McLellan.

Zai, R (1942) *The Phonology of the Morebattle Dialect* Lucerne: Räber & Co.

Zettersten, A (1965) *Studies in the Dialect and Vocabulary of the Ancrene Riwle* Lund Studies in English 34.

Zettersten, A (1985) *New Technologies in Language Learning* Copenhagen: Gyldendal; Oxford: Pergamon Press; Lund: Studentlitteratur.